Scandalous Times

Also Available from Bloomsbury

*Ethics under Capital: MacIntyre, Communication,
and the Culture Wars,* Jason Hannan
*Right-Wing Culture in Contemporary Capitalism: Regression
and Hope in a Time without Future,* Mathias Nilges
*The Reasoning of Unreason: Universalism,
Capitalism and Disenlightenment,* John Roberts
*Badiou Reframed: Interpreting Key Thinkers for the Arts,* Alex Ling
*Mathematics of the Transcendental,* Alain Badiou, trans.
A. J. Bartlett and Alex Ling

# Scandalous Times

## Contemporary Creativity and the Rise of State-Sanctioned Controversy

Alex Ling

BLOOMSBURY ACADEMIC
LONDON • NEW YORK • OXFORD • NEW DELHI • SYDNEY

BLOOMSBURY ACADEMIC
Bloomsbury Publishing Plc
50 Bedford Square, London, WC1B 3DP, UK
1385 Broadway, New York, NY 10018, USA
29 Earlsfort Terrace, Dublin 2, Ireland

BLOOMSBURY, BLOOMSBURY ACADEMIC and the Diana logo
are trademarks of Bloomsbury Publishing Plc

First published in Great Britain 2021
This paperback edition published in 2022

Cover design by Charlotte Daniels
Cover image © Cat Arch Angel / Getty Images

A catalogue record for this book is available from the British Library.

Library of Congress Cataloging-in-Publication Data
Names: Ling, Alex, author.
Title: Scandalous times : contemporary creativity and the rise of state-sanctioned
controversy / Alex Ling.
Description: London ; New York : Bloomsbury Academic, 2021. | Includes bibliographical
references and index.
Identifiers: LCCN 2020024884 (print) | LCCN 2020024885 (ebook) | ISBN 9781350068551
(hardback) | ISBN 9781350068544 (ebook) | ISBN 9781350068575 (epub)
Subjects: LCSH: Scandals. | Social norms. | Immorality.
Classification: LCC HM676 .L56 2021 (print) | LCC HM676 (ebook) | DDC 302.2/4–dc23
LC record available at https://lccn.loc.gov/2020024884
LC ebook record available at https://lccn.loc.gov/2020024885

ISBN:     HB:     978-1-3500-6855-1
          PB:     978-1-3500-6856-8
          ePDF:   978-1-3500-6854-4
          eBook:  978-1-3500-6857-5

Typeset by Integra Software Services Pvt. Ltd.

To find out more about our authors and books visit www.bloomsbury.com
and sign up for our newsletters.

*The malice of a good thing is the barb that makes it stick.*
Richard Sheridan, *The School for Scandal*

# Contents

# Acknowledgments

First and foremost, an enormous debt of gratitude is owed to Suzie Daniells and François Ladouceur, without whose constant support and generosity this book would not exist. I also want to acknowledge the help and assistance I have received from my colleagues at Western Sydney University, in particular Anthony Uhlmann, Adam Daniel, and Lorraine Sim, together with colleagues and friends from afar, notably Adam Bartlett, Barbara Creed, and Angus Taylor. Lastly, eternal thanks go to Lucy Russell and Liza Thompson at Bloomsbury Academic, for their professionalism, their support, and their patience throughout the project.

# Introduction:
# Notes on a Scandal

We live in scandalous times. Every day it seems that we are greeted with some new controversy: some daring act of provocation, some atrocious misdeed, or salacious piece of gossip makes its way to us via our chosen media, demanding our attention, our emotional investment, and, ultimately, our judgment.

> *The hedge fund manager who absconds with his clients' money ... The famous athlete whose secret doping regimen is suddenly and sensationally exposed for all to see ... The former child star who loudly proclaims her newfound adulthood by ramping up her sexuality ... The prudish politician who for years has been leading a tawdry double-life ... The boundary-pushing artist who finally takes their work that one step too far ...*

That we are easily able to attach myriad proper names to each of these generic examples—and that we can do so with hardly a second's thought—attests not only to the familiarity with which we embrace these "exceptions to the norm," but also to the fact that they now arise with such rapidity and regularity as to constitute "normalized exceptions." Indeed, of the many ironies that are part and parcel of our hyperconnected, later-than-late-capitalist society, one of the most striking is the way that scandals like these, together with the controversy that surrounds them, have become such an expected and even comforting part of our lives. Exactly how it is that these otherwise largely far-removed events and revelations have come to affect us so deeply is another.

More remarkable still is the fact that the question of what all of this actually means remains to this day largely unanswered. Or in other words: while we can certainly point to numerous fascinating and sophisticated studies of scandal—studies that have been undertaken from multiple critical perspectives (sociological, political, anthropological, historical, artistic …) and with regard to a variety of media forms (traditional, mass, digital, social …)—there has as yet been very little properly philosophical consideration of the concept.[1] So it would appear that, in this area at least, despite their undeniable ubiquity and influence, scandal is still regarded "as a subject too frivolous to warrant serious scholarly attention."[2]

And yet it is precisely this kind of theoretical investigation that is so clearly required today. For while the events themselves may at times appear trivial or insignificant (from an "intellectual" point of view, at least), the consequences they have on our everyday lives are anything but. To be sure, far from representing the meaningless "froth of social and political life,"[3] the fact is that contemporary scandals wield a truly alarming subjective power. Our contention here is then that scandals really do *mean* something (in the significatory as much as the intentional and consequential senses of the word), and this meaning is only reinforced—even intensified—by our obstinate and misguided refusal to recognize it.

None of this, of course, is in any way to suggest that the influence the scandal has over its audience has somehow passed by unnoticed in critical commentary. To the contrary, questions of identity formation and social construction, in particular in relation to moral frameworks, have long been an underlying theme of so-called scandal research. So much is this the case that they can even be said to constitute a defining and hence unifying feature of all scandal-related scholarship, Steffen Burkhardt going so far as to characterize this otherwise diverse field of research as "the systematic and comparative study of scandals as a social ritual that serve the purpose of updating normative moral models in a society and, through communication, contribute to a collective difference and identity formation."[4]

Countless examples of this "subjective" focus abound. Max Gluckman's early anthropological work on "Gossip and Scandal" identifies the latter as a powerful mechanism of social order that functions to preserve "the unity, morals and values of social groups,"[5] and which is even strategically employed in some communities "to maintain the principle of equality between all members."[6] Ari Adut's more recent work on scandal and morality similarly demonstrates how the former not only "trigger a great deal of the normative solidification and transformation in a society,"[7] but might also easily function as a "social control mechanism."[8] Burkhardt himself identifies as a central function of the contemporary scandal, "the act of upgrading the moral preference code of a social framework," such that it "negotiates social belonging and non-belonging."[9] Approaching the same idea from a different angle, Sigurd Allern and Ester Pollack point to the dangers of overzealous scandal coverage as reinforcing social conformity, whereby the media's eventual "symbolic execution" of the scandalous party only "confirms the re-establishment of the social order."[10]

Needless to say, it would hardly be difficult to extend this list further. That the bulk of the existing research recognizes the considerable influence the scandal has on the individual subject is not in question here. Our immediate concern rather lies elsewhere; in particular, it rests with the nature of the *subject* itself.

## Sovereign Public Subjects

While the "intimate" function of scandals in individual and social formation obviously represents a key concern of this book, the way we will be approaching this question differs significantly from previous studies. For one thing, as already indicated, the lens we employ here is neither explicitly political, nor sociological (nor artistic, nor historical ...), but rather philosophical. (That being said, our analysis will naturally also take in these other important areas.) To this end, while the work undertaken here is certainly concerned with identifiable historical and contemporary scandals, it is not intended as constituting "scandal research" *per se*. Moreover, the aforementioned "intimacy" of scandal—the way it so profoundly (if surreptitiously) affects its public—does not represent for us a horizon, as is the case in standard models, but instead constitutes a point of departure. Specifically, in examining the subject of scandal, our first port of call must be none other than the individual *subject* as such: not the scandalous "subject matter"—i.e., the shocking or salacious details of the event itself—but rather *the materiality of the subject on which the scandal acts*, namely, the "scandalized," as opposed to the "scandalous," subject.

Clearly some words of explanation are required here. One of the major shortcomings of existing scandal research, at least from the standpoint of philosophy, is that the bulk of these studies assumes, seemingly by default, and likely as a result of their predominantly empirical nature, an essentially uncritical or "pre-philosophical" understanding of the individual subject—even if this conception can easily be traced back to Descartes and his famous "cogito." To this end, the scandalized subject is implicitly (and even, on occasion, explicitly) conceived along the lines of an autonomous and stable entity qua "sovereign individual subject," as the prepotent "core" of the self, endowed with absolute consciousness, and representing the original and authentic source of action and meaning. This in itself is, of course, hardly surprising: as Pierre Schlag has shown (in reference to normative legal frameworks), this sovereign subject matches the conventional model of the "liberal subject" presupposed in virtually all areas of contemporary thought, and which is assumed to be "autonomous, coherent, self-directing, integrated, rational and originary."[11]

Yet this fundamentally (if perhaps unintentionally) Cartesian notion of the fully self-transparent subject—of the subject "certain that there can be nothing in him, in so far as he is a thinking thing, of which he is not aware"[12]—simply does not square with recent philosophical thought. After all, this basic concept has undergone a massive transformation over the course of the twentieth century alone. Sigmund Freud, for example, showed how the subject is riven by unconscious desires—that "we are 'lived' by unknown and uncontrollable forces"[13]—after which Jacques Lacan contrived to "invert its usage,"[14] theorizing it as a void point, the "empty waste" of the cogito. Edmund Husserl's self-declared "neo-Cartesian" phenomenology (which nonetheless managed to "reject nearly all the well-known doctrinal content of the Cartesian philosophy") further eroded its sovereign basis, dissolving "the *illusion* of a solipsism" inherent to the cogito with his theory of "transcendental intersubjectivity."[15] Following on from this, Jean-Paul Sartre showed how the subject's "existence comes before its essence"[16]—an existence which is entirely conditioned on the mediation of others—while Martin Heidegger demonstrated its basis not in the individual cogito (which "neglect[s] the question of Being altogether")[17] but in transcendent Dasein. Countless more examples present themselves: Louis Althusser held that the subject constituted an ideological fiction; Maurice Merleau-Ponty re-designated it a register of pure experience; Michel Foucault showed how it was produced within a network of power relations; Emmanuel Levinas understood it as a category of morality; on and on the list goes.[18]

This steady process of "de-subjectivization"—of stripping away the autarchic layers of the subject—in fact continues to this day with figures like Alain Badiou and Quentin Meillassoux, both of whom enlist mathematics to their cause, the former to reduce the subject to an elementary formalism—not a necessary function but rather a contingent framework; "a configuration *in excess* of the situation"[19]—and the latter in order to strip it of its enduring "correlationist" attributes such that we might thereby once again "make our way towards the absolute."[20]

While it would be easy, as before, to extend this list with further examples, the basic point should by now have been made clearly enough: from the most intimate aspect of our individual selves, to an abstract framework configuring multiple different objects, the contemporary subject would seem to bear only the most passing resemblance to its classical Cartesian conception. In a word, the subject is today but a shell of its former self.[21]

All the same, it is this increasingly philosophically obsolete subject that still underlies (and, by the same token, undermines) the lion's share of scandal-related scholarship. To be more precise, the bulk of scandal research reformulates this "sovereign individual subject" in terms of an equally sovereign public qua *collection of subjects*, a "sovereign public subject." The reason for this is itself straightforward enough, in that a scandal is, by definition, not an individual affair, but rather demands a public (typically an indignant one). Simply put, while the offending subject matter may originally be individual in nature, for it to qualify as "scandal," this material first needs to undergo some form of public revelation; it must "become public." As Robert M. Entman succinctly puts it (while glossing one of the dominant approaches to the study of scandal): "no public indignation, no scandal."[22] Or again, this time in the words of Molière's eponymous Tartuffe, "it's scandal, Madam, which makes it an offence/And it's no sin to sin in confidence."[23]

At the risk of losing our train of thought, we can derive from this basic proposition two further crucial features of scandal, such as it has been theorized in the existing scholarship: first, that in order to reach a public, the event in question must be "publicized," meaning it must undergo some form of *mediation* (which in today's hyperconnected world is almost invariably a "mass-mediation" or a "mediatization");[24] and second, that this event—which, it should be pointed out, can be either real or imagined—must in some way deviate from or *transgress* an (implicitly or explicitly) accepted social order or code of conduct.

Thus we already have at hand the three necessary conditions of any scandal, these being: (1) a sovereign public subject, (2) a (real or imagined) transgression of the social-symbolic order, and (3) a process of mediation. The combination of these three essential factors gives us perhaps the most elementary definition of scandal itself, namely, as constituting *a mediated process that fascinates the public (principally through the invocation of outrage) by proposing some violation of the given social-symbolic order.*

In point of fact, almost every definition encountered in the loose field of scandal research proposes some variation on this theme. It is this basic structure, for example, that underlies John Thompson's influential work on political scandals, in which he offers a preliminary definition of "scandal" as referring to "actions or events involving certain kinds of transgressions which become known to others and are sufficiently serious to elicit a public response."[25] Thompson further clarifies this general definition by identifying five key aspects to scandals, being: a *transgression* of accepted norms, values, or moral codes; an attempt at *concealment* by the transgressor; general *disapproval* by "non-participants" (i.e., figures who are aware of, but not directly involved in, the transgressive event); public *denunciation* by these non-participants; and some form of ensuing *reputational damage* to the transgressor.[26]

While Thompson obviously restricts his focus to explicitly political scandals, the preponderance of "generic" scandal scholarship never strays far from this basic framework. For example, even as he notes that "a general model of scandal [...] remains an unrealized desideratum," Adut nonetheless goes on to propose an admirably concise theory of scandal as "the disruptive publicity of transgression."[27] Burkhardt, for his part, characterizes scandal as "a communication process that sparks public outrage through a postulated violation of the general moral model of the social reference system,"[28] while Esser and Hartung define it in terms of "the intense public communication about a real or imagined defect that is by consensus condemned, and that meets universal indignation or outrage," and where the "defect" in question involves "some form of injury to a social norm."[29] Again, we could easily continue this list.[30]

## Real Subjective Creation

Clearly, the bulk of the existing research treats scandals as morally determinative phenomena, that is, as functioning to reproduce already-established models of social propriety. To this end, the scholarship has effectively instituted a logical cause-effect relationship, by which the transgressive event is treated as root cause, whereas the public response—both conscious (e.g., in terms of widespread offense or even distress) and unconscious (concerning the event's structural and psychological influence)—is understood as its "effect." Or more precisely: while the initial event figures as "necessary cause" (or even "pre-cause"), it is the all-important *publicizing* of this event—its mediation/mediatization—that provides its "sufficient" causal complement.[31] In any case, it is the secondary, "subjective" part of the scandal (i.e., the unsuspecting audience qua "sovereign public subject," whose ordered existence the scandal works to maintain) that amounts to the final link in the chain. Wherefore a rudimentary order has been established in the extant scholarship—one that is in equal parts quantitative and qualitative, sequential and hierarchical—such that the scandalous subject material is systematically prioritized over and above the materiality of the scandalized subject.

As already indicated, the point at which we take our leave from this now well-established model is, in effect, in our conception of the *subject* itself. Indeed, by taking this secondary, constitutive subject as the focus of our attention, we effectively turn the standard approach on its head, making its horizon our point of departure. Having said this, for practical reasons, our predominant focus will for some time not be *on* but rather *around* this subject—taking in its context and foundations—and only later will we be in a position to examine it square on. While the exact details as to how and why this is necessary will be one of the focal points of the following chapters (and to some extent, the remainder of the book), it is, all the same, important that we say one or two preliminary words here before moving on.

Briefly, our interest in the subject of the scandal is tied to the awareness of a particular form of scandal that, for reasons which will become increasingly clear as we move on, we call *real*. We distinguish "real scandal" from "ordinary scandal" (such as the kind we encountered at the very beginning of this book) on the basis of its foundational relation to the subject; that is to say, on the view that, far from being "scandalized" (hence a secondary part of the process), the subject is rather what *creates real scandal*. In fact, the creation of scandal—or, more to the point, *the scandal of creation*—is, in a certain sense, the ultimate "object" of the subject, its *raison d'être*.

Yet this fundamentally "creative" subject is, it must be said, a peculiar structure: one that stands in marked opposition to orthodox philosophical conceptions of subjectivity. For such a subject can be conceived of as neither substance, nor void point, nor invariable of presentation. Nor for that matter does it designate a register of experience, nor category of morality, nor ideological fiction. And, of course, it goes without saying that it is neither sovereign nor individual—at least, not in the classical sense.

Rather, the subject we are interested in here is, in essence—and, more to the point, in *form*—a *creative enterprise*: one that presents, as a matter of course, something profoundly, even disturbingly, *new*. We draw this conception directly from the work of Alain Badiou, whose philosophical system in fact underpins the bulk of our scandalous investigations, and who (as indicated earlier) conceives of the subject less as a living, breathing organism than as a structure we can all, given the opportunity, enter into.

Emerging only in the wake of a radical *event*—which we can think of for the moment as a sudden rupture with the laws of a given situation involving a surging forth of new possibilities that are as unassimilable as they are unprecedented—Badiou's subject *exceeds* the human animal (qua "sovereign individual subject") as a formal framework that unites, on the one hand, the lingering trace of this event's occurrence, with, on the other, the gradual materialization (or the "actualization") of the new possibilities it implied—a unification which takes the form of a *new creative body*.

To this end, far from being something we simply *are*, as in the conventional Cartesian or "liberal" conception, the subject is rather something we *might become*, something altogether *exceptional*.[32] Furthermore, to become a subject is to partake in a process of authentic creation, such that we can say "no creation, no subject" (and *vice versa*).[33] In classical philosophical terms, a subject is then far more than the mere sum of its individual parts: it is ourselves *(re)oriented toward a greater good* (with all the ethico-philosophical resonances this term carries with it).[34]

As we have already indicated, it is this properly creative conception of the subject that allows us to conceptualize real scandal as something altogether separate from ordinary scandal. Specifically, we conceive of real scandal as being the effect of a violent rupture with the order of things that results from the appearance of something radically new (and in this precise sense, *real*) in the world, hence, as *the social consequence of an instance of real subjective creation*. Or again: real scandal occurs when a public body is forced to *account for the unaccountable*. We can thus say that the subject "creates scandal," and thereby causes *controversy*—which might similarly be understood in terms of *the social affect accompanying a scandalous act*—to the extent that it *creates*, full stop. Indeed, real subjective creation—by which we obviously mean something far rarer and more extraordinary than the superficial transformations that make up conventional "novelty"—is fundamentally and incontrovertibly scandalous, in so far as it necessarily upends the existing order: in breaking not only with what is permitted, but moreover with what is *possible*, it plunges the situation, for a time at least, into *a state of chaos*.[35] All of which is to say that authentic creation, and hence authentic subjectivity, is inherently transgressive; its very being is transgression.

Yet this real scandal—which, we should add in passing, equally designates the "good" form of scandal; its positive or "ideal" model—is not, for all that, the unique object of our study. Rather, our concerns lie just as much with another, far more troubling kind of scandal—one that replicates or "mimics," at the level of both structure and effect, the chaos and disruption brought about by acts of real subjective creation, *precisely in order to counteract this very process*. This fundamentally negative or eliminative result is achieved in the main by overlaying the "authentically new" with its aseptic double: the pretense of creation qua *simulacrum of novelty*.

Such scandals, which we accordingly call *simulacral* (and which are, in truth, *anti*-scandals), in effect represent the weaponization of scandal (and in particular, the controversy which surrounds it) directly in the service of the state. It is to this end that we find ourselves today increasingly bearing witness to the production of a perverse form of state-sanctioned controversy, whereby the presentation of an almost perpetual state of *dis*order paradoxically functions to prohibit the very possibility of real disruptive creation and the scandal it occasions, and in this way functions to maintain and even strengthen the existing order. In perverting what might otherwise be a clear signal of radical innovation—i.e., the unsettling (but no less vital) social reverberations of the great "shock of the new"[36]—the contemporary "simulacral" form of scandal has managed to wholly overcome its "real" roots to become this act's determined enemy.

If real scandals are essentially prescriptive—directing, so to speak, the proverbial "winds of change"—simulacral scandals are then contrarily proscriptive, working to neutralize both the subject and the real creation it entails, and in this way preserve and even reinforce the status quo. Thus the simulacral scandal performs the most dispiriting of functions, namely, that of extinguishing the very possibility of possibility itself.

# Modus Operandi

It should by now be clear that our intention in this book is not merely to offer up a list of scandals that have been carefully collated according to their relative size and significance, thereby establishing a kind of obscene "catalogue of controversy." Nor is our goal simply to present a number of in-depth analyses of scandalous exemplars, zeroing in on preeminent historical events in order to clinically dissect them and examine their inner workings (though obviously a small amount of case study will be involved here). Nor, for that matter, do we mean to confine ourselves to a specific subsection or species of scandal, such as the "political scandal," the "financial scandal," the "art scandal," or the "sex scandal."

On the contrary, as noted at the outset, our interest is first and foremost philosophical, which is to say that we are principally concerned with establishing exactly what—and, crucially, *why*—contemporary scandal really *is*: not only how it works and what it does, but moreover what it truly means, both for *us* (individually and as a society) and, just as importantly, *in-itself*. More specifically, we are interested in those particular forms of scandal which are tied to processes of *creation*, or that have some intrinsic relation, be it positive or negative, to the idea of the *new*.

Broadly speaking, we will go about all of this by analyzing the various functions that scandal serves in society, paying particular attention to the role of the creative subject in its production, its reception, and its ramifications. More comprehensively, our aim in examining the contemporary function of creation through the dual prisms of "scandal" and "controversy" is to show:

(1) that in disrupting the operation of the "state" (broadly conceived), the advent of the authentically new is always cause for scandal, such that we can define *real scandal* as the social (or "intra-situational") effect of instances of true creation, and reciprocally (2) how the homogenizing and fundamentally "static" process of "manufacturing consent"[37] is today in large part ensured through the seemingly antithetical practice of "creating controversy," which is itself achieved via the incessant production of aseptic novelty in the form of *simulacral scandals*. Or in other words, we want to show how the problem of the sudden suspension of the state's ordinary functioning as a result of real scandal (which itself arises from acts of radical creation) has directly led to its contemporary "solution" in the form of its simulacral complement, namely, the creation of state-sanctioned controversy.

To this end, the book has been evenly divided into four separate parts, respectively focusing on "Scandals," "Foundations," "Creation," and "Controversy." "Part One: Scandals," comprising the first two chapters ("The Big Reveal" and "Chaos and Novelty"), is concerned with introducing and outlining what we identify as the four generic forms of scandal that exist today, which we designate as *revelatory*, *dissimulative*, *real*, and *simulacral* (or alternatively: "sensational," "retailing," "original," and "static"). Of these four, it is the last two—real/original and simulacral/static—that will come to occupy the bulk of our attention, for the related reasons that: (1) unlike their "ordinary" revelatory and dissimulative counterparts, both real and simulacral scandals are inextricably bound up with the act of creation, and (2) each necessarily (which is to say, automatically and axiomatically) concern the operation of the *state itself*, albeit from completely different angles, and to fundamentally different ends.

"Part Two: Foundations" begins by isolating a single, all-important element as determinative ("in the last instance") of all four forms of scandal, being none other than the nebulous category of the *real*, which we understand in quasi-Lacanian terms as simultaneously underlying and undermining individual and collective reality. Our effort to make sense of this outwardly "sense-less" category allows us at the same time to lay out the philosophical groundwork for our entire argument. To this end, the chapters that make up this section ("Grounds for Annulment" and "Making Sense of Everything") detail the simultaneously creative and chaotic role the real plays first in Lacan's influential "antiphilosophy," and then, more substantially, in the philosophy of Alain Badiou. Here the real is first reformulated in terms of multiple-being before being meticulously set out to establish a complete rational ontology: an ontology whose internal stability or overall "stasis" is only guaranteed through the systematic repression of the disruptive real, the logic of which will finally be used to schematize scandal.

The chapters making up "Part Three: Creation" ("A Terrible Beauty" and "Wresting with the Impossible") venture beyond the inner confines of this "complete" ontology to explore its properly scandalous outer limits, isolating the various fault lines and impasses where the real might in effect re-enter the system and make its chaotic presence powerfully felt. This "return of the real," which takes the form of a radical and unpredictable *event*, is then analyzed in terms of the tumultuous effects it can have on the situation—effects which have the potential (if not the authorization) to engender a new creative subject that might in turn lead to a real scandal surrounding the fabrication of what Badiou would call a "new universal truth." In detailing the transgressive nature of this entire process—from the conception of multiple-being all the way up to the creation of truth—we finally show how, regardless of their radicality, such events might only indirectly give rise to real scandal, as the latter contrarily requires for its existence a crucial mediation, which is precisely the *controversial work of the subject.*

Finally, "Part Four: Controversy," comprising the last two chapters ("Brave New World" and "The Real Problem"), focuses on how this real subjective creation is today being abrogated and substituted through the increasing production of novel forms of state-sanctioned controversy. After analyzing the classic models of state repression elaborated in George Orwell's and Aldous Huxley's dystopic fiction in accordance with the overarching system developed in Parts Two and Three, we turn our attention to the undisputed nonpareil of scandal at work today: social media. Here we "upgrade" Huxley's dark vision of "universal happiness," together with the key theses of Neil Postman's related work on the "entertainmentization" of information in the age of television, to argue that the dominant social media essentially function as "scandalizing apparatuses." In doing so, we focus on the polarizing president of the United States and putative "King of Twitter,"[38] Donald Trump, examining the ways he both uses and is used by different forms of static controversy. In closing, we sketch out a rudimentary "ethics of scandal" that might allow us to transcend the state of numbing satisfaction that defines our epoch and finally open us up to the chance of experiencing something which has become not only increasingly rare but even scandalous in its own right, which is nothing less than the possibility of real happiness.

Part One

# Scandals

1

# The Big Reveal

Clearly one of the central concerns of this book is the way that scandals have come to exert an enormous influence over our everyday lives, affecting our thoughts and actions to a degree that is both difficult and dangerous to ignore. Indeed, key to their overall "effectiveness" is the extraordinary familiarity and even intimacy of their operation. They impress themselves upon us, telling us how and how not to act, what to do and say, even what to think and feel. More and more, it is the scandal that affirms our place in the world: Are we for or against? Do we resent or approve? Is it "us" or is it "them"?

The routine, insistent nature of these scandalous impressions and affirmations is at once remarkable and plain to see. To open a newspaper is, after all, to be confronted with story after story demanding either approval or condemnation—an endless succession of calculated polemy which is in no way restricted to editorials and political analysis, but equally comprises business news, sports coverage, food and entertainment reviews, art criticism, science reporting, even fashion advice.

Much of this either takes its cue or is simply lifted whole from the increasingly caustic world of social media—doubtless *the* arch-scandalizing technological development of the twenty-first century—which, in providing both a literal and metaphorical platform for society's collective "id," has in all likelihood done more to split the human race into warring camps than anything the world has seen in a substantially long time.

All of this is of course to say nothing of politics itself, whose scandalous *bona fides* are as incontestable as they are self-evident. Suffice for us to point to the paragon of anti-virtue that is the forty-fifth president of the United States, Donald Trump, whose almost caricaturishly scandalous actions—his shady business dealings, his disregard if not outright disdain for ethical norms, his indisputable racism and misogyny (both public and private), his bellicose tweets, his blatant lies and schoolyard bullying tactics, etc.—only serve to further drive a wedge between his supporters and his detractors, effectively informing each side of what they need to condemn absolutely and what must be defended at all costs.

Now, the reasoning behind all of this is, at least on the face of it, fairly straightforward. Part of the function of scandal is, after all, to polarize—in effect, to "divide and conquer"—and the ones who best employ it, those who have, either willingly or unwillingly, been awarded the title of "celebrity" (in which we should hear both the Old French *celebrité* or "celebration" and the Latin *celebritas*, meaning "multitude" or "throng")[1] know this only too well.[2]

Moreover, looking beyond their superficially confronting nature, it is important to acknowledge the paradoxically reassuring effect these polarizing divisions have on us, the way they can imbue us with an intense sense of comfort and self-satisfaction. In point of fact, it is precisely this gratifying affect that makes the scandal one of the most powerful tools in the celebrity's already-considerable arsenal. After all, what could be more rewarding than recognizing yourself—i.e., your "true" self: your deepest beliefs and heartfelt convictions—in (or, alternatively, in sharp contrast to) the actions of some "celebrated" individual whose existence has been deemed infinitely worthier than your own?

That being said, we needn't judge ourselves too harshly here, if only for the fact that this whole affirmatory process is, more often than not, something that we only barely register, let alone have any real control over. For when first confronted with a scandal, our immediate, almost automatic reaction is hardly to carefully consider its "objective" nature (its context and defining terms, its determination as much as its possible ramifications …). Rather, it is to crudely assess its relation to *ourselves*: does it "represent" us and our worldview or, contrarily, does it offend our sensibilities?[3]

Our subsequent "rational" response is then oriented and shaped by this initial, "reflexive" (understood in both the physiological and referential senses of the word) assessment. Indeed, it is important to stress here how it is only *after* we have established our own rudimentary relation to the scandal that we might so much as begin to take stock of its broader picture. And it almost goes without saying that this ensuing account, while doubtless more considered, is nonetheless going to be deeply colored by the preceding spontaneous (or "inconsiderate") evaluation.[4] All of which is finally to say that, when it comes to scandals, first impressions really do count.

## Anagnorisis and Peripeteia

It would seem then that there is a protocol proper to the scandal, which is that they must address us before we can address them. Moreover, we also recognize that there is a certain "immediate" (meaning both instantaneous and unmediated) unconscious pleasure we take in this address: a personal gratification which lies in our initial identification or rejection, in the manner by which it re-establishes the terms on which our own identity is at once constructed and instructed (does it reflect "us," or rather, does it reflect "them"?).

Yet the satisfaction we enjoy here is by no means limited to the ways in which the scandal structures and reinforces our worldview. To the contrary, far from being confined to this initial, fundamentally narcissistic level, the comfort we find in the scandal is arguably derived for the most part from its deeply felt, seemingly incontestable, *authenticity*.

Once again, the logic here is fairly clear and straightforward. In effect, the transgressive nature of scandals leads us to understand them in "revelatory" terms, that is, as being direct *exposures of the real itself*—as the sudden "revelation of a little bit of the real."[5] In this age of public relations absolutism and around-the-clock "image management," the scandal appears to offer us a tantalizing glimpse of what *really* goes on, cutting through the multiple layers of artifice and spin to reveal an underlying, and oftentimes disturbing, "truth." (This disclosive function is especially pronounced in the case of politics, where the scandal is generally supposed to expose "the 'hidden face' of power" and in this way "bring out the duality that underlies political life: the gap between what is said and what things are, between idealized politics and down-and-dirty politics, between the norms that are publicly legitimated and upheld and actual behavior.")[6]

In any event, these sudden disclosures are then further subjected to the same logic of mediatization and sensationalism that informs our epoch as a whole. Played out before the public eye with all the spectacle and emotional intensity of the best-scripted dramas, the revelatory scandal evokes as much the multiple plot twists and dramatic reveals of contemporary fiction as the anagnorisis and peripeteia of ancient tragedy[7]—thus giving the fullest expression to the notion of its representing "a *drama of concealment and exposure*."[8]

At the time of writing, two such revelatory scandals dominate the headlines: the so-called college-admissions bribery scandal, where a group of wealthy parents (including Hollywood actors, corporate CEOs, and the like) stand accused of buying their underperforming children's way into prestigious American tertiary institutions such as Yale and Stanford, to the tune of 25 million dollars and the multiple trials and sentencings of the long-time DC lobbyist and erstwhile chairman of Donald Trump's 2016 election campaign, Paul Manafort.

That each of these scandals should induce a considerable emotional investment on the part of their "audience" relates not only to their representing peripeteic "reversals of fortune" for the key protagonists, who have themselves come to embody especially rancorous positions in the eyes of an intensely divided American public (the "liberal Hollywood elite" in the case of the college-admissions scandal and the "unscrupulous political opportunist" in the case of Manafort). Moreover, our engrossment derives from their anagnoristic function, from the fact that they each appear to expose (albeit from different angles), both for the public and for the scandalous "actors" themselves, the same tragic truth about the way that wealth and power operate in the United States—a country that invests heavily in the myth of "meritocracy" (and in particular in the fabled "American dream" of equal opportunity and upward mobility)—which is, of course, that *the game has been rigged from the very start.*[9]

Yet this "of course" leads us to ask ourselves: what exactly is so revealing about these revelations? The number of scandals that have already come and gone and, in the process, exposed the manifold ways by which the global aristocracy perpetuates its own privileged status through brazen acts of lying, cheating, and outright exploitation is simply too large to count. Indeed, it has been public knowledge for decades that admission processes at many elite universities are deeply inequitable and geared toward the rich and powerful.[10] Likewise, few can be surprised to hear of Manafort's historical criminal practices (including tax and bank fraud, conspiracy, money laundering, foreign-lobbying violations, and obstruction of justice), acts of corruption that the general public—regardless of its ingrained meritocratic beliefs—takes for granted as occurring at the highest levels each and every day.

To be sure, much of the pleasure we take in these "revelations" would appear to come not from the ostensibly "new" information they provide, but rather from the way they reinforce already-established knowledge, things that we have long been aware of, on one level or another. After all, who, today, is unaware of the fact that the scales are—and always have been—heavily slanted in favor of the already-fortunate? And who, for that matter, could fail to recognize that power and corruption so often go hand in hand?

## From Revelation to Dissimulation

Yet we also revel in the banality—in the rank ordinariness—of these scandalous events and, in particular, in the remarkable degree of insouciance and nonchalance the protagonists frequently bring to their activities. So much is this the case that, in a decidedly "meta" turn of events, the very process of recognizing this fact has become a marked feature of the way that scandals are both reported and commented upon. To take a single representative example: discussing the college-admissions scandal in *The New Yorker*, journalist Naomi Fry initially "wondered why perusing the minute interactions between [principal fraudster William] Singer and his clients gave me so much pleasure," before identifying the cause as "the sheer everydayness of the documented conversations, whose polite blandness, in the context of their apparent criminality, often led to high comedy."[11] (Fry then goes on to relate this to the "similar satisfaction" she experienced on first reading of Donald Trump Jr's "I love it" email response that led to the infamous "Trump Tower meeting"— attended by, among others, Paul Manafort.)[12]

Of course, this pleasurable banality need not always be made explicit, but can equally (and just as effectively) be inferred. To report on Trump's latest outrageous assertion or controversial tweet is, for example, equally to underscore—regardless of the intentionality behind this (or the degree to which the journalist ideologically supports or opposes the president)—both his mediocrity and his triviality, for the simple reason that these acts bely a life immersed in the duties of office and speak instead to an irresponsible obsession with television, and with Fox News in particular (to which his tweets and assertions frequently serve as real-time responses).

Needless to say, the banality that often accompanies scandals equally extends to the simple fact that we have experienced the *very same thing* countless times before, just as we will again in the future. To be sure, regardless of how incendiary both the college-admissions and the Manafort scandals may appear at the time of writing, the odds are high that, by the time of this book's publication, they will have been largely forgotten, having long ago been buried beneath mound upon mound of fresh controversy, the detritus of a thousand and more almost-identical cases that have come and gone in the intervening period.

All of which inevitably leads us to question not only the originality but, moreover, the very *authenticity* of such scandals: the simple idea that they present us with "the truth and nothing but the truth." For as enticing as they may be, we can of course equally contend that so many of these increasingly routine transgressions present nothing other than the strategic face of contemporary capitalism: calculated marketing exercises designed to stimulate consumer interest and generate increased revenue, such controversies arguably do little more than attest to the contemporary truism that "there is no such thing as bad publicity."

This fundamentally commercial logic is, for obvious reasons, especially apparent in mainstream broadcast and digital media: from the studied pugnacity and invective of radio shock jocks, to the ever-increasing supplementation of news reporting with a relentless stream of turgid commentary in the form of fatuous "hot takes" and reliably contentious roundtables (which, in disguising opinion as journalism, only serve to further erode the already problematic distinction between "editorializing" and "reporting"). Here, the dual logics of scandal and capital—or in traditional publishing terms: of "editorial" and "marketing"—perfectly coalesce in the never-ending pursuit of greater audience share or "traffic," the measure of which is provided in the form of "ratings" and "clicks" (or "likes" or "shares" ...), which will then finally be parlayed into advertising revenue.

The same underlying logic of course equally applies to the participatory and accordingly self-promotional world of social media, where the principal unit of quantification becomes that of "followers," and where "marketing is no longer a separate function from editorial—the editorial is the marketing."[13] Yet in cultivating the transformation of individuals into so-called personal brands, social media goes one step further than its more traditional counterpart, by not only facilitating but actively encouraging a practice of *self-scandalizing* (a practice which, regardless of its superficially devaluing effects, is clearly pecuniary in intent).

While we could easily cite myriad examples of this process (of which the now-clichéd "celebrity sex tape" is perhaps the most well known), its perfect distillation is arguably found in the carefully choreographed and drawn-out spectacle of the modern social mediated "celebrity feud." To take a single and obvious example, the extent to which superstars Kanye West and Taylor Swift have been able to leverage their infamous encounter at the 2009 Video Music Awards (during which West interrupted Swift's acceptance speech for "Best Female Video" to declare Beyoncé the "rightful winner") into an ongoing and highly profitable succession of social mediated scandals—perhaps the most notorious centering on West's track *Famous* (with its graphic video and baiting refrain "I made that bitch famous")—and thereby propel their respective brands into overdrive has been nothing short of remarkable.

In short, while a significant number of scandals doubtless come to light only involuntarily, without the consent of the scandalous party—and to this end, may indeed divulge some underlying "truth" (a term we will have cause to think about in some detail shortly)—many more are deliberately constructed before being foisted upon us, harnessing the allure of transgression and provocation in a self-serving attempt to increase "brand awareness" and revenue. All of which is to say that if there is indeed such a thing as an "art of scandal," it is none other than *the dark art of marketing*.

Having now sketched out two elementary "forms" of scandal—one authentic and revelatory, the other cynical and dissimulative—it is important to recognize that the practice itself exists on a spectrum, with considerable latitude to be found between one end and the other. Moreover, these positions need not even be mutually exclusive: that a scandal reveals something authentic does not necessarily mean that its exposure was altogether uninfluenced by market forces, just as a commercial product specifically designed to scandalize might still address something of real value. We see this perhaps most clearly in the case of art, whose historically provocative nature (at least since the nineteenth century) ensures that its greatest scandals might easily fall into both camps at the same time.

Take Andres Serrano's infamous 1987 artwork *Immersion (Piss Christ)*, which ignited a major congressional debate in the United States over public arts funding in the late 1980s. That this 60 x 40-inch photograph depicting a plastic statue of Jesus on the cross submerged in the artist's own urine was intentionally provocative is beyond doubt, as is the fact that the controversy surrounding it benefited the artist enormously. (Serrano himself cites as the "high point" of his career "being a completely unknown artist denounced in Congress.")[14] Yet the scandal of *Piss Christ* can comfortably be placed in both the dissimulative and revelatory categories, for while clearly designed to provoke, the work nonetheless has significant artistic and intellectual merit— indeed, the one and the other are inextricably entwined. Thus we can agree with Serrano's claims that his work represents a criticism of the "billion-dollar Christ-for-profit industry" and a "condemnation of those who abuse the teachings of Christ for their own ignoble ends,"[15] while at the same time leveling this same criticism back at him; both are equally as valid as they are scandalous.

It is furthermore unlikely to have escaped the reader's attention that the examples we have been pursuing up to this point—the college-admissions bribery scandal, the multiple crimes of Paul Manafort, the self-promotional social mediated celebrity feud, the reliably controversial actions of President Trump, etc.—each constitute fundamentally *negative* instances, in that they all involve either outright corruption or, at the very least, a significant degree of duplicity. Yet we need to understand that just because a scandal might only follow the public revelation of a transgression, this does not necessarily mean that the material it brings to light must itself be corrupt or even duplicitous. Indeed, to assume otherwise would be to make the mistake of conflating "transgression" with "corruption" (which, to be clear, only represents one particular form of transgression).[16] Moreover, it is not difficult to recognize how in certain situations, material which might otherwise be seen as scandalous would hardly raise an eyebrow, while in others it may even be considered laudable.

With all of this in mind, it is worth examining the distinction between the two models of scandal encountered thus far in just a little more detail before we move on to more "fundamental" matters. In doing so, we will consider two well-known examples drawn from the field of art and separated from one another by a period of exactly one hundred years.

## Blurred Lines

In February of 1913, the artist Marcel Duchamp entered his painting *Nude Descending a Staircase No. 2*—the same work which had only recently caused rumblings of discontent among orthodox cubists at its initial showing at the *Salon des Indépendants* (so much so that the artist withdrew the painting from the exhibition)—in the International Exhibition of Modern Art held at the armory quartering of the 69th Regiment of the National Guard in New York City. Intended to introduce the American public to "new trends in European art," the Armory Show (as it came to be called) scandalized US audiences accustomed solely to realist art and largely unfamiliar with the avant-garde movements of Cubism, Futurism, Fauvism, and the like. At the center of this outrage was Duchamp's *Nude*, whose geometrical, mechanistic rendering of the rhythms and flows of its eponymous nude—establishing what the artist called "a static image of movement"[17]—both bemused and shocked the assembled public.

The critical backlash was hard and fast. Duchamp's painting immediately became the subject of countless parodies—*The New York Evening Sun*, for example, published a cartoon depicting "The Rude Descending the Staircase," while a contemporaneous exhibition included a work titled "Food Descending a Staircase"[18]—and was variously likened to "an explosion in a shingle factory" and "a collection of saddlebags."[19] Even President Theodore Roosevelt joined in the fray, attacking the work in a letter to *The Literary Digest* in which he unfavorably compared it to his own bathroom rug.[20]

Regardless of its notoriety, however, it is important to not lose sight of the fact that Duchamp's painting did not actually present its audience with anything authentically *new*. Whereas in breaking with the previous mimetic representational system several years earlier, cubism itself had introduced an element of real chaos into the artistic world—which is to say (in our own terms) that it caused a *real scandal*—the same can hardly be said of *Nude*, which contrarily essentially followed a number of already-established cubo-futurist ideas without really contributing much to them.[21] Indeed, were it not for the fact that it became the de facto "face" of the Armory Show, *Nude's* canonical status in the history of modern art would be far from assured.

Certainly, both *Nude Descending a Staircase No. 2* and the Armory Show more broadly redefined for a mass audience exactly what might constitute "art," exposing the preponderant myth of realism for the artificial construction it was. Yet the fact remains that the *real* chaos which accompanied Duchamp's painting pre-existed the work by a number of years. Indeed, we need to bear in mind here the difference between, on the one hand, art, and on the other, its audience (however "mass" this may be). For *Nude* itself did not give us anything new in terms of *art* per se. Rather, it pulled back the curtains on the broader "art world," revealing to its blushing audience how its body of works had sagged with age, and its pretenses toward grand ideals like "creativity" and "originality" now served to disguise a decidedly conventional outlook. In short, by publicly stripping art of its realist garb, *Nude* exposed the artifice that lay at the very heart of artistic practice.

Exactly one hundred years after the scandal of *Nude*, in March of 2013, musicians Robin Thicke and Pharrell Williams released the single *Blurred Lines* from Thicke's new album of the same name. The song quickly became the subject of intense controversy following accusations not only of plagiarism (Marvin Gaye's family would go on to successfully sue for copyright infringement of his 1977 song "Got to Give It Up," awarding Gaye the dubious distinction of posthumous partial songwriting credit) but moreover of sexism and misogyny. And for good reason: the song's lyrics—which Thicke half-joked were intended to be "completely derogatory toward women"[22]—can, at best, be described as a paean to the clichéd virgin-whore dichotomy, at worst, a justification for, and even endorsement of, date rape.

The controversy surrounding *Blurred Lines* only intensified with the release of its "uncensored" music video in which three female models—naked save for skin-colored G-strings—dance, strut, and act flirtatiously, while the fully clothed male musicians watch on wearing expressions variously affecting bemusement and bravado. Less than one week after its release, the video was taken down from YouTube—only to be reinstated three months later—while the song found itself subject to multiple bans from various public institutions (including numerous university campuses).

The *Blurred Lines* scandal did not peak however until later that year, when Thicke joined tween icon and former Disney star Miley Cyrus onstage to perform the song at the 2013 MTV Video Music Awards. While Thicke, suited and wearing sunglasses, essentially reprised the "cool" persona he had affected in the video, Cyrus stripped down to a nude latex bikini and spent the duration of the song twerking and gyrating against Thicke's crotch, simulating masturbation and doing her level best to kill off her wholesome "Hannah Montana" image. That the broadcast continuously cut to shots displaying the stunned and occasionally aghast faces of the celebrity audience only added to its impact. The effect on social media was immediate, with Cyrus and Thicke's performance generating upward of 360,000 tweets per minute, making it the most tweeted-about event since Twitter's inception in 2006.[23] The song itself would then go on to become the US' longest-running number one single of 2013, and one of the biggest selling singles of all time.[24]

Needless to say, as with Duchamp's *Nude*, *Blurred Lines* clearly presents us with nothing truly new. To the contrary, its sexual provocations merely repeat a well-established marketing formula (the obviousness of which hardly bears analysis), the song, music video, and VMA performance each being explicitly designed to attract controversy and "go viral": Thicke's manager conceded he intended the song to be banned quickly since "getting something banned actually helps you,"[25] while the video's director Diane Martel freely acknowledged that, far from being artistic, her motivation was expressly commercial and driven by marketing potential.[26]

Moreover, in order to forestall in advance some of the more damaging effects this controversy was sure to generate (while simultaneously adding fuel to the fire), the song even factored in a "plausible deniability" defense, by which it would be justified as "feminist" in intent. Williams, for example, repeatedly claimed that "if you're looking at the lyrics, the power is right there in the woman's hand," while simultaneously pointing out how "the visual [...] was written and directed by a woman. And it was her concept."[27] In cynically decrying sexism while delivering the very quintessence of misogynistic exploitation, *Blurred Lines* truly epitomizes the capitalist ideal of "having one's cake and eating it too."

While the respective scandals surrounding *Nude* and *Blurred Lines* certainly share many striking points of similarity—not least concerning their perceived immorality and vulgarity ("How could the quasi-reverential figure of the nude be so aesthetically disrespected!"; "How can such gratuitous nudity and sexual suggestion be exhibited in respectable public fora!")—it is clear that they nonetheless each represent fundamentally different forms of scandal. For whereas Duchamp's *Nude* exemplifies its essentially revelatory function (in a way that can hardly be understood as "corrupt"), *Blurred Lines* contrarily presents its dissimulative counterpart, in the distillation of one of capitalism's most basic tenets, namely, the simple fact that "sex sells."

Or again, if *Nude* takes us "behind the scenes," exposing realism as only a single *kind* of artistic practice (and not its alpha and omega), what *Blurred Lines* "reveals" is that there really is nothing "behind" capitalist interest: the "secret" is that there is no secret; profit literally *is* everything. Thus the controversial passage from *Nude* to *Blurred Lines* equally marks a second, no less contentious movement, being the scandalous succession of "revelation" with "retail."

## Different Perspectives

While recognizing that scandals exist on a spectrum and are themselves nuanced phenomena, let us nonetheless agree for now that the two ostensibly opposed conceptions of scandal we have thus far put forward constitute the dominant forms by which the phenomenon is generally understood to operate today. On the one hand, we have the scandal as revelation of some secret underlying "truth," as "throwing open the gates" and allowing us to see what has been hiding behind the walls.[28] While on the other, we have the scandal as serving to mask the very absence of truth: the fact that there is no truth to begin with, that everything that takes place is simply "business as usual" (and this "business" is finally nothing other than the relentless pursuit of profit).

If the former, revelatory model constitutes what we might think of as the ordinary or "intuitive" conception of scandal, that is, its immediate, uncritical (or even *pre*-critical) acceptance, then the latter, dissimulative version—by which the scandal fulfills the function of "retail" pure and simple—figures its more cynical and, we might even say, "academic" understanding.

Needless to say, we do not intend this rudimentary uncritical or cynical division to be understood as a value judgment. Nor, for that matter, is it put forward here as being in any way absolute or exhaustive. As we have already seen, it is perfectly possible, even common, for a scandal to fall into both camps at the same time. The presidency of Donald Trump represents a case in point: on the one hand, the innumerable scandals surrounding Trump reveal time and again a character of astonishing ineptitude and ignorance masquerading behind a façade of singular omnipotence and omniscience; at the same time, however, fewer would argue that this constant stream of scandals is not "good for (his) business," and that they in fact function to maintain—and even to a large extent *are*—his business model (together with that of countless other industries, including the otherwise endangered art of journalism itself).

Rather, by "uncritical" and "cynical," we are simply recalling what we said earlier concerning our spontaneous evaluation of scandals, and the way this serves to color our experience both *of* them and *in relation to* them. In practical terms, the division here refers to the degree to which this coloring takes effect. Whereas the revelatory model—with its emphasis on ideas like deception and disclosure (and, by extension, justice)—is in some ways the more "natural" position to assume, and to this end might even be characterized as naïve, the alternative "retailing" model contrarily adopts a deeply critical view, to the extent that it recognizes the scandalous revelation *as* dissimulation, and accordingly sees as its goal *the exposure of the exposure*, or the revelation of the dissimulation.

That we qualify this second position as "academic" simply reflects the fact that this "double exposure" is the remit of a good deal of academic criticism. And indeed, there are countless variations on this dissimulative theme spread throughout the whole of contemporary critical theory and philosophy—even while little of this work can accurately be classed as "scandal research"—from the ascetic and acerbic writings of Theodore Adorno and Max Horkheimer, through the divergent postmodernisms of Jean Baudrillard and Fredric Jameson, all the way up to the reconstituted dialectical materialism of Slavoj Žižek.[29]

And yet, for all their apparent differences, we can nonetheless observe how in both cases the underlying structure remains fundamentally the same, to wit, *a rupture with established social protocol is suddenly and fascinatingly made public*. To this end, the key difference between the revelatory and dissimulative models of scandal would seem to come down to a question of *intentionality*, that is, of which party has the most to gain from the exposure and, reciprocally, which has more to lose: the *scandalous* or the *scandalized*? Speaking in very broad terms, the revelatory model excoriates the former while enlightening the latter, whereas the dissimulative model contrarily enriches the former at the expense of the latter. (Obviously the degrees and modes of this excoriation, enlightenment, enrichment, and expense will vary considerably.)

This dual logic is in fact already present to some degree in orthodox scandal research, which likewise conceives of scandal simultaneously in terms of an authentic—and therefore justly *consequential*—event, and as a carefully orchestrated "staging process" where the "emotional mobilization of the public plays a crucial role."[30] Adut, for example, recognizes two dominant intellectual perspectives on scandal that roughly correspond to our own revelatory and dissimulative models, which he designates the "objectivist" and the "constructivist" positions. Briefly, the former, objectivist approach places greater weight on the transgressive component (which it effectively— if erroneously—reduces to a form of "corruption") and accordingly "treats scandals as the proverbial iceberg tip—as events in which the usually concealed corrupt components of social systems are revealed to the public."[31] By contrast, the latter, constructivist view "regards scandals as socially constructed phenomena and thus puts the stress on the public reactions to transgressions," an emphasis that, at its most extreme, recognizes scandal as "a moral panic fashioned or exploited by elites to manipulate mass perceptions."[32]

While each of these models has their attendant problems, and neither can be said to in any way provide a "full" account of scandal, they nevertheless fit neatly into the rudimentary definition of scandal we put forward earlier, namely, as "a mediated process that fascinates the public by proposing some violation of the given social-symbolic order."

Authentic revelation, objective phenomenon, social construction, cynical dissimulation: not only are each of these conceptions easily subsumed under the elementary logic of scandal, but, when taken together, in effect cover its entire spectrum, from naïve truth to cynical deception.[33]

# Chaos and Novelty

While we have thus far focused our attention on what we take to be the standard conceptions of scandal (as genuine revelation and as cynical dissimulation), the argument we will be pursuing from this point forward represents a significant break with this orthodox logic. The reasons for this are manifold. For one thing, while it is of course crucial that we are able to grasp the complicated mechanics underlying the process, simply pointing to the fact that scandals are, more often than not (and regardless of their relative authenticity), "good for business" can hardly be said to qualify as new information. Few would be surprised to hear, for example, that media advertising trades in unreasonably heightened and deliberately provocative sexual imagery, or that a salacious headline in an online newspaper will garner more clicks and drive up page traffic. Likewise, even the target audiences of tabloid and yellow journalism are at least to some degree aware of the sensationalist or even fabricated nature of the content they consume. We all know that "sex sells." We all know how clickbait works. We all know that "fantasy" and "framing" have a part (however large or small) to play in all news reporting—not least when the subject in question is a celebrity and, as such, already exists to some extent in the fantastical realm. There is accordingly little to be gained from rehearsing these arguments any further here.

More to the point, we have already said that the logic of scandal extends far beyond the basic intuitive and academic models outlined above. Indeed, regardless of whether we are talking "revelation" or "retail" (or "objective phenomenon" or "social construction" …), crucial to our argument is the idea that none of these conceptions should be understood as in any way constituting the essence or the true nature of scandal. For when we look closely, we can see how all of these entirely legitimate kinds of scandal are themselves, to a large extent, derivative of another, altogether more fundamental—and, it should be added, fundamentally rare—form of disruption, a disruption which, in its simultaneously revelatory and repressive force, essentially constitutes a kind of *chaos*.[1]

This is in fact precisely the word—"chaos"—that the great twentieth-century thinker Gilles Deleuze used for it, which he related to the necessarily creative work of philosophy, of science, and of art, areas of thought which, when practiced properly, "tear open the firmament and plunge into the chaos,"[2] bringing back with them concepts and ideas that disrupt and discredit contemporary doxa, throwing established opinion into turmoil.

Yet so too does it provide the conceptual (and, for that matter, etymological) background to the contemporary philosophy of Alain Badiou and, in particular, his theory of the "event"[3]—a key concept we have already touched on, and which we will return to throughout this book—which similarly deposes opinions and constituted knowledges, and which announces the arrival of something that is both radically *new* and immediately *universal*.

What we are talking about is the pure chaos that arises when something truly and utterly unexpected comes to pass, and in so doing causes the everyday order of things to not simply go awry, but in fact fall completely off the rails: when, philosophically speaking, there occurs something like a "kink" in the ontological order; when we come up against something—an object, an event, even an idea—that radically breaks not only with the status quo, but moreover with the very *state of things*, which is equally to say, with *the state itself*.

This notion of breaking with the logic of the "state"—and, correspondingly, the idea of there being an equivalency between the "state of things" and the "state itself"—is a point as crucial as it is complex. It is accordingly worth briefly pausing here to ask what the term actually means for us. So, to be clear, we are conceiving of the "state" here and throughout the book not simply as a straightforwardly political mechanism—the so-called machinery of the state comprising the government, bureaucratic and legal systems, the military, etc.—but rather as a broader homeostatic principle, namely, as *the stabilizing function proper to a given situation*. (It is for this reason that we will repeatedly make use of the cognate term "static," which so effectively captures this stabilizing property.) In this, we again follow the work of Badiou, for whom the "state" represents a crucial ontological category, designating the set of mechanisms that govern and dominate any given situation (political or otherwise), or the means by which an essentially static "regime of repetition"—a system which can only offer the *illusion of change*—is both established and maintained.

While we will examine this fundamentally structural conception of the state in some detail in Part Two, our immediate interest resides uniquely in its sudden *failure*, in the point at which it (or at least, a *part* of it) crumbles and collapses, causing the situation it oversees to descend into a temporary "state of chaos." Such is, after all, the disruption caused by the unexpected appearance of something truly new and unprecedented, that is, by an extraordinary moment of *real creation*.

To be sure, is there anything more scandalous or straightforwardly polemical—more immediately and enduringly *controversial*—than the historical existence of radical novelty itself? Be it a formal innovation that forces a total reassessment of the limitations as much as the possibilities of art (as for example in the cases of cubist and abstract painting), or a new scientific theory which compels us to fundamentally change our understanding of the world (such as the successive theories of relativity and quantum mechanics), or even an unforeseen amorous encounter that abruptly turns our life upside down (as so many of us have experienced when falling in love). Instances of real novelty such as these don't simply disrupt, but rather completely shatter existing economies of knowledge, bringing about a revolution in the way we understand the world.

This is in fact a basic rule of any and all authentic innovation, or what we have here been calling "real creation," so as to differentiate it from other, less divisive forms of "creativity" (on which we will have more to say shortly): the arrival of something truly and absolutely new demands that everything already established as "known" must now be reassessed and reordered in relation to its unexpected having-come-to-be. In effect, the "new" cannot take its place in the order of things without fundamentally disrupting or "chaoticizing" this order, and thereby ushering in a *new* (and as-yet undetermined) *order*.

Yet this radical upheaval—this sudden chaos brought about by the advent of the new—equally implies that, far from providing a sense of comfort and satisfaction, an encounter with real novelty is contrarily going to be a profoundly unsettling, even *traumatic*, experience: in shaking our foundations—in uprooting us from our "proper place" and re-placing us somewhere unfamiliar, somewhere "improper"—the "new" confronts us with the anguish of uncertainty, of unknowing, of unpreparedness, and of unfamiliarity.

All of which is to say that real creation—which, to be absolutely clear, we are here taking to be the *fons et origo* of authentic or "real" scandal, or what we might even call (given its "creative" roots) *original scandal*—is nothing less than the stripping away of our security blanket: the point where the brakes lock and we lose control of the vehicle, where all coordinates vanish and we can no longer tell "up" from "down," "left" from "right"[4]—in short: vertigo, impotence, *chaos*.

## Nothing Comes from Nothing

At the risk of interrupting our focus, it is worth momentarily pausing here to acknowledge the fact that many readers will immediately object to this idea of real creation (and, *ipso facto*, the concomitant notion of "real scandal"). They will object on the basis of a fundamental insight regarding the course of history itself, which is that everything, no matter how revolutionary or unexpected, can be shown to have a precedent: while it may be vague and indistinct, a path leading up to the event can always be mapped out after the fact. History is, after all, not a discreet series of disconnected episodes, but rather a continuum—one that advances according to an unfailing logic of cause and effect, and which subscribes to the ancient principle of *ex nihilo nihil fit*: "nothing comes from nothing."[5]

In addressing this, it is necessary to acknowledge a subtle but crucial philosophical postulate underlying our general argument, one that relates to the very idea of "nothing," and which boils down to the following: to declare that "nothing comes from nothing" is, so far as we are concerned, equally to affirm that *everything* comes from nothing (or even: that the one in effect means the other).

This is a complicated point—one around which many dense philosophical tomes have been constructed[6]—and something that we cannot hope to satisfactorily address here and now. Suffice for the moment to say that, far from being an essentially negative principle of pure inactivity or existential stasis, the thesis "nothing comes from nothing" is for us contrarily an assertion of radical productivity, less a statement of what *is not* than of what *is*—and, more importantly, of what *can be*.

Obviously, the last thing we want to do at this early stage is bog ourselves down in the complex line of reasoning that leads us to adopt this seemingly contradictory position. So rather than prematurely tying ourselves in knots with convoluted theoretical excurses, we will instead simply note that our overall philosophical approach is grounded in the idea that each and everything that is presented to us—or that is "given to experience"—originates from an unlocalizable and unrepresentable point of absolute a-substantiality and a-particularity, a point that can be said to constitute *absolutely nothing*. "Being," "chaos," "void," "real": these are just some of the names and concepts that have historically been used—and that we ourselves will be employing here—to make sense of this critical point, names and concepts which, while in no way equivalent, nonetheless exhibit a certain correspondence in so far as they each figure different ways of giving meaning to *nothingness itself* (or of making "sense" out of "ab-sense").[7]

To cut to the chase, our position is very much that things *do* happen, that every now and then, something actually *does* come from nothing, and that this not only takes place suddenly and randomly, but moreover does so with a complete and total disregard for social protocol and individual well-being. In fact, not only do we contend that these chance happenings are of crucial importance; we even go so far as to argue that they are, quite literally, the *only* things of any real consequence—strictly speaking, when it comes to the question of actual authentic creation, *nothing else matters*.

Yet this raises another possible point of contention, this time concerning the supernatural connotations attached to the concept of "real creation" or—it means the same thing—"radical novelty." The key problem being that these terms can easily be interpreted as camouflaging an essentially mystical occurrence that might otherwise be categorized under the antiphilosophical heading of "miracle." To this end, it is especially important that we be crystal clear on the following point: that the "new" is *radical* does not in any way mean that it is *miraculous*. We are not at all proposing here a form of divine or alchemical *creatio ex nihilo*. Quite the contrary, although it may at first sound incongruous or even outright illogical, the idea of real creation qua radical rupture is in effect ultimately grounded in a principle of *continuity*.

Indeed, contrary to its common acceptation (and seemingly flying in the face of much of what we have already said), the principal model on which we are basing our conception of real creation—this being Badiou's philosophy of the event and his formulation of the subject—should *not* be understood as proposing a straightforward or naïve division between conservative continuity and radical rupture. While each and every "event" involves a radical break with the "state of things," this does not mean that it entails a total disconnection from the broader context in which it takes place. Simply put, an event represents a rupture with the *state* of the situation, not the situation itself. To employ a sporting metaphor, while the state of play may be suspended or even upended, the field on which the game is played remains, for all intents and purposes— for a time at least—the same.[8]

But we are clearly getting ahead of ourselves, touching on ideas and concepts for which we cannot as yet provide adequate justification. And so, in drawing this section to a close, let us simply spell out the following: first, that one of our central philosophical concerns throughout this book will be to pay very close attention to what it really means to be *nothing*; and second, that one of our key assumptions is that while the new assuredly breaks with the old, this does not mean that it emerges from some mysterious "elsewhere"; rather, our contention is that the one is *immanent* to the other. Needless to say, we will be looking at all of this closely in due course.

## Creating Controversy

Returning once again to our general argument, how then do we move from the fundamentally traumatic experience associated with radical novelty or real creation—where we are confronted with the angst of absolute uncertainty and instability—to the essentially comforting and reassuring conception of scandal we were discussing only moments ago?

It is at this point that we arrive at the real meat of the matter. For one of the key conceptual hypotheses underlying this book is that the converse conceptions of scandal we put forward above as figuring the dominant forms by which this phenomenon is generally understood to operate today—i.e., as "revelation of the real" and as "dissimulative marketing exercise" (conceptions we argued broadly echo the chaos brought about by instances of real creation)—are today increasingly being supplemented with, and even supplanted by, another, far more pervasive and altogether more insidious form of scandal, one that is concerned less with the direct accumulation of capital, and still less with exposing the hidden maneuverings and manipulations that take place behind closed doors, than it is with shoring up the base mechanisms of power in the form of *control* and of *regulation*.

What we are talking about here is the fabrication of controversy not simply in the place of, but moreover *in the form of the real*—controversy manufactured *as* real. Or in other words: less the inauthentic reproduction of a "genuine" scandalous revelation (as per the standard dissimulative model) than the calculated—and fundamentally counterproductive—*reproduction of the original scandal's very authenticity*, not "real scandal" but *the scandal "as" real*.

Now, as with our earlier interjection concerning the "state," the difficult and potentially obscure nature of this last point begs a question, which in this instance is: what exactly do we mean by the "real"? So, just to be clear: we understand the "real" as referring not to "objective reality" (which might in any case be better rendered, with Deleuze, as the "actual"), but rather to something closer approximating "anobjective" reality, or better yet *an objection to* reality. Indeed, the "real" designates what is constitutive of reality *without being represented as such*; it is, in effect, the elusive rock on which "reality" is both founded and founders. Here we follow the thought of Jacques Lacan in particular, who conceives of the real in terms of both "*anti*-meaning" and "*ante*-meaning,"[9] as that which "resists symbolization absolutely"[10] while at the same time allowing signification to proceed in the first place. Moreover, the real is also what *interrupts* or "chaoticizes" this process by the fact that it "admits something *new*."[11]

While we will of course be exploring this critical concept in some detail in the coming chapters, for now it is enough to recognize how, in saying that this supplementary mode of scandal adopts the *form of the real*, we contend that it paradoxically mimics a schismatic act of radical transformation precisely in order to (re)produce its very opposite, namely, *stasis*: the static calm of pure continuity. Or to be even more exact: the phenomenon of controversy is here used to replicate the disruptive *affects* of radical creation—of an actual encounter with the rawness of the real—without, for all that, actually presenting us with anything truly new. To the contrary, what we bear witness to is nothing other than the production of the simulacrum of novelty—where "simulacrum" is understood in the classical Platonic (as opposed to, for example, the Baudrillardian) sense[12]—the sole purpose of which is to stand in for, and thereby short-circuit, if not outright eliminate, the very possibility of real creation and the threat this entails. In short, it is an attempt to *annex the real itself.*

Key to our overall argument then is this idea of the simulacral scandal as marking a direct response to the real; that while the chaos and disruption which accompany real scandals make them anathema to the prevailing order, this sudden suspension of the state's ordinary functioning has in turn led to its contemporary "solution" in the form of the simulacrum of novelty: a kind of static production of controversy which is sterile, sanitized, and toothless; one that mimics the affects of creation without delivering any of its effects, giving us "novelty" devoid of "newness," "reality" minus the "real," and, fundamentally, "controversy" without "scandal," the creation of an ironically scandal-less controversy.

This ineludibly static fabrication of controversy will of course constitute one of the principal concerns of this book. In particular, our focus will be on the ways that the powers that be (whatever form these forces may take), in failing to accommodate or comprehend acts of radical creation—acts which are, in their eyes, both illegal and incomprehensible—instead work to pacify them by simulating a single, albeit crucial, aspect of such novelty, being its violent rupture with the laws governing the situation, by producing a kind of *state-sanctioned controversy.*

Creativity without creation, form without content, affect without effect: in the conservative fight to maintain the status quo, it is controversy that is winning out over consensus, and the engine of this victory has been none other than the scandal itself.

## The Blind Man

It is high time that we once again attempted to clarify much of what we have been saying through recourse to historical illustration. In doing so, we will reprise the approach taken in the previous chapter by considering two separate artistic examples separated from each other by a timeline of exactly one hundred years.

First let us rewind to April of 1917, where the Society of Independent Artists is about to stage its first annual exhibition at the Grand Central Palace in New York. Following the precedent set by the Armory Show four years earlier, the lead up to the event has seen the Society—of which Duchamp is a founding member—effectively proclaim its independence from the artistic status quo (or the "state of art"): its slogan is "no jury, no prizes," while its regulations effectively state that each of its members (meaning anyone who paid the six dollar membership fee) is obliged to exhibit a work in the show. The stage is perfectly set for Duchamp—who by this point had not only moved to America but also resolved to "stop being a painter in the professional sense"[13]—to give birth to the "readymade."

Unlike *Nude*, however, this time the labor had been long and involved. As Duchamp would later recall, it was four years earlier (around the time of the Armory Show) that he first "had the happy idea to fasten a bicycle wheel to a kitchen stool and watch it turn,"[14] establishing (if only for himself) what might retrospectively be considered the first of these infamous objects, *Bicycle Wheel*. While other similar works were "produced" by Duchamp in the intervening years—e.g., 1914's *Bottle Rack*, 1915's *In Advance of a Broken Arm*, and 1916's *Comb* being three now well-known examples—none of these were put on display as such, but rather remained gathering dust in his private studio.

And so it was not until 1917 that the readymade truly came into existence, when, working under the pseudonym "Richard Mutt," Duchamp attempted to enter an industrially fabricated urinal he had christened "*Fountain*" into the Society's inaugural exhibition. While appearing at first as little more than a failed prank—not only was the urinal refused entry, but it was almost immediately lost (all that remains of the original "work" itself is a photograph taken by Alfred Stieglitz)—this (non)exhibition is now generally understood to be, alongside the great inventions of cubism and abstraction, one of if not *the* defining artistic event of the twentieth century, one that did not simply introduce us to a new mode or form of artistic practice, but rather fundamentally changed the very idea of art itself.[15]

Exactly how this came to pass is testament to the scandalous nature of real creation. For when Duchamp's attempt to exhibit *Fountain* proved unsuccessful, this immediately gave the lie to both the Society's "avant-garde" credentials and its supposed "independence" from the artistic establishment, in as much as *Fountain*—or, more specifically, its *rejection,* its "illegality" in the eyes of the state—made the jury's hidden presence only too explicit: the work's refusal clearly contradicted the "democratic" claim of the exhibition and revealed the Society's underlying conformity with, and lack of genuine independence from, the very institutions that represented the current "state" of art.

While all of this only took place (quite literally) "behind the scenes"—the work itself remaining secreted behind a partition for the duration of the exhibition[16]—it quickly became a public scandal after a brief article defending the work appeared in the publication *The Blind Man* which not only articulated the philosophy behind the piece, but also included a photograph of the rejected work captioned "The Exhibit Refused by the Independents."[17] In this way, Duchamp paradoxically did succeed in exhibiting his urinal, in a manner of speaking, through the very act of denouncing the fact that it was not exhibited in the first place. Or in other words, the article in *The Blind Man* essentially ensured that the non-appearance of *Fountain* would be retroactively rendered intensely apparent through the subsequent *exhibition of its very non-exhibition.*

Of crucial importance here is the fact that the reasons given for *Fountain* being rejected in the first place—namely, that the object was not fabricated by the artist and that it was not even an original (i.e., unique) work at all[18]— were the very same reasons Duchamp gave for its being accepted *as* art. For what the work revealed is that all of the bits and pieces that go into making an artwork—all of those base elements which, while absolutely present (as its material substrate), nevertheless fail to be *re-presented* in the completed "work of art"—are themselves, in a very real sense, readymade objects.[19] This is, after all, Duchamp's fundamental point: the readymade lays claim to being a work of art for the simple reason that, on a quasi-ontological level, *all art is necessarily readymade.*

Not content with breaking with the state and redefining the identity of art, the readymade then equally serves as a treatise on the idea of *creation* itself. Because what *Fountain* so perfectly demonstrates is that impurity is in fact a necessary condition—even a fundamental law—of art, for the simple reason that "real" art—which, we should point out, is an extraordinarily rare commodity—always involves the formalization or the coming-into-form of what was previously formless, the radical becoming-art of what had heretofore been considered non-art (or what, according to the artistic world in question, *did not previously exist*).[20]

It is moreover precisely for this reason that any real artwork will, of necessity, appear in the situation at first as absolutely and unfathomably *abstract*, hence as an object of scandal. After all, real art, in its essential novelty, necessarily appears in the first instance as something wholly abstract to the world in which it emerges—such abstraction deriving from the fact that it falls outside of the realm of available knowledges.[21] (Suffice to recall here *The New York Times* initial assessment of cubism as comprising "pictures before which descriptive adjectives retreat in disorder.")[22] And as we have already seen, it is precisely this unknowability that underlies a real artwork's controversial nature, in as much as real scandal figures the immediate effect—or the "social consequence"—of a sudden rupture with the state of things, due to the arrival in the world of something which is fundamentally chaotic and unassimilable, in the form of the radically *new*.

As Guy Debord would write almost fifty years later in his "Situationist Manifesto," "under the existing dominant society, which produces the miserable pseudo-games of non-participation, a true artistic activity is necessarily classed as criminality. It is semi-clandestine. *It appears in the form of scandal*."[23] Accordingly, that *Fountain* was so scandalous had less to do with its vulgarity, its audacity, or even its banality, than with the fact that it proclaimed—of and for itself—a single, inadmissible truth: that it *really was art*.

## A Convenient Truth

Exactly one hundred years after *Fountain*'s rejection, in late February of 2017, the eighty-ninth Academy Awards found itself, for the third year in a row, the subject of intense scrutiny over the question of racial diversity among its nominees in the major categories. That not a single actor of color had received a nomination in any of the main acting categories over the past two years had prompted a major social media backlash under the hashtag #OscarsSoWhite, leading to calls to boycott the ceremony. Yet the 2017 event had seen a record-breaking six black actors put forward, together with one of Indian descent, amounting to at least one minority group being represented in each of the four main acting categories. Moreover, the all-important "best picture" award was shaping up to be a competition between Damien Chazelle's homage to all-things-Hollywood, *La La Land*, and Barry Jenkins's coming of age drama, *Moonlight*.

The firm favorite leading up to the event was *La La Land*, having landed a record-tying fourteen nominations (matching the number set by Joseph L. Mankiewicz's 1950 meta-drama *All about Eve* and James Cameron's 1997 blockbuster *Titanic*), while *Moonlight*—which featured an all-black cast, dealt with LGBT issues and, compared to its eight fellow nominees, had grossed the smallest amount in terms of box office—was the clear underdog.[24]

Needless to say, that *La La Land* was the Awards' favorite came as no surprise. An unthreatening pastiche of the Hollywood musicals of the 1940s and 1950s, the film's use of jazz as a metaphorical substitute for the cinema itself allowed it to offer up a commentary, in equal measure melancholic and hagiographic, on the latter's increasing anachronism in the digital age. Few could doubt that the Academy would relish such a self-congratulatory (and equally self-pitying) fairy tale.

Yet in substituting "cinema," a medium whose historical milestones have all-too frequently been marked by overt racism (think of D. W. Griffith's 1915 panegyric on the Ku Klux Klan, *The Birth of a Nation*), with "jazz," a quintessentially African-American art form which, given the context, ineluctably evokes Alan Crosland's 1927 blackface "talkie" *The Jazz Singer* (another example of cinema's stunningly racist milestones)—and in featuring in the lead roles the alabaster pairing of Ryan Gosling and Emma Stone (who had only recently attracted controversy for playing a woman of part-Chinese, part-Hawaiian ancestry in Cameron Crowe's 2015 film *Aloha*)—*La La Land* equally opened itself up to multiple charges of "whitewashing."

Thus the final showdown was set to be a literally "black–and–white" affair, in which a critically lauded African-American film dealing with traditionally "difficult" subject matter faced off against an audience-pleasing celebration of all-things-Hollywood explicitly designed to rekindle within the movie-going public a sense of the forgotten magic of cinema.

Given the stakes, it seemed fairly obvious to everyone which of the two films the Academy would rather come out on top, and fewer were surprised when *La La Land* was announced the winner. Yet even as the film's key players were finishing their acceptance speeches, the stage erupted into chaos with members of the law firm Price Waterhouse Coopers interrupting proceedings to frantically whisper to the assembled cast and crew, before one of the film's producers finally seized the microphone to declare *Moonlight* the "true" winner.

The entire scene could hardly have been scripted better: that Jenkins's *Moonlight*, the ultimate underdog, with its all-black cast and LGBT themes, should win out over Chazelle's snow-white *La La Land*—and under such dramatic circumstances—was almost too perfect to be true. And that the error was immediately picked up and selflessly rectified by the very same honorable white men whose film synecdochally represented Hollywood as a whole—and, moreover, that they did so at the expense of their own personal glory—only heightened the drama. All in all, the event appeared to radically upend and transform the situation, finally setting right the Academy's previous eighty-eight years of shameful bigotry and racial discrimination, and elevating "liberal Hollywood" over and above the prevailing Trumpian politics of hatred and division.[25] Real sportsmanship, real honor, real transformation: amid all the chaos and scandal that had engulfed the Academy (and indeed, the whole of America), finally, Hollywood succeeded in creating a real moment of grace.

Or at least, this was how the narrative surrounding the event played out. Yet if the case of Duchamp's *Fountain* teaches us anything, it is that real creation only takes place when something that was radically suppressed—such that it altogether fails to appear (and thus counts *as* nothing)—suddenly, somehow, finds absolute expression. That this "revelation" is necessarily scandalous and generates controversy arises, we have said, from the twin facts that, on the one hand, its sudden presentation is utterly unsanctioned (i.e., it radically breaks with the strictures of the state) and, on the other, there exists no framework according to which it might be judged. Artistically speaking, it falls "outside" of aesthetics; it is, as Badiou might put it, fundamentally *inaesthetic*.

Now, on a superficial reading, this is of course precisely what took place at the Academy Awards: with *Moonlight*'s dramatic win, the situation of African-American cinema, which had till this point been consistently suppressed or "unpresented" by the "state of cinema" (as embodied by the Academy), suddenly achieved maximum representation. Yet it is, at the same time, essential to recognize that this "absolute expression" did not in fact occur on its own terms, but rather was endorsed by—and even a *direct product of*—the state itself, insofar as this declaration obviously reflected a conscious decision made on behalf of the Academy's governing body.

More than this, far from existing beyond judgment—which, as we have seen, is the *sine qua non* of real creation (and hence real scandal)—*Moonlight*'s win can contrarily be understood to mark the *triumph of judgment itself*. After all, what is an "Awards Show" if not a celebration of the fundamental transparency of "judgment"—its absolute, objective, "measurability"? To employ another of Badiou's technical terms, what we see here is a case of absolute "excrescence," or of statist representation *without self-presentation*—something that is further hammered home by the fact that the award was benevolently "re-gifted" by the very people whose work represented or "stood in for" the state itself.

While the scandal of Duchamp's work concerned the fact that it took the neglected non-artistic foundation of art itself and literally placed it on a pedestal, the scandal of the Oscars "best picture" award contrarily revolved around the mollifying recognition that *there was no scandal*: that African-American cinema *was* indeed being well represented at the state level, and that there was, accordingly, no cause for concern, that the issues raised by *Moonlight* (and, more broadly, the #OscarsSoWhite movement) could now be quickly forgotten. In a word: that despite the controversy, there was "nothing to see here." The contrast with our preceding example is especially stark: what *Fountain*'s "loss" exposed, *Moonlight*'s win concealed.

To this end, far from being a victory for African-American cinema, the Academy's awarding the best picture to *Moonlight* contrarily represented the triumph of the existing order. This "victory" took place on multiple levels. First and most obviously, it served to re-legitimize the Oscars (thus consolidating its own power) by declaring their universal *inclusivity* (and, of course, by generating an enormous amount of scandal-related free publicity). Second, it functioned to re-legitimize Hollywood cinema more broadly, rendering it once again "contemporary" and "culturally relevant" (thus accomplishing exactly what its erstwhile rival, *La La Land*, had set out to do). And third, it ensured that, in a volatile situation demanding that real change take place, *nothing would actually happen*. Rather, what the world bore witness to was the mere *appearance* of transformation in the guise of state-approved controversy.

Ultimately, the scandal of the eighty-ninth Academy Awards was that there was no real scandal, only its simulacral variant. What took place—regardless of the intentionality of the people and even (perhaps) the organizations involved—amounted in the end to nothing less than a re-legitimization of the prevailing order through the fabrication of a state of chaos, the pretense of scandal masquerading as the façade of change.

Part Two

# Foundations

# Grounds for Annulment

We have said that scandals, in the generic sense—together with the controversy that surrounds them—have come to exert a paradoxically tranquilizing effect on our lives. Such is the great irony of our times, where what once marked a site of disruption—a point where established rules and conventions broke down, or where the "law" had clearly (if covertly) been transgressed—now increasingly functions as a form of regulation, instructing us on how to act, think, and even feel.

This is arguably the case irrespective of their constituent form: regardless of whether we are talking "revelation of the real" or "dissimulative marketing exercise," the end result is hardly distinguishable, being essentially *more of the same*.

To be sure, the scandalous "revelation" today almost invariably marks not the exception to the rule but rather the rule itself: that the hedge fund manager steals his client's money is not an aberration but rather a confirmation of the substratal law of greed and self-interest under advanced capitalism; likewise, that such-and-such politician is caught leading a double-life only confirms the hypocrisy and duplicity inherent to the functioning of party politics (and the system of representative democracy more broadly). Similarly, to take up another still-recent concrete example, while disgraced Hollywood mogul Harvey Weinstein's gross abuses of women and power are certainly abhorrent, they are in no way aberrant, as the enormity of the allegations that have galvanized the #MeToo movement makes only too clear.

"Revelation" or "retail," "exposure" or "enterprise": either way, we always find ourselves on the end of a sales pitch, one that essentially sells us the system as it stands—the self-same system whose constitutive inequities and aporiae not only allowed for but moreover *generated* the scandal in the first place.[1] This is, in fact, precisely how Badiou conceives of scandal, namely, as "something which is useful to the system because it presents, as an exception, the rule itself."[2] It is furthermore for this very reason that "from time to time a scandal is required, not at all as a revelation of the real, but as the staging of a very small piece of the real itself *in the role of an exception to reality*":[3] what the scandal signifies, in so far as it represents an exception to the rule, is that the rule itself—i.e., the system as it stands—is fundamentally good and honest. In this way, the scandal serves to perpetuate the very system whose corruption it presumes to expose.

## System Failure

And yet, every now and then, the system really does break down. Once in a proverbial blue moon something truly and shockingly unprecedented *happens*, short-circuiting these promotional activities and showing them up for the covert advertisements they actually are: an authentically scandalous event— an instance of real, disruptive creation—unexpectedly and inexplicably takes place, and the inferior product is exposed for what it truly is by the sudden arrival of the Real Deal.

This injection of actual chaos into the world marks something like a moment of "system failure," a point where the state—if only for a moment— loses control and is forced onto the back foot. That this crisis of authority should bring about something akin to a state of emergency is, moreover, less a likely eventuality than an inevitability, even a structural requirement. For just as chaos is the enemy of stasis, likewise the new is anathema to the state: a cancer on the system, it must be immediately identified and excised; all trace of it must be eradicated.

The basic reasoning here is, as we have seen, fairly straightforward: in disrupting established economies of knowledge, the new presents a clear and present threat to the "natural order" and must be dealt with accordingly. Yet this is obviously far easier said than done. After all, how to deal with something which is absolutely unforeseeable, that is both radically unknown and completely unprecedented? (These being, after all, the very hallmarks of "real" or "authentic" novelty.) This is the immediate challenge faced by the state in confronting the *real scandal*, the "skandalon" or "stumbling block" of the new[4]: how to prevent or rule out something that is itself not subject to rules, that is *inherently unruly*?

The answer, we have suggested, has been to hijack the process itself. Hence the principal argument orienting this book, namely, that (1) the fundamentally conservative function of much contemporary scandal is ultimately a result of the statist fabrication of controversy not simply in the place of but moreover in the form of the real, and (2) the purpose of such regulative or "state-sanctioned" controversy is finally to stand in for—and thereby neutralize—the very possibility of real creation and the threat it entails, thus to *cover over the real itself*. Simply put, by laying claim to the very idea of "creation," the state has effectively staged a hostile takeover of the real, replacing actual chaos with a kind of camouflaged order—a "counterfeit chaos" that has real method in its madness.

If this predicament sounds vaguely familiar—as it undoubtedly will to readers familiar with any number of the canonical works of critical thought of the past century (from Herbert Marcuse's denunciation of late-capitalist "one-dimensional thinking," to Jean-François Lyotard's influential analysis of the "postmodern condition," to Baudrillard's infamous assessment of the first Gulf War)[5]—this is because it represents the continuation of a project that has in fact been steadily underway for some time now. Indeed, if the total submission to commercialist demand that came to increasingly define the twentieth century led to the substitution of the "radically new" with the more market-friendly (albeit syntactically nonsensical) "new *and improved*"—such that continuity could be strategically concealed behind a mask of endless "innovation"—then the contemporary supersession of the authentically new by the simulacrum of novelty marks not only this project's ultimate realization, but furthermore its *absolutization*, its extension to every single aspect of contemporary existence.

So while it is hardly "new" to observe the ongoing substitution of genuine innovation with bogus novelty in the service of capital—and here I am of course pre-empting obvious criticism of my own claim to originality[6]—there is, nevertheless, a pressing need to disclose the trifold relation that obtains between the practice of (both real and simulacral) *creation*, the operation of the *state*, and the form and function of *scandal*.

This in turn will allow us to see how the universal expansion of the longstanding commercialist (or, more simply, capitalist) project of "pacifying the new"—aided in no small part by game-changing developments in technology (in particular, the rise of the internet and media and communications industries)—not only constitutes the key statist development of the still-nascent twenty-first century, but has moreover led to the effective substitution of the controversial "creative act" with the essentially static act of "creating controversy."

All of which is to say that the foremost scandal of our times—the "scandal of scandals," if you will—is nothing other than the statist appropriation or annexation of the scandal itself.

## Encircling the Real

Before proceeding down this path any further, it is obviously essential that we define our key terms so as to bring some precision to our investigation. In particular, it is crucial that we develop a firm grasp of what it means for something to (suddenly, incalculably …) *happen*—as well, of course, of why exactly this leads to a "system breakdown." Yet in order to come to terms with any of this, we first need to have an understanding of what the "system" in question actually *is*. Clearly there is much ground to cover here.

To this end, the bulk of this section will be given over to presenting the philosophical foundations of our argument, so as to provide us with a firm basis on which to build our case. And where better to begin this process than by zeroing in on the most elementary (and indeed, elemental) of our key concepts—the one that, in effect, determines, both in theory and in practice, all four of the forms of scandal we have encountered thus far—namely, the *real* itself: what exactly do we mean by the real? And what, for that matter, makes a scandal "real"?

As is so often the case, the best way to go about answering a question like this is to first consider what it is *not*—not least because, as we will see, one of its simplest formulations is the one given by Jacques Lacan in the very first of his famous "seminars," in which he identifies the real as the point at which meaning itself falters, as being that which "resists symbolization absolutely."[7]

For one thing, the real is not at all the same as "nature": it is not some idealized authentic or harmonious state that has been successively eroded and elided by the administrative and technological excesses of modern life. To the contrary, nature is as much a component of "reality" (which, as we suggested previously, should not be confused with the real itself) as is its transformation and corruption through human industry.

Yet neither does it represent the world's overriding organizational logic, the regulatory framework that governs our very existence (whether through consensus or coercion). Indeed, were this the case, then, in the current global context, it would mark the real out as being nothing other than the *economy*, under whose all-powerful sway any and everything is now held (not least of all politics, which we know, does nothing but cede to the demands of "economic reality"). Let us be perfectly clear on this point: the economy is, categorically and unequivocally, *not* the real.[8]

Nor does it refer to the "true" shape of the contemporary world, its allegedly anemic and atrophying condition, obscured from view by layer upon layer of simulation (the monotonous generation of wall-to-wall advertisements, digitized distractions, and so on). No, we are not envisioning here some devastated, apocalyptic version of reality, such as the dystopian "desert of the real" of contemporary science fiction and postmodern philosophy alike.[9]

Nor, for that matter, does the real point to some hidden seat of power issuing orders from the shadows, manipulating the highest levels of elected office and steering global affairs in its own desired direction. It would, for example, be a gross mistake to misperceive the real as representing the conspiratorial "deep state" of paranoid ideologues on either side of the political divide. Likewise, we are far from the insidious world of public relations propagandism, what Sigmund Freud's nephew Edward Bernays famously prescribed as the means of ensuring "the engineering of consent [toward] socially constructive goals and values."[10]

Finally, and somewhat repetitiously (if only so that we might truly hammer our "non-empirical" point home), the real is most assuredly not just another name for constitutive reality, that is, for the elementary of the situation, or what is simply given to experience (even if this is not always explicitly presented to us as such).

Rather, when we speak of the real, we are concerned first and foremost— though this is not at all to say *exclusively*—with what we might think of as reality's "abstract essence": its seemingly indivisible and inaccessible core, or what we earlier referred to in terms of "anobjective reality." This is, more or less, the general way we understand the real today: as constituting what the early twentieth-century chemist and philosopher Emile Meyerson—who Lacan himself invokes in his first published use of the term (and in a work approved by no less than Albert Einstein)[11]—called "an ontological absolute."[12] Philosophically speaking, the real must then be integrally related (though this is not to say *identical*) to the question of *being*.[13]

Now, "being" itself is an ancient philosophical concept. Indeed, according to Aristotle, it is the principal object of "First Philosophy," or of ontology proper, in so far as ontology designates the study of—or the discourse on—being qua being.[14] In substance, it refers to the most general or basic characteristic that any and every thing possesses in order to exist or to *be*, that is, to be counted as *a* being, or as a single and unique entity. "Being" is then, quite literally, the most abstract of concepts; if it is anything at all, it is, as Hegel says, "pure indeterminateness and emptiness."[15] Or again: concerning being, "there is *nothing* to be intuited in it"; technically speaking, it is not "something" but "is in fact *nothing*, and neither more nor less than *nothing*."[16]

To this end, one of the easiest ways to come to grips with the concept of being is through a simple thought experiment, such as the following: imagine an object, any object—a small dog, a mountain range, a patch of wallpaper, a cloud, your best friend, a soccer ball, a glass of fine wine. Now imagine that we can strip away each and every one of this object's properties, everything that establishes the object as *this* object and not another, abolishing its entire identity and gradually annulling it to the point of its being, in effect, nothing. Void and vacant, emptied of all content, all that can now be said of this de-objectified object is that it simply *is*. This indistinct remainder is precisely what marks out the very *being* of the object, its underlying existential elementarity. So "being qua being" (i.e., being itself, or being *as such*) is then basically another way of saying "pure being," or being that purely and simply *is*, divorced from all of its particular qualities and attributes.

As indicated above, the way that we will be using the term "real" throughout this book is integrally related to this notion of indistinct, anonymous being, and is for the most part derived, on the one hand, from the influential structuralist psychoanalyst (and self-described "antiphilosopher")[17] Jacques Lacan and, on the other, from the contemporary philosophy of Alain Badiou. Broadly speaking, our position is that while it is Lacan who most immediately and insistently calls our attention to the real, it is Badiou who finally "makes sense" of it.

Accordingly, we must begin our search for an answer to the question "what does the real mean" with a difficult and seemingly tangential theoretical excursus (though its relevance will increasingly become clear), by first considering Lacan's own formulation of this key concept, before diving headlong into Badiou's intricate philosophical system to examine the crucial role it plays therein.

## Impossible Nonsense

To cut straight to the chase, it is well known that Lacan, in his teachings, distinguished between three registers or "orders" of experience, which he conceived of as the imaginary, the symbolic, and the real. While these orders are themselves fundamentally heterogeneous, all three are nonetheless inextricably bound together in a manner analogous to that of a Borromean knot (where if one of the three strands or orders were to somehow become separated from the others then the whole knot would fail, effectively causing the entire structure to collapse).

Reductively, the imaginary can be said to designate the realm of constructed appearance or of (re)semblance, or as Lacan succinctly puts it, "everything that is artificially reproduced."[18] Psychoanalytically speaking, the imaginary is accordingly the domain of the ego and of specular identification—things that are precisely what analysis seeks to problematize (though it must be said that, for all the controversy it generates, actual psychoanalytic practice is itself of no real interest to us here).

The symbolic, on the other hand, designates the structural field that underpins the imaginary, literally composing it through the function of language. As such, it constitutes the level of law and order, being, at base, the extensive network of signifiers which provides the coordinates that determine what we ("imaginarily") experience as "reality." Or in other words, if the imaginary designates "everything that is artificially reproduced," then the symbolic is this *artificial production itself.*

Taken together, the imaginary and the symbolic can then be said to comprise the whole of "reality" as such: its form and its content (or alternatively: its signifier and signified, or its base and superstructure …). In addition to this, it is important to note that both orders (once again, quite literally) *make sense* not simply because they are in equal measure logical and comprehensible, but more importantly due to the fact that they are themselves exactly what generate intelligible meaning or "sense" in the first place. Strictly speaking, it is meaningless to posit something as standing outside of, or apart from, these registers, for the simple reason that their interaction is what defines and delimits meaning in the first place.

Yet this is precisely where the real that we are interested in is located: outside of the imaginary-symbolic matrix, thus *outside of sense*. As a matter of fact, as we intimated earlier, it is this radically non-sensical property which serves as one of the real's most elementary definitions, namely, as a direct obstacle to sense (or more specifically, as "the logical obstacle of what, in the symbolic, declares itself to be impossible").[19] It is for this reason that Lacan variously refers to it as a "blind spot," an "end point," a "point of impact and of aporia," and—most tellingly for us—a "stumbling block."[20] Without getting too far ahead of ourselves, this last point in particular speaks directly to the scandalous nature of the real itself: to the fact that the one necessarily implicates the other, even to the possibly tautological nature of *"real scandal."*

But more on this later. For now, let us simply note how, lying beyond both the imaginary and the symbolic, the real emerges as what simultaneously *exceeds* and *precedes* these orders. Or as Lacan explains (with somewhat uncharacteristic clarity and concision), "the real must be conceived as the expulsion of meaning, as the *impossible* as such, the repulsion of meaning; even the repulsion of meaning into *anti*-meaning or *ante*-meaning."[21]

And yet, in spite of its non-sensical, meaningless nature, the real nonetheless does have a key role to play in the constitution of reality (in addition, of course, to its inaugural function as *ante*-meaning), one that derives from its fundamentally ruptive or "scandalous" relationship with the symbolic. In short, unlike the symbolic—which essentially comprises "a chain of signifiers that repeats"[22] and is accordingly governed by a logic of "the same"—the real admits the possibility of *radical change*. On this point, Lacan is once again mercifully clear: the real is distinguished from the symbolic (and, by extension, the imaginary) "by the fact that its economy admits of something altogether *new*, which is precisely the *impossible*."[23]

To explain: while the real functions as an absolute and insurmountable obstacle to meaning (qua signification), it nonetheless can, on occasion, make its presence powerfully felt, specifically in the form of a disruptive and disturbing *encounter*.[24] This chance encounter with the real—"the impact with the obstacle,"[25] where meaning and anti- or ante-meaning collide—interrupts repetition, short-circuiting the otherwise automatic unfolding of the symbolic by introducing an element of pure contingency into the otherwise staid level of necessity[26]: all of a sudden, something completely unprecedented *happens*, and things can never be quite the same again.

Yet the very nature of the real (as "impossible stumbling block" qua "obstacle to sense," as absolute non-sense or "ab-sense")[27] means that this novel encounter is not only necessarily *missed*, but moreover experienced in the guise of *trauma*. To quote Lacan again, "The function [...] of the real as encounter—the encounter in so far as it may be missed, in so far as it is essentially the missed encounter—first present[s] itself [...] in the form of that which is *unassimilable* in it—in the form of the trauma."[28] (Forecasting yet again, we can already see here how the real as impossible—now hypostasized as *the* impossible, or as the radically and disturbingly new—is intrinsically related to the concept of scandal as an effect of the introduction of authentic novelty.)

That our individual or subjective experience of the real takes the form of a traumatic missed encounter is then a direct result of its objective (lack of) determination. It is "missed" because, being radically un-symbolizable, it cannot be apprehended as such; it eludes or "misses out" on being grasped as meaning (which, as "absent cause," it nonetheless instigates). And it is "traumatic" in so far as, in disturbing the (fundamentally repetitive) functioning of the symbolic, it violently upsets the order of things, establishing a state of intense *dis-order*.

So to sum up, the real is for Lacan intrinsically *meaningless* (it simultaneously exceeds and precedes meaning) and hence *impossible* (or rather, it introduces the possibility of something *new*, something "other" to what is already known or "makes sense"). Moreover, it takes the shape of a radically contingent (and necessarily "missed") *encounter*, which, in disrupting the established order, is endured as a *trauma*. Or to put all of this another way: our sole experience of the real comes in the form of *a traumatic encounter with an impossible ab-sense*.

On a final note, as both anti- and ante-meaning, the real is for Lacan only intellectually (as opposed to experientially) discernible *retroactively*, on the basis of its resistance to symbolization. That being said, it can nonetheless be approached through mathematical formalization or, more specifically, through "an *impasse* of formalization"[29]—through mathematics' inscription of its own constitutive gaps and aporiae. We will return to this important idea shortly.

## The Scandal of Being

We have said that the properly philosophical (as opposed to antiphilosophical) articulation of the real is found in the question of *being*. Far from being settled, however, this question is itself the subject of no small amount of controversy. It is, after all, not for naught that Heidegger begins his magnum opus, *Being and Time*—arguably the defining philosophical work of the early twentieth century— by lamenting how the question which animated the work of Plato and Aristotle and persisted through to Hegel "has long since become trivialized," to the extent that "a dogma has been developed which not only declares the question about the meaning of Being to be superfluous, but sanctions its complete neglect."[30]

This scandalous "forgetting of being," Heidegger reasons, results foremost from the indistinct nature of the question, not simply from the fact "that the question of Being lacks an *answer*," but moreover because "the question itself is obscure and without direction."[31] Accordingly, if the question of being is to be revived, "this means that we must first work out an adequate way of *formulating* it."[32]

Curiously enough, this question of formulation also weighs heavily on Lacan. Indeed, even while explicitly rejecting the need for an ontology— arguing that "what truly belongs to the order of the unconscious [...] is neither being, nor non-being, but the unrealized"[33]—Lacan nonetheless has frequent cause to address the problem of its *question*, and in particular the difficulties raised by the concept of the "One," or of the ultimate unity of being. Three moments in particular stand out here. Speaking of Plato's

*Parmedides*, he notes that the "hypotheses on the relations of the One and of Being remain [...] an object of scandal."[34] Elsewhere he identifies the real itself as "the stumbling block to the establishment of being and the One."[35] Finally, in approaching the *Parmedides* through the mathematical framework of set theory, he recognizes how, according to the logic of the "empty set," "it appears that the One begins on the level at which there is one missing."[36]

While the foregoing does have the definite advantage of further establishing the connection between scandal, being, and the real, we note it here principally so as to foreground the debt that Badiou's own ontology owes not only to the German philosopher—who he readily acknowledges as the figure who single-handedly "brought the question of being back into the space of contemporary philosophy"[37]—but moreover to the French antiphilosopher. For as we have already made clear, it is neither Heidegger's nor Lacan's but rather Badiou's painstaking formulation of the question of being that is of interest to us here, and in particular his embrace of what we might call the *real of being*.

To be sure, beyond the essentially linguistic and significatory (or "meaningful") concerns of Lacan's original conception, it is precisely the *form of its formulation*—namely, its doubly formal and retroactive logic—that informs Badiou's *anti*-antiphilosophical understanding of the real. For it is this very logic which allows him to deliver a real that not only is far more closely aligned with being itself, but can even be said to be—at least to some extent—*knowable*.

Indeed, in sharp contrast to (even while explicitly drawing on) Lacan, who held that "the notion of being, as soon as we try to grasp it, proves itself to be as ungraspable as that of speech,"[38] Badiou maintains that we are in fact eminently capable of providing a comprehensive schema of being—a complete rational ontology—in terms of the mathematics of set theory. So great is his conviction on this point that his entire philosophical system can easily be shown to rest or fall on the assumption of this very possibility, which he articulates in the form of a single sweeping axiomatic declaration: that "mathematics is ontology."[39]

This equation of mathematics with ontology must of course not be taken to suggest that being is itself mathematical, or that it is composed of mathematical objects (much in the way Lacan's insistence that "mathematization alone reaches a real"[40] does not mean that the real can itself be "mathematized"). To claim as much would be to make the mistake of conflating ontology, which, as we know, designates the discourse on being, with the object of this discourse, namely, being itself. No, being is not mathematics; rather, mathematics is what *thinks* being—it is the sole coherent means we have for thinking what being actually *is*. In a word: it is the rational formulation of the question of being.[41]

Having said this, in the interest of our own argument, it is worth temporarily bracketing the question of mathematics to instead begin by observing how Badiou holds being itself to be nothing other than pure or "inconsistent" multiplicity. This is an important point that will have significant ramifications further on: contra Parmenides, the putative "father of metaphysics"—indeed, contra the entirety of classical metaphysics—being is not "One," in the sense of an indivisible, ungenerable, immutable, and all-encompassing substance qua "Being."[42] Yet nor is it, strictly speaking, plural or "multiple," such that it would come in many forms (or, as Plato would have it, in "the form of the many").[43] Rather, being is *pure* multiplicity, with the emphasis falling squarely on the qualifier "pure," not the multiple itself, but the "multiple 'in-itself.'"[44]

While the distinction here may appear subtle, this does not make it any less significant. Certainly, any and every thing, regardless of its essentially multiple nature, is given to experience or "presented" *as* unified, that is, as a "consistent multiple" qua collection of "ones." This is, after all, just a simple fact of existence: all the individual things that we perceive are ultimately unified, composing either a coherent "whole" or group of related wholes. And yet, if we recognize this unification as constituting not a starting point but rather a *result*—a structural outcome or *effect*—we are thereby able to retroactively determine the multiple *in-itself* as being anterior to this "one," that is, as figuring pure (or *in*consistent) multiplicity, what we might otherwise think of as the "multiple-*without-one*."

Radically withdrawn from unification, such "pure being" is, like the Lacanian real, at one and the same time *anti*- and *ante*-one, simultaneously exceeding and preceding any and all consistency or "one-ness."

In practical terms, what this means is that once we divest an object of everything that goes into making it a unique or "consistent" thing—once we isolate it from its context and strip away all of its qualitative determinations— what remains is essentially *a multiple of multiples*. There is no intrinsic determination to this multiple multiplicity; it is not a multiple of "this" or of "that"; rather, it is purely—or it purely *is*—multiple.

Nor, for that matter, will we find any "atomic" halting point to this de-compositional process: what we eventually arrive at is not some form of primordial unity that might accordingly be designated, with Parmenides, "Being" or the "One" or the "All." Rather, our journey only ends with the *void*, that is, with nothingness itself, with the in-finite dissemination of multiple multiplicity. And as we have already seen, it is precisely this pure multiple remainder—*in*-finite, *in*-different, *in*-determinate, *in*-consisting—that marks the *real being* of the object, the elementary "there is" underlying everything that "is there."

It is on the basis of this fundamental intuition that Badiou is able to establish an entire ontology, which he then correlates to a "logical phenomenology" or "science of being-there"[45] (although, given our "real" concerns, it is the ontological sphere that will occupy our attention here).[46] Exactly how this is accomplished represents a true philosophical tour de force, which serves to formalize not only the real's retroactive logic, but moreover its scandalous opposition to sense, or its status as both *anti-* and *ante*-meaning.

Having said this, the undertaking itself is intricate and involved, with the upshot being that even our cursory examination here will take more than a few pages. Once completed, however, we will not only be in a position to present a full schema or conceptual framework of the logic of real scandal, but furthermore be able to demonstrate exactly how and why it is of such paramount importance today.

4

# Making Sense of Everything

Our aim in this chapter is straightforward enough, namely, to delve into the same ontology that will provide the foundation for our own broader argument in order to grasp something of its essential structure. In particular, we need to present the conceptual background to what we earlier called the "stabilizing function of a given situation," namely, its organizational *state*, which in effect accounts for the "whole" of being, or for everything that can possibly be given to presentation (and hence, the limits of possibility itself). The reason for this should be equally clear: if we are to understand what it really means to scandalously break with the state of things, we first need to recognize (1) what the state actually *is* and (2) just how absolute its control of the situation can be.

That being said, there are still two things we need to address before proceeding any further. First, it is important to point out that even though we are drawing our philosophical foundations directly from Badiou's work, at no point does he himself propose anything so much as approximating a productive theory of scandal. To be clear, on the sole occasion that he does engage with the concept—in his short book *À la recherche du réel perdu*[1]—this is only in order to reject it as a possible articulation of the real. As we have already noted, Badiou conceives of scandal here as something that "always presents itself as the revelation of a little bit of the real."[2] To this end, the scandal takes on the appearance of an isolated case—an anomaly of the system in the guise of "a scandalous exception."[3] Yet it is precisely in its apparently "exceptional" form that the scandal functions to mask the fact that it directly embodies the system as a whole, or that it actually represents not the exception but rather the rule itself. The power of scandal then resides in the way that it stages "as" real (hence as an exception) the guiding logic of the situation, in its "theatricalization of a tiny fragment of the real as a denial of this real itself."[4]

What is clear from this is that Badiou is only able to conceive of scandal as a negative concept and, in particular, as a fundamentally static exercise. Hence his identifying *corruption* as constituting the "essential name" of scandal[5]—a conflation we have already recognized as unnecessarily reductive. Scandal then functions for him solely as a scapegoat or, at the very least, as a calculated act of misdirection, as "the use of a little piece of corruption to escape [...] the reasonable idea, that corruption is everywhere."[6] While we do not deny that this "exceptional" logic represents a key feature of contemporary scandal (having already argued that both of the standard models ultimately function to sell us the system as it stands), obviously we in no way limit ourselves to such a static and monolithic conception.

In fact, we might immediately supplement Badiou's "little piece of the real" by considering its relation to the different modes of scandal we ourselves put forward in Part One. We already know, for example, that scandal in the form of real creation directly delivers us the *actual real*, in all its traumatic and chaotic glory. (Note that such real scandal clearly represents the very converse of Badiou's model, the *actual* exception of the real.) The revelatory model, for its part, presents us with a sort of "laicized" real—a real that corresponds not to transformative but rather transparent or, more accurately, *translucent reality*. Accordingly, we will say of its dissimulative counterpart that it serves to cover over or *opacify* this same real, denying the very possibility of any animating cause outside of the all-powerful market. Finally, we have the simulacral form of scandal, which, in failing to extinguish the real, instead appropriates it for its own static ends, annexing the real itself through the *simulation* of its effects.

Actualization, translucence, opacity, and simulation: clearly the idea of "corruption" is inadequate to account for all of these differentially productive forms of scandal. Our task here is then, first and foremost, that of working through Badiou's ontology so as to establish a *positive* conception to scandal— even if this is only in order to better grasp its controversial negation.

Yet we also need to address an apparent paradox inherent to our taking up of the real as an explicitly philosophical concept. For in constituting an "impossible ab-sense," the real would equally seem to comprise the antiphilosophical core of Lacanian thought, a point that is intrinsically repellent to rational critical inquiry. Indeed, Badiou himself pinpoints Lacan's quarrel with philosophy in terms of its representing, in his eyes, "a pretension of thought to dispense with the real altogether."[7] How then can we speak, for example, of "the real of being,"[8] without succumbing to antiphilosophical practice?

The difficulty here arises primarily from Lacan's formulation of the real as constituting a realm which is fundamentally inaccessible to knowledge. Not that the problem is that of inaccessibility *per se*. (Indeed, as will only become increasingly clearer, what constitutes for Lacan a logical stumbling block qua "impossibility of knowing" instead marks for Badiou—whose philosophy contrarily affirms that "everything *can* be absolutely known"[9]—a point of direct inscription and perfect legibility.) Rather, the issue would seem to reside in the notion of "realm" itself, in so far as this term carries with it problematic connotations of location and of place, and thereby leaves the real in danger of being hypostasized as a kind of "transcendent beyond" in the form of an "other place": a "place outside of place" or "dis-place" replete with quasi-mystical properties. (This confusion is hardly aided by Lacan's repeated insistence on a "mysterious *jouissance*,"[10] which is a concept that will be given a wide berth here.)[11]

To avoid this antiphilosophical trap, it is therefore imperative that we prohibit any and all such objective determinations of the real. Not for a second do we hold that the real *is* being or, indeed, that it is anything else at all. As we have already intimated, the real is not a thing: far from being a place or an object or position to be taken up, the real can better understood as an extra-ontological principle which takes the form of a limit or an impasse—an unbroachable "absolute" (as in Meyerson's formulation) beyond which there is, strictly speaking, *nothing*.[12]

That we cannot contend that the real *is* being does not, however, prohibit us from holding that *being is real*. Or to put this another way: while we can certainly speak of "the real of being"—or, simpler still, "real being"—we cannot identify "a being of the real." Certainly, the relationship between these two terms is extremely close, even intimate. But it would be a fundamental mistake to suppose that this closeness implies anything approaching reciprocity or identity. Ultimately, we cannot draw a strict equation between being and the real: the one is irreducible to the other; while things can *be* real, nothing is *the* real.

# A Stumbling Block

While there is obviously more to be said here (and indeed, this will be far from our last word on the subject), it is high time that we rejoined our broader ontological argument. So, picking up where we left off: after having recognized real being (qua being) as pure multiplicity, devoid of any instance of the One, Badiou goes on to surmise from the simple fact that "oneness" exists (or that even things which are multiple are nevertheless presented to us *as* unified), that this unification must be nothing other an *effect* of presentation, a process by which pure multiple multiplicity is "counted-as-one."

This process of unification (or "one-ification") produces what he terms a *situation*. A situation is then, in effect, the *E pluribus unum* of ontology and can accordingly be defined as *any presented (or "one-ified") multiplicity whatsoever*: a telephone conversation with a friend, a city along with all of its inhabitants, a business meeting, Hollywood, the internet, a collection of artworks, ontology, the North American political system, this book.

Now, to add yet another term to our rapidly expanding ontological lexicon, Badiou designates the actual operation behind this—i.e., the situating (or "presentational") process itself—the *count*, for the simple reason that it "counts" certain elements (i.e., multiples) as *belonging* to the situation, while reciprocally "discounting" others. The count is then what initially structures the situation—in fact, it literally *is* the structure of the situation—and is to this effect indistinguishable from the situation itself: they are for, all intents and purposes, one and the same.

This question of distinction, however, proves to be of critical importance here. For we cannot avoid the fact that, in keeping with its "real" roots, the underlying "being" of a situation—its "un-counted," pure multiple foundation—cannot itself be presented, for the simple reason that all presentation necessarily involves unification: to be "situated" is nothing more nor less than to be (both literally and figuratively) "counted," or to be subjected to the unifying process of the count.

But this of course leads directly to a fundamental paradox: given that all knowledge is necessarily "situated" (in so far as for anything to be *known* it must first be *counted*), it follows from this that the in-consistent being which underlies all consistency must itself be, strictly speaking, unknowable.

Meaning that any knowledge of what *precedes* the situation is itself rendered null and void simply by virtue of its situatedness. Or in other words, we cannot truly know what came before the situation, since the situation represents the limits of knowledge itself. Consequently, we can say that inconsistency designates *the real of presentation*, or the precise point at which knowledge butts up against its own limit: as a point of radical (and literal) unaccountability, inconsistency announces itself as the stumbling block or the original scandal of being.

We would appear to have reached another impasse: having annulled the One, pure multiplicity proves to be just as impenetrable a ground of being. Yet this does not mean that we are done here. For while we cannot escape the fact that the inconsistent substructure of a situation is itself fundamentally ungraspable, the simple fact that presentation is a process or an *operation* tells us that there must first be something on which this operation operates. Meaning that the count, by its very nature, retroactively posits a corollary "to-be-counted," a pre-operative "before-of-the-count" that necessarily differs in some way from—or fails to fully coincide with—its situated result (else it too would be "counted") and can accordingly be said to "in-consist" in the situation in the form of a "phantom remainder."[13]

Precluded from presentation itself (i.e., the "counted" result) yet included in the presentation *in-itself* (i.e., the operation of "counting"), the pure multiple must really *be nothing* in the situation. However, as Badiou is careful to point out, "being nothing is by no means the same as not-being."[14] Indeed, this "nothing" (qua residual "phantom of inconsistency")[15] not only subsists but even *insists* within the situation in two immediate guises: in the very operation of the count (which itself remains uncounted) and in the pure multiple on which the count operates (which, we know, differs in-itself from its situated, or consistent, result).[16]

To cut a long and complicated story short, pure multiplicity can be shown to "in-consist" (or be "un-presented") in the situation in the form of the *void*, the multiple of nothing that is, technically speaking, neither "one" nor "multiple." The void thus designates "the name of being—of inconsistency—according to a situation."[17] It is this void that we recognize as the "phantom remainder" of the original uncounted multiple, which, as multiple of nothing, "haunts" the presentation and designates the "subtractive face of the count."[18]

*Qua* unlocalizable, unknown, unpresented point of every presentation, the void can then be said to constitute, in Lacanian terms, the very juncture between "symbolic structuration" and its "primitive real."[19] Or as Badiou would have it: the point at which the structured situation is "sutured" to its inconsistent being.

Of the many important theses arising from this key proposition—namely, that the void marks the point at which a situation is sutured to its underlying being (or where the symbolic and the real intersect)—the one that most concerns us here relates, unsurprisingly, to its infinitely "creative" function, that is, to the simple and unavoidable fact that everything that *is*—which is to say, *creation as such*—"is woven from the proper name of the void."[20] (This of course returns us once more to our earlier discussion of the concept of "nothing" and, in particular, our "productive" understanding of the principle of *ex nihilo nihil fit*: that "nothing comes from nothing.")

It is hard to overstate the importance of this crucial ontological postulate, namely, that any and everything is woven out of the void (or alternatively, that "everything comes from nothing"). While we obviously do not have the space to explore the full reasoning behind it here—although its mathematical justification, which rests on the axiom of the empty or "void" set, can actually be provided with considerable ease[21]—we will suffice ourselves by saying it boils down to the fact that if ontology necessarily proposes a theory of the void (which, as we have just seen, it most assuredly does) then it follows that "ontology, in a certain sense, can *only* be theory of the void."[22] For in supposing that ontology also presented other, non-void or "full" terms, the resulting distinction would necessitate the void itself being counted-as-one (in order for this differentiation to take place), thereby effectively "voiding" its empty status, in so far as it would now be illegally "filled." As such, "the only solution is for *all* of the terms to be 'void' such that they are composed from the void alone."[23] Or in other words: nothing does indeed come from nothing, *and this alone is what gives us everything.*

Thus we finally arrive, by way of this retroactive intellective movement (from the "impure" One to the "pure" multiple and back again), at the infinitely generative core of structured presentation itself: the void of being that constitutes the pure chaos of creation.

## The State of Things

Regardless of its existential absoluteness, however, the void of being nonetheless presents a real threat to the prospect of systematic, structured presentation. For were a situation to actually encounter its void—were it to, in effect, scandalously *present* its inherent in-consistency—this would logically bring about "the ruin of the One"[24] and the ensuing reign of chaos.

It is for this reason that every situation, as a matter of course, subjects itself to a structural *re*-count or a "count of the count," thereby establishing a reinforced meta-structure which ensures that *everything* in the situation is present and accounted for. This secondary count by which the very structure of a situation is itself "counted as one"—such that each and every one of its constituents can be said to be both *presented* and *represented*—is finally what Badiou calls, for its "metaphorical affinity with politics"[25] (and not for any literal connection), the "state of the situation," or simply the *state*. Understood in this way, far from being a rigidly political complex, the state simply designates the meta-structure that accounts for a situation's stability (or even its "metastability"), guaranteeing it a certain equilibrium such that it does not fall into chaos.

As we have already indicated, it is this fundamentally homeostatic conception of the state that we are employing throughout this book, namely, as an ontological ordering principle that conserves the structural integrity of a given situation (whatsoever it may be) *precisely by delimiting its creative function*. For the state, Badiou tells us, "is not simply what governs reality"; more than this, the state is what enjoys an absolute monopoly on *possibility itself*, such that it "pronounces that which is possible and impossible."[26] Or to put it once more in distinctly Lacanian terms: the state is what ensures that the "chaotic and [...] primal"[27] real (considered here in terms of pure being) does not disturb symbolic/imaginary experience; it is what keeps "reality" running smoothly.

Obviously there are a number of important points arising from all of this that need to be addressed before we can move ahead, first and foremost being the fact that such a structural conception of the state implies that it is not only *apolitical* but moreover *ahistorical*. For one thing, as a key ontological criterion—as the guarantor of existential consistency—there can obviously be no straightforwardly Marxian question of "the withering away of the state" (or at least, not of the *real* state). The state has always existed and will always exist; while its *placeholders* may vary, it itself remains perennially *in place*. Needless to say, the list of organizations and regulatory frameworks that can occupy its structural *position* is virtually limitless, encompassing not only governmental and legal institutions but also things like art auction houses, limited liability companies, and religious organizations, extending all the way out to entrenched patriarchal structures and even linguistic rules such as grammar and syntax. Yet none of these can be understood to constitute *the* (final and absolute) state. Rather, these variegated and essentially administrative bodies—"administration" being for Badiou "homogenous to the state of the situation"[28]—might be better designated "state representatives" (or "state actors"), in view of the fact that they constitute effective but ultimately *provisional* mechanisms for establishing and maintaining situational order.

Another important takeaway here is that, in so far as the state is essentially a matter of structure and not conscious intent, we cannot escape the fact that each and every action it takes must be understood as being, strictly speaking, *unintentional*.[29] To be sure, as an automatic and autonomous process whose sole functional criterion is to maintain structural order, the state cannot really be shown to *mean* anything (at least, in the purposive sense of the word). Accordingly, any intentionality we can attach to the state must be ascribed to its representative within the situation.

That the state lacks a sense of purpose or intent does not, however, mean that it is entirely disinterested. Indeed, a final crucial point arising from all of this relates to the fact that, as the structural mechanism by which the situation is kept under control—therefore as the ontological expression of *power* itself (an expression which, we will shortly see, is as much literal as it is metaphorical)—the state is by definition profoundly caught up in the functioning of the situation. To be sure, its very existence is intrinsically linked to the situation's relative stability: as Badiou observes, "the state is an entity that has only one idea: to persevere in its being,"[30] and this persistence relies as much on the consistency as the constancy of the situation as a whole. One of the more interesting and important inferences we can draw from this is that the most consequential contemporary state representatives—the ones that have the biggest impact on the functioning of our so-called global society—will not be, strictly speaking, political, but rather capitalistic in nature, being composed of those bodies that have the strongest monetary interest in maintaining and even strengthening the status quo. We will return to this key point later.

So to sum up: in designating the ontological superstructure of the situation, the state is accordingly irreducible to its political namesake, being rather the "re-count" by which the very structure of a situation is itself "counted as one," thereby ensuring that there is both (situated) presentation and (static) *re*presentation. Having said this, while the "real" state (qua structural re-count) remains, as we have said, "unintentional," the same need not apply for the various organizations—such as the parliamentary state—which function as its placeholder, and thus occupy a concrete position in the situation they oversee.

## The Mathematical Turn

We have by this point isolated three distinct ontological orders: first, we have the level of *pure multiplicity* (or of real being qua being); second is the level of the *presented situation* (or of structure and consistency); and third, there is the level of *state representation* (or of order and power). (Note that, in Lacanian terms, only the first of these can be directly correlated with the category of the real, while the second and third jointly configure the symbolic register.) Together, these three levels—multiple-being, structured situation, state power—constitute the foundations of reality as such. Finally, it is these orders which comprise the philosophical grounds on which we can construct our overall argument.

The initial means of this construction are, however, not so much philosophical as they are mathematical. Here we reencounter the fundamental axiom we briefly passed over above, namely, Badiou's declaration that "mathematics *is* ontology." For if ontology figures the discourse on being, and if being itself is pure multiplicity (as Badiou claims it to be), then we cannot escape the fact that the sole area of thought capable of providing the minimal and sufficient structure necessary to articulate such real multiple multiplicity is none other than *mathematics*. Indeed, this is precisely what mathematics and, more specifically, axiomatic set theory—which is the particular branch of mathematical logic that Badiou equates with ontology[31]—does.

While taking care to not run away with ourselves, certain aspects of this relationship demand at least some comment. So, first of all, let us note that set theory "thinks" real multiplicity in a number of immediate ways. For one thing, a set has no "essence" other than that of being a multiple; it is determined neither externally (nothing constrains the way it seizes another thing) nor internally (a set is entirely indifferent to what it collects). Meaning a set, thought in itself (i.e., outside of what it "collects"), *in-consists*: it consists (or is composed) of nothing, its sole predicate being its multiple nature. To this end, a set is, quite literally, inconsistent multiplicity; it is the mathematical expression of in-consistency itself.

More than this, each of a set's elements constitutes another set, meaning every multiple-set is itself a multiple of other multiples, without reference to any originary unitary element (or primordial "One"). So a set is likewise radically without-one; it is, in its essence, *uncounted* multiple multiplicity.

To cut to the chase, we can easily ascribe an immediate set theoretic correlate to everything that we have examined thus far in terms of the structure of being. A situation, for example, is obviously a set, in as much as a set, in its most elementary definition, is simply "a plurality thought as a unit."[32] Likewise, the state of the situation (qua structural reinforcement or "count of the count") is mathematically expressed in the axiom of the power set, which tells us that, for every set $A$, there also exists a superior set of all the possible subsets of $A$.

Moreover, set theory admits of a single and sole relational function, which is that of *belonging* (written $\epsilon$), and this alone dictates what composes or "one-ifies" a set (in so far as what "belongs" to a set is what is "counted" in it). This of course further establishes the fact that the set itself possesses no unary predicate, no essence other than its being a multiple/set. This itself leads us in turn to another crucial correlate, in that the axiom of the empty or "void" set—which constitutes the sole existential axiom of set theory (and which simply states that "there exists a set with no members")[33]—means that any "first" set must be a set to which no elements belong (written Ø). All of which means that set theory equally premises existence itself on the void; it is a "universe generated, as it were, out of nothing."[34]

While we could easily go on like this, the point should by now have been sufficiently established as to why it is Badiou and not Lacan who can be seen to "make sense" of the real. Although Lacan certainly recognizes that "mathematization alone reaches a real"[35]—even going so far as to define mathematics itself as "what can be taught of the real"[36]—it nonetheless remains for him a site of impossible ab-sense, designating not the triumph but rather the "*impasse* of formalization."[37] As Badiou summarizes: "The real, in its Lacanian conceptual content, is what absolutely resists symbolization, whether carried out by means of mathematics, logic, or topology."[38] This is moreover precisely why Lacan pursues formalization to its absolute limit, in order to isolate the exact point of its breaking down, "where something that evades and unravels it surfaces,"[39] or where the real makes its disturbing presence felt.

For Badiou, by contrast, in grasping the multiple as "not a (formal) concept, transparent and constructed, but a real whose internal gap, and impasse, [is] deployed by the theory"[40]—ergo as the process of directly inscribing and manipulating pure multiple-being—mathematics ensures as a matter of course the real's perfect legibility—without, for all that, diminishing in any way its simultaneously creative and destructive power.

For us, however, this "perfect legibility" marks a significant problem. Because once it has been equated with ontology, mathematics—in its complete rationality, objectivity, and apodicticity, or in its *total mastery of its terrain*— demonstrates more than anything just how firm and inflexible the state's grasp over the real truly is: the seemingly unqualified, even unqualifiable, reign it enjoys over its situation. In other words, the equivalence of mathematics and ontology only serves to further confirm the absolute indomitability of the state.

Where in such a world—which is, after all, our own (if on an abstract level)— is there even the slightest room for real scandal (which we have explicitly aligned with real creation or with what breaks free of the state's grasp), let alone for any activity that might so much as approximate "the scandalous"? For to engage in truly scandalous behavior, it would seem that it is not only necessary to escape prying eyes moreover, we need to defy the very laws of mathematics. And yet, as we will see in the following section, this is precisely what real scandal manages to do.

## On the New

Before moving on to the next stage of our investigation, given the extraordinary strictures of the system we have outlined thus far, it is worth taking a moment to think about the one thing that remains, according to its logic, wholly unaccounted for. This leftover quantity is, of course, nothing other than that of the *new*. For while our ontology is clearly capable of "making sense" of the real, it does not—and more to the point, *cannot*—allow any space for the radically new. How exactly are we then to understand the coming-to-be of the new, or the process of real creation as such? How, in short, are we to account for the wholly unaccountable?

The first thing to note here is that the truly new has been very much out of favor for a long time now. Few ideas, after all, could be more antithetical to postmodern thought, which still in many ways constitutes the dominant philosophy of the present era (certainly with regard to the question of radical creation) and which effectively understands our world as destined to serve up "endless varieties of what *already exists*."[41] Accordingly, far from representing anything *real*, the new is today understood as being entirely contained within the replicatory logic of the symbolic (i.e., the great "chain of signifiers that repeats").[42] While the idea of the new of course persists and even *insists* today, we can nonetheless clearly see how it has, on the whole, long been reconceived in line with the familiar "new and improved" of advertising discourse, that is, as the endlessly *renewed* (*recycled*, *remade*, *reworked* …).

In short, the new that exists today is, for the most part, an aseptic or ersatz new—a new that has in effect been downgraded to the status of *novelty* (in the "fashionable" sense of the word). Needless to say, the reason for this demotion is less philosophical than straightforwardly capitalistic. For contrary to common assumption, markets do not thrive on the actually, authentically new, but rather operate on the *conceit* of newness: on the "like new," the "as new," the "almost-but-not-quite new"; in a word, on the "novel." Doubtless, it is a basic law of economics that the market "requires that new products be turned out endlessly in order to generate ever-higher products."[43] And of course we understand perfectly well that capitalism cannot flourish when it is confined to what already exists; that it "is by nature a form or method of economic change and not only never is but never can be stationary";[44] and that for it to survive it must continually transform itself, opening up new markets and new products in an ongoing process of "creative destruction." Yet the fact remains that, like the states they function to support, markets can only accommodate partial or incomplete ruptures with their logic— hence their oft-remarked upon correspondence to quasi-stable or metastable states[45]—whereas the disorder instituted by the radically new is, at least initially, simply too much to bear. In a word, while novelty may drive the market, the new crashes it.

Earlier in this chapter we noted that the dominant state representatives today are not necessarily political but rather capitalistic in nature, owing to the fact that the state constitutes the organizing principle of a situation, and this principle is almost invariably ultimately reducible to that of *capital*. Yet this would seem to raise an immediate contradiction. For while the state obviously functions to maintain a level of stasis, capitalism demands a constant process of creation and destruction. Indeed, the aforementioned phenomenon of "creative destruction" has long been recognized as "the essential fact about capitalism"; as its original theorist contends, "It is what capitalism consists in and what every capitalist concern has got to live in."[46]

Yet the contradiction here is, in truth, only superficial, for the fact remains that while capitalism demands regular bursts of novelty, it nonetheless requires, at its highest level, an overall stasis. Indeed, creative destruction names the very process by which local instabilities serve to establish global stability (of the market itself). In effect, both capitalism and the state require the sheen of constant disruption and discontinuity—or the incessant production of novelty—precisely in order to ensure that things *stay the same*. This fundamentally conservative logic is perhaps most perfectly encapsulated in Tancredi's famous lines from Giuseppe di Lampedusa's *The Leopard*: "If we want things to stay as they are, things will have to change."[47]

Of course, in saying all of this, we are hardly breaking fresh ground. Theodore Adorno, for example, long ago called attention to the fact that "what parades as progress in the culture industry, as the incessantly new which it offers up, remains the disguise for an eternal sameness."[48] Likewise, Guy Debord saw only too clearly how "in the domain of culture the bourgeoisie strives to divert the taste for innovation, which is dangerous for it in our era, toward certain degraded, innocuous and confused forms of novelty."[49] More than a half-century after Adorno's and Debord's analyses, we still see this in almost every aspect of culture: in the sad fate of contemporary cinema, which now subsists almost exclusively on a steady diet of remakes, reboots, sequels, prequels, "origin stories," and the like; in our associated obsession with the "franchisable," the "personalizable," and with "immediate brand recognition"; in the endless stream of upgrades and redesigns of already-available goods and gadgets that we only rarely actually need; on and on the list goes.

This pressure for the continual production of novelty (precisely in order to maintain an overall stasis) without running the risk of introducing the *actually new* has, moreover, seen the substitution of the idea of real creation with the more nebulous notion of "creativity." Indeed, few concepts are more fetishized today than that of creativity, while, reciprocally, few ideas are more derided than that of "creation." It is, for example, now commonly assumed that "there are more people being more creative, seeing it as part of their identity, than ever before"[50] and, correspondingly, that "creativity and its business-like cousin innovation are the most interesting and the most profitable areas of the economy."[51]

Today we recognize all manner of fundamentally static things in "creative" terms: we willingly incorporate ourselves into the "creative economy," we invest in the "creative industries," we work to sustain "creative ecologies," and so on.[52] Everywhere we look, we are surrounded by a mix of self-identifying "creatives," "disruptors," "innovators," "content creators," and the like—indeed, it has even become routine these days to speak of a "creative class," whose "distinguishing characteristic [...] is that its members engage in work whose function is to 'create meaningful new forms.'"[53]

This recasting of "creation" as "creativity" would then seem to mark the final victory of the market (and, accordingly, the state) over the very possibility of the new, as the latter is entirely overtaken—or, in its own terms, "improved"—by the inexorable logic of advertising and marketability.

Again, these static developments have been in the works for some time. It was, after all, this same stifling process that Deleuze and Guattari railed against almost three decades ago when they declared that "the most shameful moment [for philosophy] came when computer science, marketing, design and advertising, all the disciplines of communication, seized hold of the word *concept* itself"—which, as a slice of "chaos" given form and meaning, had previously constituted the creative core of philosophy—"and said: 'This is our concern, we are the creative ones, we are the *ideas men!*'"[54] Far from being restricted to the philosopher, however, the shame felt today resonates around the world. For in reducing the truly new (which is, in effect, what the Deleuzian "concept" designates here) to the level of communication, we effectively relegate it to the position of what is *already known*. Indeed, what is authentically "new" is by definition precisely what *cannot* be immediately communicated, for the simple reason that it does not yet make sense: it stands in excess of what is known and hence expressible.

It is against this backdrop—against the absolute power of the state and its "monopoly of possibilities,"[55] against the reign of market-adjusted novelty and the creativity fetish—that we must somehow position our own concept of the *scandalously new*: as marking a point, which remains out of reach of the state; as intrinsically tied to the intrusion of the real; as "traumatizing" the situation by shattering existing economies of knowledge and plunging the situation into a state of chaos and emergency; as demanding that everything already established as "known" be rethought in relation to its unexpected appearance; as the sudden liberating possibility of what was hitherto impossible—in short, as the *fons et origo* of real scandal and the true generator of controversy. Exactly how all of this might be accomplished will be the subject of the following section.

Part Three

# Creation

5

# A Terrible Beauty

To make things simple for us, we will begin this chapter by boiling down the previous section's principal findings concerning the structure of being and the real into the following key statements.

*The real is (the) impossible.* The real exceeds and precedes—and is therefore inassimilable within—"reality." Its intrusion into this field is then experienced as a traumatic encounter which introduces the possibility of something new.

*The real is expressed as being.* While not strictly equivalent, the historical articulation of the real takes place in the discourse of ontology, or the study of being qua being.

*Real being is pure multiplicity.* Being is not unified or "One": once we have denuded an object of its context and its content, what remains is nothing other than a multiple of multiples.

*Being is unified in (and by) a situation.* The presentation of pure multiplicity— its structuration or "counting-as-one"—constitutes a "situation." A situation is accordingly any presented multiplicity whatsoever.

*The presentation of pure being is (a) real.* All presentation entails a regime of structuration. Yet pure being (as inconsistent multiplicity) escapes capture by the One. Inconsistency is then the real of being, the "unaccountable" hence scandalous point at which the "count-as-one" fails.

*Existence is woven from the void. (Or: "everything comes from nothing.")* Given that what *is* is pure multiple, while what is *presented* is multiple/one, being can only be presented *as* nothing. Pure multiplicity thus in-consists in the situation in the form of the void, which marks the point where the situation is sutured to its underlying being.

*Every situation has a state.* To preclude the potentially disastrous presentation of its void, every situation is "re-counted" such that its structure is itself counted. This recount, which ensures situational stability through the suppression of the void, establishes the state of the situation.

*Mathematics is ontology*. It is not philosophy but axiomatic set theory which gives us the science of being qua being, or of being subtracted from all of its particular qualities and attributes. Mathematics is then the writing of the real.

Having come to grips with these key postulates, we now arrive at a crucial turning point in our investigation of the real. Thus far our analysis has focused on its essentially objective qualities—characteristics which, while certainly productive (not least in the case of the void), nonetheless remain essentially, even hopelessly, passive. Indeed, considered as an ontological substrate—as being qua pure multiplicity—the real that we have come to "know" here functions all-too literally in the service of the state: far from being active, this is a real that is entirely acted upon; an overborn and wholly subjugated shadow of its true self; a real that has been thoroughly *accounted for*.

Yet this is of course only half the picture. To explain: having identified the real as the determinative element of scandal—in terms of either its translucence (in revelatory scandal), or its opacity (in dissimulatory scandal), or its actualization (in real scandal), or its simulation (in simulacral scandal)—clearly our aim in the previous section was to "make sense" of this real by stripping away its Lacanian vagaries and clarifying its content. Thus, for example, the dual properties Lacan identifies as "anti-meaning" and "ante-meaning" were respectively formalized in terms of "pure multiplicity" (in its diametrical opposition to knowledge) and "structural void" (as unpresented ground of all presentation). Moreover, Badiou's set theoretic ontology not only has been shown to account for the idea of the real's being mathematically formalizable, but moreover perfectly demonstrates its retroactive determination.

In limiting our examination to this "objective" side of the real, however, we fail to take into account its crucial *subjective* characteristics and, in particular, its inherently impossible and traumatic nature. Missing from our description then is the all-important idea of the real's constituting a disruptive and disturbing encounter with something absolutely "other" in the form of the radically *new*. Or to put this another way, we have till now neglected to confront the truly *scandalous* side of the real. To account for this, we now turn our attention to the decisive (and decidedly controversial) idea of the "event": the critical concept which Badiou himself recognizes as constituting no less than "the bedrock of my entire edifice."[1] For it is a key contention of this book—so important, in fact, that it both underpins and orients our entire argument—that such events are not only *real*, but, moreover, quickly become scandalous affairs.

## The Return of the Real

Before we can detail the event itself, however, we need to think just a little longer on a specific postulate which we have only recently put forward, being the idea that the axiom of the power set provides us with the properly ontological (i.e., mathematical) expression of the state of the situation. What this axiom tells us, in effect, is that, for every set $A$, there also exists a "superior" set of all the possible subsets of $A$. To spell this out, it means that, if we designate $A$ the set {a, b, c}, then the "power set" of $A$—written $p(A)$—establishes the demonstrably larger set {a, b, c, {a, b}, {a, c}, {b, c}, {a, b, c}, $\emptyset$}.

There are two important things that need to be noted here. The first is that the void or "empty" set $\emptyset$ is *included* in—or is a *subset* of—every single set (which returns us to our earlier discussion of the "phantom remainder"). And the second is that the total number of subsets derived from the original set can be very easily measured by the formula $2^n$, where $n$ designates the number of elements in the initial set. So, for example, in the above case we have $2^3$ or 8. (Accordingly, if we designated $B$ the set {a, b, c, d, e}, then we can calculate the number of sets established by its power set simply by following the formula $2^5$, which of course gives us 32.) We can therefore say that $2^n$ measures the size or the "cardinality" of the state/power set.

Yet things are far less clear cut when we are dealing with *infinite* situations. And the fact of the matter is that, in the last resort, "every situation is ontologically infinite."[2] Indeed, this general situational infinitude would appear to be an immediate consequence of the fact that the One is not. As Badiou explains: "Since there is no immanent limit anchored in the one that could determine multiplicity as such, there is no originary principle of finitude. The multiple can therefore be thought of as in-finite. Or even: infinity is another name for multiplicity as such."[3]

Now, as we have seen, the amount by which the state "dominates" its situation would be readily calculable were it simply a question of finite quantities: all we would need to do is follow the rule $2^n$. Things are markedly different, however, as soon as we realize that we are dealing with infinite quantifications. For under ordinary (infinite) circumstances, the amount by which a state dominates its situation is, for all intents and purposes, both absolute and beyond determination. All of which leads us to a difficult but unavoidable law of representation, which is that the size of the power set lies in irremediable excess over its initial set.

Suffice to say that the indeterminate or "immeasurable" nature of this quantitative excess results from two key ontological theorems: the first being the still unproven—though, in the estimation of at least one of its most famous theoreticians, "*obviously* false"[4]—*continuum hypothesis*, which posits that "the cardinality of the real numbers really is the next infinity up from the cardinality of the natural numbers"[5] (that is to say, no other infinite quantity exists between them); and the second being "Easton's theorem," which, building on Cohen's work, effectively tells us that in order to designate the value of $p(C)$, where $C$ is an infinite cardinal, it is entirely consistent to simply choose *any* superior successor cardinal of $C$ (meaning that the amount by which $p(C)$ exceeds $C$ is, in effect, *unknowable*).[6]

Needless to say, the still-undecided nature of the continuum hypothesis—and even more so, the infinite errancy resulting from Easton's theorem—will have enormous ramifications on the relation of a situation to its state. For regardless of how accurately we can measure the situation, or how perfectly it can be "known," no reliable means exists by which we might estimate the extent to which its state "exceeds" it: that "the logic of the excess is *real*, insofar as it is impossible to limit it,"[7] means that the gap between structure and metastructure (or between the situation and the state) is, in effect, incalculable.

This unexpected encounter with incalculability within the regime of the countable—an encounter which "introduces randomness into the heart of what can be said of being"[8]—thus marks the precise point at which the real makes its destabilizing reappearance. This scandalous "return of the real" then testifies to the existence of a second ontological stumbling block (following the in-consistency of being as marking the real of presentation) in the form of "the impasse of being,"[9] which can be stated as follows: given a (measurably) infinite situation, we cannot know but rather can only *decide* the size of its state.

(The irony to all of this, of course, is that the same state whose function it was to *prohibit* or "void the void" ultimately facilitates its re-emergence at the very juncture between itself and the situation over which it presides. Which is to say that the state—whose power is, as we have just seen, *literally incalculable*—nonetheless fails at its most basic task.)

In designating a mathematical real (or a point of radical unaccountability), this ontological impasse, which "causes the quantitative excess of the state to err without measure,"[10] cannot be overcome using only those tools expressly belonging (or immanent) to mathematics. To the contrary, it requires recourse to an extra-mathematical anomaly, to something that, while operating within the general parameters of mathematics, nonetheless breaks with its most fundamental rules. It is to this critical anomaly that Badiou gives the name *event*.

## The Clamor of Being

Having finally raised the specter of "the event," only to declare it external to ontology, we might well ask what exactly it is that we are talking about. A rough and ready response would be to say that an event refers to a momentary and unpredictable rupture with the state of things, thus to a sudden "perturbation of the world's order."[11] A more detailed answer would add to this that it involves the unexpected arrival on the scene of a radically *un*-known—and thus, for all intents and purposes, altogether *new*—element, whose address is (for reasons we will examine shortly) immediately universal, and whose consequences are such that they can be shown to impact upon the whole of the situation.

As we will see, each of these crucial properties—unpredictability, unknowability, universality, novelty—directly results from the event's testifying to a sudden upsurge of being itself in the space of the situation. Meaning an event is, in a sense, doubly real, in that it figures the illegal presentation of real being: as both being and its direct presentation, the "realness" of an event extends as much to its form as to it content. Accordingly, far from being a contained affair, we might say that an event contrarily signifies—to repurpose Deleuze's expression—the great "clamor of being"[12] that reverberates around the world.

Yet in spite of their potentially momentous effects, events are in reality as rare and fleeting as they are fragile. Indeed, an event might be best conceived of as "a tear opening up in the texture of the situation"[13]—a tear which, if left unattended to, will be quickly patched up by the immeasurably powerful state. Now, that the state must immediately quash the event is itself a direct—and, we should remind ourselves, unintentional (the ontological state being, as we have said, a matter of structure, and not conscious intent)—consequence of the latter's very novelty, which, in rupturing with the static laws of the situation, identifies itself as illegal and hence a threat. Or to put this in our own terms, the state's role here is that of expeditiously accounting for the sudden presence of the unaccountable—the brief revelation of the secret underside of the situation—precisely in order to prevent a real scandal from taking shape.

As such, if an event is to have any real and lasting effect, then its happening must be somehow *affirmed*. This affirmation ensures that even though the laws of the situation dictate that the event itself must vanish, a mark of its having-taken-place nonetheless remains, in the form of an "evental *trace*." As an immediate and lasting consequence of a vanished event, the trace need be little more than a pronouncement about the radical possibilities it implied; an indication, however vague, that something which had been adjudged impossible *can now be*.

Yet this is far from a straightforward business. For one thing, in siding with the illegal event, this agent of affirmation—which, to forecast just a little, marks the first iteration of what we will come to recognize as the *subject of scandal*— effectively declares itself an "enemy of the state." Moreover, it turns out that we can in no way know for certain of an event's occurrence, since in falling outside of the statist order—which is equally to say: outside of "knowledge" *per se* (in so far as everything that is "known" is necessarily known *by the state*)— an event is thereby completely withdrawn or "subtracted" from all predication. Complicating matters still further is the fact that its radically un-known and hence indiscernible status means that its very happening must be, properly speaking, *undecidable*: any decision regarding its having taken place or not will be, strictly speaking, "pure," being made in the absence of any criteria of judgment.

So, to sum up, a real event, which is both indiscernible and undecidable from the point of view of the situation, illegally "interrupts repetition" by breaking with the laws of ontology (or, as Lacan would have it, in rupturing with the symbolic) to introduce something altogether new in the form of a heretofore unimaginable *possibility*. All of which ultimately means that it is the impossible itself—understood in its "absolute" sense, namely, as "that which *exceeds the possible*"[14]—that introduces us to the very possibility of possibility.

## Reflexivity, Revelation, Resonance

While this description of the event and its radical consequences may be all well and good, the fact remains that we have not yet said what it actually *is*. One of the principal reasons for this is because, as we have already noted, the very nature of the event means that it escapes mathematical thought: as an "exception to [ontological] constraints taking the form of an incalculable origination,"[15] any attempt to say what it *is* is hampered by the inconvenient but unavoidable detail that, technically speaking, it *is not*. Indeed, despite the fact that it involves the direct revelation of being—or more to the point, precisely *because* of this fact (i.e., its illegality)—the event ultimately falls on the side of "that-which-is-not-being-qua-being."[16] This is, after all, as we have already suggested, why an event should be understood as being "doubly real," in so far as it designates something like "the real of the real" or "the impasse of the impasse."

Seemingly making matters even more difficult is Badiou's contention that an event cannot be thought outside of its immediate context, or what he designates its "site," which itself constitutes a very peculiar, albeit essential, part of the situation. For while a site is itself a presented or "situated" multiple, this is not at all the case for any of the elements that belong to it. To be sure, from the situation's perspective, a site is effectively empty, being constituted solely of unpresented, which is to say, *void* multiples (hence its being said to lie "on the edge of the void")[17]: so far as the situation is concerned, there is literally nothing to be found beneath the site.

But of course there is more to it than this. In point of fact, it is precisely its being built on "nothing" that makes the site so important to the situation. For being a consistent multiple composed exclusively of what in-consists (i.e., its unpresented or "void" multiples), the site necessarily amounts to the minimal effect of structure conceivable. Meaning that, far from being insignificant, it is to the contrary *foundational*: incapable of resulting from any internal reshuffling on the part of the situation, the site requires for its existence only the minimal effect of the count. All of which is to say that the site actually "founds" the very situation of which it is a term. Thus our first key "evental" point: an event is inextricably tied to its site (hence the composite term "event-site"), which founds the entire situation on the basis of the void alone.

Now, one of the central assertions of Badiou's "complete" philosophy is that, far from receding to an essentially passive or inert state of being—and this in spite of the fact that its contents are, strictly speaking, void—an event-site contrarily contrives to *reveal itself*. That is to say, the site "summons its being in the appearing of its own multiple composition" and thereby "*makes itself appear*."[18] Two important things follow from this. The first is that, in giving its very being a value of existence, a site involves "the instantaneous revelation of the void that haunts multiplicities."[19] And the second (which is, in fact, derived from the first) is that, by bringing forth the constitutive void of the situation (or the "ante-situation"), the event-site literally presents us with something that had hitherto lacked any and all form of representation.

Ergo our second key evental point: in emerging from the site, an event invokes the foundational void of the situation and, in doing so, produces something that is, for all intents and purposes, radically new and altogether unaccountable. Moreover, as we will see, this is what allows us to conceive of an event as revealing a hidden "truth," in so far as it exposes the unpresented or in-visible cornerstone of the situation—the linchpin that holds everything together. For it is precisely this simultaneously disavowed yet constitutive content that constitutes the essential nature of the situation: its underlying *truth*. (We have in fact already seen this process play out in some detail in our examination of *Fountain* in Part One, where the scandalous non-exhibition of Duchamp's work exposed the non-artistic foundation of art which would otherwise remain unpresented in an "ordinary" completed artistic work.)

Moving on now—and still taking care to limit ourselves to the abstract level of being—technically speaking, in convoking its own being or its "void," an event-site $x$ proves itself paradoxical in so far as it constitutes a *reflexive multiple*, which is to say it is an element of itself (i.e., $x \in x$). In its counting of itself *in itself*—or in its *accounting for itself*—it therefore comprises a supernumerary term, making it, by virtue of the axiom of foundation (which effectively prohibits a set's belonging to itself), ontologically illegal. Hence its aforementioned fragility and transience: in transgressing the laws of being, the event-site must accordingly vanish; it "appears only to disappear."[20]

Yet we must once again exercise caution here. For while an event-site's inevitable transience certainly indicates its constituting something of a "disappearing act," this should in no way be taken to mean that it is inconsequential. Indeed, one of Badiou's basic contentions is that a site only qualifies as (or "becomes") a real event if, in convoking its void, it reveals something radically new that *has profound consequences for the situation in which it takes place*. To be clear: much in the way that one of the scandal's basic conditions is its mediatization (or its "mass-mediation"), likewise a site only becomes an event in so far as it exhibits maximal (or "mass") consequences—consequences which, as we know, are encapsulated in the "trace" affirming the new possibilities opened up by the vanished event, and which have accordingly been drawn directly from the void. (Thus we might rephrase our earlier Deleuzian appropriation and say that an event *only* raises the clamor of being in so far as it resonates throughout the world.)

This brings us to our final and crucial evental point, which is that by relating to the situation from the basis of the void alone, an event can not only be shown to reveal the underlying truth of the situation, it can moreover be said to immediately address itself *universally*. For in constituting the "absolute neutrality of being," the void is the only thing that "neither excludes nor constrains anyone."[21] Or in other words, in speaking from the position of the void, the event addresses each and every one of us in a single voice—a voice that, in defying all characterization and rejecting all distinction, can lay claim to being truly universal.

Thus we see how an event, in emerging from a foundational site, invokes the void of the situation to produce something that is at once radically new, fundamentally true, and immediately universal. Furthermore, we can recognize the ontology of the event-site as consisting of three essential points: (1) it takes the form of a reflexive multiple, (2) it involves the revelation of the void, and (3) its consequences resonate throughout the situation. It is no doubt worth adding here, as we draw this pivotal section to a close, how the ontological illegality of the first two of these points—and the inherently disruptive and controversial nature of the third—only serves to underscore the event's proto-scandalous nature.

## The Real of the Real

That our discussion of the event has thus far taken place almost exclusively on the level of ontology, despite the fact that the event itself constitutes an extra-ontological phenomenon, is clearly a paradox that warrants further explanation. So first off, let us reiterate that Badiou is absolutely unequivocal about the fact that while mathematics provides us with the thought of being, it does not—and indeed *cannot*—give us the thought of the event itself. As he himself puts it: "If real ontology disposes itself as mathematics by evading the norm of the One, then unless this norm is re-established at a global level there must also be a point wherein the ontological (hence mathematical) field is de-totalized or remains at an impasse. I have named this point the *event*."[22] Moreover, it is for precisely this reason that we can say that "philosophy is, perhaps above all else, the general theory of the event, or the theory of what subtracts itself from ontological subtraction. Or the theory of the impossible proper to mathematics."[23]

In a nutshell, mathematics—which, as ontology, figures the science of the real—can only "think" the event to the extent that it can think *its own real qua impasse*. Or again: mathematics only grasps the event in so far as it axiomatizes, or establishes *as a rule*, its own incomplete, aporetic structure. The reason for this is straightforward enough: an event represents an incursion of the real into the space of the social-symbolic (or the mathematizable situation), and "we reach the real not by way of formalization—since this is its impasse—but by exploring what is impossible in this formalization."[24] While we can see this formalized impossibility clearly in a number of the crucial mathematical theorems which we have already cited—in the axiom of foundation as well as in Cohen's and Easton's work on the continuum hypothesis (and indeed, in Georg Cantor's original hypothesis)—nowhere is it more clearly expressed than in Kurt Gödel's famous "incompleteness theorems."

As is well known, these propositions irrevocably changed our perception of mathematics. For what Gödel's work so clearly shows is that, contrary to what we suggested earlier, mathematics does not, and indeed *cannot*, enjoy total mastery of its terrain: within any sufficiently complex formal axiomatic system, there will always be pieces of information which cannot be accounted for: things that are "undecidable" by virtue of the fact that they can neither be proven nor be disproven from within the system—in short, things that are *fundamentally un-known*.[25]

Lacan himself came to explicitly articulate his own conception of the real on the basis of Gödel's celebrated work, noting how

> it has been demonstrated that, in arithmetic, something can always be stated—whether or not it is put to logical deduction—which is articulated as though it stood *in advance* of the very things which premises, axioms, and grounding terms, whereby the said arithmetic can find a base, enable us to presume to be provable or refutable. Here, in a domain that in appearance is the surest, we put our finger on what stands in opposition to the entire grasp of discourse, of logical exhaustion, which introduces a wide, irreducible gap here. *This is where we designate the real.*[26]

Now, as we have seen, Lacan explicitly rejects the need for an ontology, characterizing his own conception of the real as "pre-ontological"[27] and as being solely "affirmed in the *impasses* of logic."[28] We, on the other hand, in following Badiou's demonstration of the mathematical inscription of the real, can contrarily conceive of the Gödelian impasse as *extra*-ontological—as *interrupting* this writing of the real—and therefore as marking, in effect, a "reflexive real": an internal real or a *real of the real*.

It is precisely in these interruptive spaces of ontology—these points where the real makes its disturbing return—that we can begin to think *about* the event. We say "about" because, while mathematics cannot directly deliver us the thought of the event itself—since, as "that-which-is-not-being-*qua*-being," it resists full ontological expression—this does not mean that it has nothing whatsoever to say about it. Indeed, one of the immediate upshots of ontological de-totalization is that, although mathematics would appear to have little to say concerning the event's constitution (outside of illegal formulas like $x \in x$), it nonetheless allows a *space* for an event to, as it were, *be*: a space which lies precisely in its logical gaps and blind spots, in its inconsistencies and aporiae. In fact, the work of Gödel in particular, but also that of Easton and Cohen, ensures such an evental space *as a rule*. Otherwise put: while the event itself will never be welcome at the mathematical table, its seat is always reserved.

6

# Wresting with the Impossible

At the center of this book is a simple idea, which is that from time to time, and under certain exacting conditions, moments of real disruptive creation take place, and these instances are broadly recognized in the form of *real scandal*. That they are understood to be "scandalous" results from two related facts: first, that in figuring the sudden revelation of something radically *un-*known—something which we could not or were not supposed to have been aware of—what presents itself as radically new will initially be, from the standpoint of the situation in which it appears, not only incomprehensible but in fact inconceivable, and for this precise reason, illegal; and second, that this event's incomprehensibility, inconceivability, and illegality mark it out as a subject of intense controversy.

Yet in detailing the nature of the event itself, we have identified it as "proto-scandalous"—as the necessary (but not sufficient) condition of real scandal—and seen how, regardless of its consequences, its own fate is nonetheless to immediately disappear. Moreover, while we have just now seen how the impasses of mathematics open up a space for the event, giving us, in effect, its *shape* but not its *thought*—and while we know that an event, in turn, opens up a space for the realization of hitherto impossible possibilities, in the form of real novelty and universal truth—what we have not yet seen is exactly how we contrive to *pass* from the one to the other. For the simple fact is that this critical passage—from static situation to eventual rupture to radical creation—is clearly not something that takes place of its own accord, but rather requires some form of active engagement or external support.

All of which finally brings us to the last and arguably most important piece of our ontological puzzle—a piece that we identified early on as all-important to our investigation, and yet have actually heard little from since. We refer here to the figure of the *creative subject* (or, alternatively, the *real subject of scandal*, the "scandalous subject"). Our aim in this section is accordingly to chart a course from potentiality to actuality, and in so doing transport us from evental possibility to subjective—and consequently, scandalous—fact.

## The Fabrication of Truth

We know already that a truly creative subject is not something that can be conceived in any of the standard ways (e.g., in terms of substance, void point, moral category, or ideological fiction), but rather must be understood as constituting a formal imposition or a "formalism." Indeed, Badiou has come to define the subject simply as "any fora which organizes the connection of the consequences of an event."[1] Constructed both in and *out of* the aftermath of an evental rupture, the subject is, in essence, an overarching framework that connects the trace of a vanished event, on the one hand, with the materialization of the new possibilities it implies, on the other. This gradual "objectification" of the subject appears in the form of a *new creative body* which is principally composed of the manifold *works* that it produces (where a "work" is defined as "a finite set of consequences of an event").[2]

On this account, far from being something that we inherently are—as in the conventional "autonomous, coherent, self-directing, integrated, rational, and originary" model of Schlag's reckoning—the subject is rather something that we might enter into: to become a subject is, in effect, to subject ourselves to something much more than what we are; it is to submit to a *greater good*. While this classical term "good," with its concomitant moral and ethical significations, will come to take on real significance in our final section, for the present it is enough to know that Badiou equates the term with his own conception of "truth," which, so far as he is concerned, is the principal object of philosophy proper. Thus a "good" subject—one which is *subjected to the good*—is a subject oriented toward a truth.

While this last term has taken something of a back seat in our considerations thus far, it is in fact in the concept of "truth" that we hit upon the most scandalous aspect of our overall philosophy: the part that—alongside the "real" in its various guises (pure multiplicity, impasses of ontology, event)—arguably authorizes our use of the word "scandal." For what, after all, is more scandalous than the sudden revelation of some inadmissible thing that had long been hidden deep beneath the surface of the situation? And more to the point, what could be more controversial than the announcement that this repressed content constitutes its ultimate *truth*, the truth of the situation as such? Such is, in a word, the *real scandal of truth*: if the original disruptive event constitutes, in effect, a first indication of the secret underside of the situation (hence its "proto-scandalous" status), then the controversial truth that emerges out of this represents the full extent of its unconscious depths.

All of which of course only begs the question of what a truth actually *is*. Needless to say, the truth we are concerned with here differs from its classical understanding as "aletheia" (or, for that matter, as "correspondence"). For a truth is less a disclosure of what *is*, than a construction—literally a *fabrication*—of what *will be*. To be precise, a truth constitutes an *infinite generic set*, which is actively composed by a subject using only those recourses which are immanent to a given situation and whose material is made up of the consequences of a vanished event.

Without going into excessive detail, we will say that a truth's being *infinite* means not only that it is (in the cautious language of Cantor) a "transfinite"[3] set, but also that its subjective production entails an essentially endless sequence of possible consequences. Similarly, of its being *generic*, we will say that this means that it is a special kind of multiplicity, one which "evades" every criteria of discernment the situation has at its disposal, and thus "cannot be integrated according to any of the predicates available in the language of the world in which it appears."[4] To this end, the sole "characteristic" of a truth is precisely the *absence* of any characteristics, or its being radically *un*characteristic.

Yet, as we saw in our initial consideration of the question of being (as well as in our subsequent discussion of the event), this absence of properties also means that it effectively identifies with the situation *as a whole*. Truths can then be said to speak "for" the world—which is to say, *universally*—in so far as "their being can be considered to be identical to the simple fact of belonging to this world."[5] Or in other words, a generic subset is identical to the situation in its entirety—it is immediately and intrinsically universal—for the simple reason that "the elements of this subset—the components of a truth—have their being, or their belonging to the situation, as their only assignable property."[6] This is, after all, precisely what "legitimates the word 'generic': a truth attests in a world to the property of being in this world. The being of a truth is the genre of being of its being."[7]

While ensuring its universality, the genericity of a truth at the same time presents a significant problem for the state. In particular, that a truth is absolutely "*indiscernible and unclassifiable* for knowledge"[8]—or that it is wholly *unaccountable*, that it "eludes knowledge at the level of its being"[9]—means that the state will be totally incapable of recognizing it for what it truly is. Nor, obviously, can it know anything about it; so far as the state is concerned, a truth *makes no sense*.

Yet it *does* make sense to the subject. Indeed, the very reason for a truth's being "true" ultimately lies in the fact that, far from embodying some kind of abstract non-sense, it actually says something very *particular*—however paradoxical this may at first sound—about the situation whence it emerges. In fact, as we have seen, a truth is only a truth in as much as it directly identifies the previously unidentified or repressed "foundation" of the world in question, or what we earlier designated its "site."

That a truth *is* a "truth" then results from the fact that, in emerging from the site, it convokes the foundational void of the situation. For it is precisely this simultaneously disavowed yet constitutive content that is revealed as the truth of the pre-eventual situation.

## Overcoming the Impasse

That a truth poses such a considerable problem for the state—or that, in failing to recognize or account for it, the state thereby loses its grip over the situation—stems not only from the former's genericity, but also from the very impasse of ontology (i.e., the errancy of its power over the situation) that it itself institutes. Indeed, Cohen's difficult generic set theory—which was in fact originally developed precisely in order to overcome this problem of errant excess—not only provides us with the mathematical expression of a truth, but it also effectively tells us that "the being of a truth [...] is to be situated in the very space opened up by the impasse of ontology."[10] So it is the very same scandalous impasse that not only allows for, but actually fosters the subject; as

Badiou himself observes, "the impasse of being, which causes the quantitative excess of the state to err without measure, is in truth *the pass of the Subject*."[11]

Yet this obviously presents us with an immediate problem. On the one hand, we know that the evental origin of a truth precludes its being mathematically explicable. Yet on the other hand, we have also said that a truth itself *is* ontologically expressible, taking the form of an infinite generic set. The question that remains, then, is how exactly this is the case: how to reconcile ontological expression with its own exception?

In addressing this, we first need to recognize that, being counted by the state, yet having no discernible or expressible property, the entire being of a truth resides in the fact that it is composed of multiples which are themselves presented in the situation. Such an indiscernible inclusion, we have already seen, can then have no real "property" other than that of referring to the fact of its *belonging*. Moreover, as this property—which is, of course, nothing other than that of being itself—is obviously shared by each and every term of the situation, the indiscernible subset in effect possesses the properties of any set whatsoever: of the generic subset, "all one can say is that its elements *are*."[12] It is, after all, in this precise sense that the generic set presents the universal truth of the situation, in as much as the indiscernible subset grasps and exhibits "as one-multiple the very being of what belongs insofar as it belongs."[13]

Yet this leaves us with a decidedly passive view of truth: one that is both detached and impotent (especially when contrasted with the immeasurable power of the state). For if all that we can say of such a set is simply that it *is*, then this hardly leaves us much to work with. While there are obviously advantages to conceiving of a truth as generic—in terms of its being immanent, infinite, universal, and foundational—we cannot get around the fact that, in remaining radically "subtracted" from knowledge, or in constituting "a hole, or a subtraction, in the field of the nameable,"[14] then for all its bluster, it does not actually *say* anything—or at least, nothing comprehensible. If this essentially mute truth is then to have any real effect, clearly we need to find a way to overcome its innately passive, detached, and impotent nature. That is to say, it needs to be *forced* upon the situation, such that a new "extended" situation will be established: a "generic extension" in which this new part will be discernible (which is to say, "knowable"). In other words, it needs to be forcibly *made public*.

Such "forcing" is however not simply a figure of speech; to the contrary, it is a mathematical reality. Indeed, it is precisely this ontological process of forcing—developed (once again) by Cohen to establish the independence of the continuum hypothesis—that constitutes for Badiou "the fundamental law of the subject."[15] While it goes without saying that the actual mechanics of forcing are both difficult and involved, its general "idea" can thankfully be grasped with relative ease.[16] In substance, it shows how an initially indiscernible subset of a situation (i.e., a generic multiple) can actually come to be discernible by "forcing" certain otherwise undecidable statements about this multiple to be recognized as either "true" or "false."[17] (Or in our own terms: how an otherwise unaccountable part of a situation is forced to be publicly taken into account.)

While we do not want to get caught up detailing the intricacies of this now-standard mathematical practice, the fundamental importance of the process not only to Badiou's conception of the subject but to our overall argument is such that it demands at least a few more words. To this end, let us note how, in rendering the indiscernible subset discernible (thus forcing it "to *be*"), clearly the very language of the situation, meaning the sum total of its presented terms, must itself be transformed, such that the "new" subset will come to "make sense" (or be "taken into account") therein. Thus the subject sets about re-signifying or "consequentializing" various terms which are already present in the situation, connecting them, piece by piece, to the trace of the vanished event.

Obviously, from the situation's point of view, these newly "consequential" terms will not yet make any sense (hence their controversial nature). Yet the wager of the subject is that they *will have been* comprehensible once the new situation (i.e., the "generic extension" of the old situation) has been established. It is this anticipatory logic—this de-temporalization or "flattening out" of the future anterior inherent to the process of forcing (a logic which puzzled even Cohen at first)[18]—that is key to the operation of the "good" subject, such that, by following its fundamental law, it "names a point in a situation where the situation's inconsistency will have been exposed,"[19] a space where its truth *will finally have been made clear.* Thus, "in the absence of any temporality, thus of any future anterior," Cohen not only "establishes the ontological schema of the relation between the indiscernible and the undecidable," but in doing so "thereby shows us that the existence of a subject is compatible with ontology."[20]

All of which brings us to a point where we not only recognize how a true subject forces the situation "to dispose itself such that this truth […] be finally recognized as a term, and as internal,"[21] but can moreover present a more comprehensive definition of subjectivity itself. Thus, we understand the subject as being a fundamentally anterior function, in as much as it only comes into existence in the wake of an aleatory event. More than this, we know that, in spite of its formal nature, the dimensions of the subject can nonetheless be conceived of as both *dynamic* (with regard to the event and its consequential trace) and *extensive* (concerning its material support, that is, the "body of works" composing it). Furthermore, by way of its fundamental law (i.e., the forcing of indiscernible terms), the subject locates itself precisely "at the intersection […] of knowledge and truth"[22]: oriented toward the "good," the subject is what traces out, in the situation in question, "the becoming multiple of the true."[23]

Ultimately, the creative subject is a *synthetic function*: a means of integrating the possible and the impossible, or of fusing "reality" with the real. It is the subject that finally brings together being *and* event, ontology *and* inconsistency, knowledge *and* truth, such that all of these things might not only *make* but moreover *create sense*.

## The Subject of Scandal

We finally have at our disposal not only a "rational" theory of the real in the form of a complete coherent ontology, together with its unaccounted for (or "incoherent") excess, but moreover a functional theory of true creation that feeds directly into our own model of real scandal. To help us along, we can once again condense all of this into the following key statements.

*There is an impasse of ontology.* Mathematics (hence ontology) is necessarily structurally incomplete: it exhibits its own real (thus a "real of the real"). Specifically, it is impossible to measure the amount by which a state quantitatively exceeds or "overpowers" its situation.

*Situations harbor sites which can become events.* In presenting nothing other than its void, a site "founds" the situation of which it is a part. When this void presentation is maximally consequential, a site becomes an event.

*An event announces something radically new.* In convoking the foundational void of the situation, an event produces something hitherto unrepresentable or absolutely un-known, in the form of a *real new possibility*. An event thus declares the impossible *as* possible.

*An event is extra-ontological.* As the illegal or "unaccountable" revelation of its own being in the space of the situation, an event violates the fundamental laws of ontology and accordingly "appears only to disappear."

*A subject draws forth the consequences of a vanished event.* Established in the wake of an event, a subject is a formal framework connecting an evental trace with the gradual actualization of the possibilities it implies in the form of a new truth. A subject is thus what *accounts for the unaccountable*.

*A truth is an infinite generic set.* It is infinite because it is both "transfinite" and, in principle, incompletable. It is generic because it "evades" all available criteria of discernment; its sole "characteristic" is then the absence of any characteristics (hence its immediate *universality*).

*A truth is the creation of a subject.* Neither being nor the event delivers a truth. In forcing the indiscernible consequences of an event to become discernible— or in accounting for the unaccountable—the subject creates, piece by piece, a new truth. Creation is then the exclusive preserve of the subject.

We might add to all of this a final, critical point, which is that the subject qua agent of real creation, or as composer of a new universal truth, engages as a matter of course—which is to say, *axiomatically*—in a fundamentally scandalous enterprise.

We can register this last point even when we limit ourselves to the conventional understanding of scandal as simply involving the discovery of some violation of the social-symbolic order (such as we see in the "ordinary" revelatory and dissimulative models). Indeed, transgressivity is clearly suffused throughout the entire ontological process, from its elementary foundations all the way to its ultimate truths. We see it in almost every stage of its development: in the instrumental yet secretive role played by an unpresentable real; in the simultaneously disclosive and explosive phenomenon of the event (which itself "transgresses the laws of being");[24] in the tendentious yet objectively incomprehensible nature of the subject's undertaking (which exploits a generic set's "transgressive capacity");[25] in the disquieting revelation of the situation's hidden truth.

More to the point, however, the specific model of subjectivity put forward here perfectly correlates with our own model of real or original scandal, understood in terms of the social reverberations of instances of real creation whereby something absolutely "unaccountable" is forced to be publicly taken into account. This correspondence is easily recognized in the way in which the momentary revelation of the situation's foundational void is taken up and painstakingly accounted for by a new (or "true" or "creative" or "good" or "scandalous" ...) subject, whose inevitably controversial efforts ensure that the consequences of this brief exposure not only are made transparent, but moreover come to be recognized throughout the situation as *true*.

Thus we see a significant shift away from the dominant causal logic of scandal that we identified at the very beginning of this book, such that while the transgressive event continues to figure as necessary "pre-cause" (hence its "proto-scandalous" status), it is now the subject itself which provides its "sufficient" causal complement. Indeed, we can at this point take the three basic conditions of scandal outlined in our introduction—namely, a sovereign public subject, a transgression of the social-symbolic order, and a process of mediatizaion—and substitute for these a *static situation*, an *event*, and a *subjective procedure*. This conceptual exchange allows us finally to reformulate our initial generic definition of scandal (as figuring a mediated process that fascinates the public by proposing some violation of the given social-symbolic order), so that real scandal will be said to constitute *the intra-situational effect of a post-eventual process of real subjective creation*.

This scandal of real subjective creation—or alternatively: the subjective creation of real scandal—is in actual fact something that is borne out in the very mathematics we have been using to build our case. Consider, for example, the controversy generated by Georg Cantor's invention of set theory, following the publication of his deceptively titled 1874 paper "On a Property of the Collection of All Real Algebraic Numbers."[26] It is almost too easy to appreciate the scandalous nature of Cantor's work and, in particular, his quantification of the infinite, since it so obviously flew in the face of the general conception of infinity (the tone for which had been set in 1831 with Carl Friedrich Gauss's assertion that "the infinite is only a *façon de parler*, in which one properly speaks of limits").[27] So controversial was Cantor's project that numerous influential mathematicians would go on to denounce it before his findings were eventually accepted, among them Henri Poincaré (who conceived of transfinite numbers as a disease to be cured)[28] and his own former professor, Leopold Kronecker, who would accuse him of being a "scientific charlatan" and a "corrupter of youth,"[29] and go to considerable lengths to hamper and discredit his work.

Yet Cantor was also personally scandalized by his discoveries, in particular by the troubling spiritual consequences not only of his initial mathematization (and hence laicization) of the infinite, which had heretofore been considered the exclusive province of God, but far more acutely by his enumeration of multiple such quantifications, that is, by his discovery of plural infinities. For it was this, more than anything, that might confirm the traumatic fact that "God is really dead."[30] It was Cantor's piety, after all, which kept him from holding that his multiple quantifications of infinity spelt the death of transcendence, to the extent that he mobilized the term "transfinite" in place of "infinite," in deference to the latter's divine connotations.

So great was this private scandal that Cantor would go on to argue— seemingly against his own work (as well as the logical absurdity of there being a set of all sets)—for the existence of an *actual infinity*, insisting he was "so in favor of the actual infinite that instead of admitting that Nature abhors it, as is commonly said, I hold that Nature makes frequent use of it everywhere, in order to show more effectively the perfections of its Author."[31] To this end, Cantor proved himself to be at once a scandalizing agent of real creation, literally introducing a new infinite subject, and, paradoxically, a staunch defender of the inherently static idea of the One. Indeed, in claiming the multiple infinities he had uncovered actually only "increased the extent of God's dominion for they had no upper bound: there was no 'biggest' infinity."[32] Cantor philosophically aligned himself with none other than Plato—that other great "corrupter of youth"—in his fundamental belief in "the *unity of all to which we ourselves belong*."[33] All of which marks Cantor out as a supremely divided subject, his own deeply theistic beliefs remaining forever at odds with what his unconscious ontology knew to be the case.

## A New Way of Thinking

To be clear, we could just as easily demonstrate the scandalous nature of Gödel's and Cohen's revolutionary creations.[34] (Indeed, we might even show how Badiou's own mathematical ontology, which he explicitly conceives of as a "Platonism of the multiple," would have scandalized Plato himself!)[35] What is crucial to recognize in all of this, however, is that real scandal is in fact not so much an immediate as it is a secondary effect of a real transgression. Or again, regardless of the temptation to draw a straight line between "event" and "scandal"—such that we would literally have a "scandalous event"—it is important to understand that real scandal does not in fact arise directly from an event (which is, in any case, immediately dealt with by the state), but rather only emerges *indirectly*, through the actions of the subject. In a word, it is not the event but rather the subject (which is nonetheless actuated by the event) that causes real scandal.

The reason for this, as we have repeatedly said, is that real scandal is intrinsically tied to creation and, in particular, to the subjective creation of truth. Indeed, our very definition of real scandal is premised on the idea that such acts radically upend the existing order by breaking with the established laws of what is possible and impossible and, in doing so, plunge the situation into a state of chaos. This is, after all, why real creation must be understood as being *essentially* scandalous: in confronting the situation with a "construction that actuates a *new way of thinking*,"[36] one which might be able to "account for the unaccountable"—as we see not only with Cohen's method of forcing, but also with Gödel's laws of incompleteness and Cantor's quantification of the infinite—the previous regime of thought is (literally) forced to undergo an exhaustive and ultimately traumatic restructuring, where long-established theoretical and conceptual models must be radically remodeled or rejected, while seemingly logical ways of understanding the world are exposed as not only irrational but even deleterious. That such wholesale transformation would take place without intense resistance is risible to say the least.

That it is the subject and not the event which "causes" scandal then lies in the fact that an event is itself not so much a creation as it is a *promise*: while the event (which we have repeatedly described as "proto-scandalous," or as the necessary condition of real scandal) announces how "the possible *will be* wrested from the impossible,"[37] it is only with the subject that this wresting actually takes place, such that this new possibility might become a reality. (Hence its functioning as "sufficient cause" for scandal.) Certainly, the event is inherently transgressive, but the state ensures that it is so only for the briefest of moments. As creator of a post-eventual truth, however, the very being of the subject *is* transgression; it is, in effect, nothing else. It is only with the subject that the order of the possible and the impossible is truly transformed, such that we can finally proclaim "all changed, changed utterly: A terrible beauty is born."[38]

Part Four

# Controversy

# Brave New World

We have spent the last chapters establishing the philosophical basis for a conception of real scandal as the social consequence of authentic creation. This should not delude us, however, into supposing that the extraordinary profusion of controversy we are bearing witness to today—or the simple, inarguable fact that we live in "scandalous times"—is in any way indicative of our inhabiting an especially creative environment. To the contrary, our present is, if anything, marked by a potent conservativism and ever-increasing authoritarianism; we have reached a point where "the ratchet effects of modernization appear to have lost their force in the most diverse spheres of activity" and, far from moving forward, instead "we are witnessing a reversion to an earlier stage of 'civilized conduct.'"[1]

This reactionary ethos is apparent in all aspects of modern society. Extreme right-wing populism, with its anti-elitist, anti-establishment rhetoric (often spoken by elite members of the establishment) and aggressively nationalistic outlook, is the political flavor of the moment and looks to remain so for years to come. Science does not seem to be faring much better, with the threat of anthropogenic climate change still being answered at the highest levels by a doubling down on those industries most responsible for the production of greenhouse gasses through the combustion of fossil fuels. Everywhere we turn, from the alternately pleasing and polarizing works of contemporary art to our much-feted information technology industries, we bear witness not to processes of real creation but to the steady beat of *progress*; to so many extensions, repetitions, recyclings, and superficial transformations of forms of knowledge that are, in effect, already circulating within the situation, and which inevitably function to reproduce the dominant order.

While scandals are doubtless multiplying under these conditions, fewer and fewer can be said to be *real*. The goal of this final section is accordingly that of establishing how and why this is the case and, most importantly, what it all means.

## The Other Big Brother

From the mid-twentieth century on, two ominously prophetic works of literature have vied for the dubious honor of having their dystopian vision become reality. On the one hand, George Orwell's *Nineteen Eighty-Four* forced upon us Big Brother, the Ministry of Truth, and the Thought Police, describing a world where societal "integrity" is maintained through brutal repression: a controversial "picture of the future" in the form of "a boot stamping on a human face—for ever."[2] Aldous Huxley's *Brave New World*, on the other hand, in gifting us with *soma*, the feelies, and orgy-porgy, presented an essentially hedonistic vision of suppression through satiation: a subtler (though no less effective) method of maintaining order where society has in effect been seduced into *repressing itself*.

Each of these visions has cast their considerable shadows over our modern lives, such that for a long time the question was "which template would win?"[3] "Hard" power or "soft"? The closed fist or the sensual caress? Big Brother's terrifying visage, or the infantile delights of Centrifugal Bumble-Puppy? Of course, on a certain, immediate level, the answer has been *both*. That in their eternal pursuit of order and stasis the powers that be (i.e., our foremost state representatives) are perfectly capable of encompassing, at one and the same time, brutal oppression and total permission, is so obvious that it hardly bears mentioning. The penitentiary and the shopping mall, the detention center and Amazon: regardless of their evident experiential differences, each nonetheless ultimately represents alternate forms and degrees of imprisonment and social control.

Yet in the current climate of increasingly authoritarian rule and populist politicking, it is Orwell's vision that appears to have finally edged out Huxley's. This ostensible victory, fueled by an overwhelming sense of fear and mistrust on the part of the general public, is even directly reflected in terms of book sales,

*Nineteen Eighty-Four* topping the Amazon best-seller list in early 2017[4]—sixty-eight years after its original publication—following White House Counselor Kellyanne Conway's claim that the Trump Administration was justified in delivering "alternative facts."[5] (Huxley's novel reached number twenty-eight on the same list at the same time.)[6] So we would seem to be witnessing precisely what Orwell's totalitarian mouthpiece O'Brien predicted, namely, the final triumph of a world of brutal oppression—where insurrection is directly answered with torture, and where the ruling Party is prepared to use any and every means to "squeeze you empty, and then […] fill you with ourselves"[7]—over "the stupid hedonistic Utopias that the old reformers imagined."[8]

Of course, that *Nineteen Eighty-Four* would eventually win out in the minds of the general public is, in itself, hardly surprising, and in fact supports our own argument concerning the structure of power and the uses of scandal—in particular, as a potent tool of misdirection or obfuscation. For compared to Huxley's vision, Orwell's blueprint is not only infinitely easier to recognize and even accept as a real possibility; it is, at the same time, far simpler to reject.

That Orwell's vision is easier to accept as a potential reality rests on the fact that it immediately corresponds to the threat so many of us see as standing directly in front of us: a world of "alternative facts" and total surveillance, "a world of fear and treachery and torment […] which will grow not less but *more* merciless as it refines itself."[9] Likewise, looking back over our own argument in Part Two in particular, we can easily identify multiple connections between Orwell's highly regulated society and our own ontological argument. The calculated restrictions of Newspeak, for example, clearly point to the way that the state (or in Orwell's terms, the "Party") exerts absolute control over the situation by reducing its "discernible" terms to a bare minimum—or again: the way that language "governs" being by "subordinating existential judgment to finite and controllable linguistic protocols"[10]—such that the state is able to ensure "the monopoly of possibilities."[11] Similarly, it is hard not to register the correlation of Orwell's characterization of the Party, which "is not concerned with perpetuating its blood but with perpetuating itself,"[12] with our own "unintentional" understanding of the state as an entity whose single and sole idea is "to persevere in its being."[13]

More important than the ease with which we are able to accept the prospect of Orwell's vision, however, is the fact that it is even easier to *reject*, and thus actively oppose. Indeed, one of the reasons we can identify it so easily lies in the fact that it is so immediately hostile to our own ideology (regardless of our political persuasions). After all, the destructive philosophy of the Party leads directly to a world in which everything that we hold dear has been annihilated: a world where "the sex instinct will be eradicated," where the orgasm is abolished, where there is no loyalty, no love, no laughter, "no art, no literature, no science," no curiosity, no enjoyment—in short, a world where "all competing pleasures will be destroyed."[14]

Regardless of its structural similarities, Orwell's world is then primarily recognizable by virtue of the fact that it remains an *other* world: a world that doubtless exists elsewhere, but is never quite *our* reality; an ever-present threat to the otherwise tried and true democratic values that this "other threat" in effect functions to affirm (if only through negative example). Orwell's vision is then, finally, less a straightforward diagnosis than a clarion call, a demand for eternal vigilance in the face of external powers that would threaten our otherwise "good" way of life.

## Mond's Monde

Huxley's hedonistic dystopia, by contrast, would seem to suffer from the fact that it hits *too* close to home. For the Huxleyan idea that we might end up effectively amusing ourselves into a docile state of indifference—that Western democracies will ultimately "dance and dream themselves into oblivion"[15]—while simple enough to comprehend, is far more difficult to accept, and even harder to reject. After all, the brave new world Huxley describes is one where pleasure is not destroyed but rather paramount, where the sex instinct is promoted and the orgasm is celebrated, and whose ultimate mandate is "self-indulgence up to the very limits imposed by hygiene and economics."[16] To recognize such things as constituting an inherent danger to society is then to reject a core part of our psychical makeup; indeed, it is to reject the Western way of life.

Similarly, to oppose and thereby attempt to overcome the peril that lies at the very heart of Huxley's world—to turn our back on the coercive power of pleasure—is to acknowledge that this dystopia has in fact already taken hold: if Orwell's vision represents an incipient but still unrealized threat, Huxley's is an already-existing reality. That is to say, while *Nineteen Eighty-Four* demands that we remain ever watchful of those people and ideas that would tread upon our core values, *Brave New World* contrarily identifies these very values *as* the problem; that the threat resides not in the other but in what we hold most dear (or, to invoke a well-known horror trope: that the call is actually coming from *inside the house*).

It is to this end that the enormous ideological force of Orwell's *Nineteen Eighty-Four*—the extraordinary resonance that its immediately recognizable system of domination still has with the general public—paradoxically functions to consolidate the more insidious aspects of *Brave New World*'s own model of oppression, drawing our attention away from the more intimate danger identified therein and toward an altogether different target, a target which is both easily identifiable and fundamentally "other." This is, in a sense, the most scandalous aspect of *Nineteen Eighty-Four*: in eclipsing Huxley's prophesy with his own, Orwell's text only serves to disguise the truth of the other more completely.

That Huxley's work can be seen to provide a literary blueprint for our current malaise equally extends—and this is where his writing becomes especially significant to our own argument—to its diagnosis of the problem of real creation (which we ourselves have correlated with real scandal), as well as to the static "solution" it puts forward. Indeed, few figures have managed to articulate more clearly the difficulty posed by real novelty than *Brave New World*'s "World Controller" Mustafa Mond, who, like Orwell's O'Brien, functions as the personification of the state (or, as Huxley would have it, the "World State").

To this end, the eventual meeting between Mond and the novel's principal characters serves the purpose of providing definite answers to the many questions that have built up over the course of the narrative, and accordingly takes the form of a long scandalous revelation (in the "ordinary" sense in which we have been using the term). Here, Mond candidly acknowledges the incompatibility of things like "truth" and "beauty" to the proper functioning of society, which he admits operates on a principle of stasis that is itself only maintained by ensuring the ongoing "happiness" of its constituents. As he puts it, "Universal happiness keeps the wheels steadily turning; truth and beauty can't."[17] It is, as always, this "steady turning"—this uninterrupted *repetition* of the social-symbolic order—that is key to the whole process. As Mond avers, "We have our stability to think of. We don't want to change. Every change is a menace to stability."[18]

Of especial interest to us is how Mond then zeros in on the question of scientific invention—and here we should bear in mind our recent examples of the transgressive mathematics of Cantor, Gödel, and Cohen—reasoning that since "every discovery in pure science is potentially subversive," it is of vital importance that it be kept "most carefully chained and muzzled."[19] Moreover, the simple fact that science is what has allowed for the current order to take hold (genetic engineering in particular being "the foundation on which everything else is built")[20] only underscores its inherent danger. As Mond openly admits:

> I'm interested in truth, I like science. But truth's a menace, science is a public danger. As dangerous as it's been beneficent. It has given us the stablest equilibrium in history. [...] But we can't allow science to undo its own good work. That's why we so carefully limit the scope of its researches—that's why I almost got sent to an island. We don't allow it to deal with any but the most immediate problems of the moment.[21]

In raising the threat of seeing science "undo its own good work," Mond articulates the crux not only of the static view of science, but of authentic creation more broadly. For "real science"—the kind that Mond himself engaged in before becoming World Controller (hence his almost being "sent to an island")[22]—means real creation, which in turn means change, which of course means instability, and "instability means the end of civilization."[23] After all, real science is, at its core, a fundamentally revolutionary enterprise—a radical program of thought that not only lays down the "rules of existence," but might also, at the same time, overturn and dismantle them. To allow such a powerfully creative thing to proceed unchecked is, in the eyes of the state, not simply to tempt fate, but to cede control of it altogether.

## To Overturn the World

As a process of creation, real science is then antithetical to stability. Here we might think of Cantor's famous declaration that "the essence of mathematics lies in its freedom"[24] or Thomas Kuhn's work on the structure of 'scientific revolutions'[25] (or, more recently, Carlo Rovelli's contention that "rebellion is perhaps among the deepest roots of science: the refusal to accept the present order of things").[26] The reason the state cannot abide creation is therefore not simply because it introduces something new, but more importantly, it is because in doing so *it undoes what came before it*.[27] This creative "undoing"— the scandalous core of the subjective process—is, in the final analysis, the only thing that poses any real threat to state power. For as we have seen, the new is not simply built *on* the old; more precisely, it is built *out of* the old. Hence its upending of the situation: in reclaiming and refashioning the very material out of which the situation is both constructed and statically *re*structured, the new undermines the statist order and, in so doing, establishes a radically new order: an order which is fundamentally out of reach of the state, or that "puts the State at a distance."[28]

This restructuration is, after all, a basic law of real creation. In fact, we would do well here to briefly review one or two things that we already know. First, recall how an event, as we have defined it, figures the revelation of the hidden void of the situation. Now, in its foundational capacity, this void is obviously something that was there (i.e., in the situation) from the very beginning, even though it was never presented as such and accordingly "counts for nothing." So, while an event is an exception to the *rules* of the situation, it is still very much immanent to the situation, in so far as it is part of its basic material (hence its representing "an immanent exception to the laws of a given situation").[29] To this end, as we said at the very start of this book, while an event is without doubt an extraordinary occurrence, it should not be understood as being in any way "miraculous." Likewise, the universal truth that is created by the post-evental subject is fabricated entirely out of materials which, while initially indiscernible (and hence *controversial*), are nonetheless strictly immanent to the world in which it takes place.[30]

All of which is to say that the entire creative procedure—the vanished event, the indiscerning subject, and its infinite truth—represents nothing less than a radical reconstruction of the entire situation from the ground up using only its available means, a process which starts out by undermining its foundations only to gradually advance further and further outward, such that, like Winston's idealized proles, it "would one day overturn the world."[31]

Returning to *Brave New World*, Mond's emphatically statist response to this real danger is, unsurprisingly, to curtail invention and promote in its place a carefully delimited and intentionally misunderstood science, doled out as "hypnopaedic platitudes" and an endless array of technological gadgets, coupled with an equally debased art, principally in the form of the "feelies." In practice, this of course means a drastically reduced—and hence legally "acceptable" or *uncontroversial*—version of truth and beauty, a circumscribed model that has been wholly stripped of its transgressive qualities. Like the actual drug *soma*, these prudently sanitized versions of art and science effectively function to medicate the populace, lulling them into a state of stupefied contentment and rendering them numb to the very desire to create anything new.

It is, to be sure, this pacification-through-satiation—this numbing appeasement that Mond calls "happiness"—which is the primary source of the novel's horror, both for Huxley and for the contemporary reader. Indeed, it is hard not to register the manifold parallels between Mond's world and our own (together with its worrying political implications). As with the World State and its citizens, we as a society lionize science as the sole arbiter of truth—albeit only up to the point where this "truth" comes into conflict with the operations of the state (as, for example, in the case of climate science).[32] Likewise, our existence is so suffused with hi-tech gadgets that our every gesture seems to be both mediated and modulated—and, by the same token, registered and regulated—by technologies that we only rarely understand. The same can be said of our engagement with art, which is likely to oscillate between binge-watching television series via online streaming services and following the arbitrary trends of an artificial art market which we know "has done more to alter and distort the way we experience painting and sculpture […] than any style, movement, or polemic."[33]

Ultimately, what Huxley grasped so much clearer than Orwell was the extraordinary effectiveness of this satiatory program: the fact that direct force pales in comparison to the power of indulgence and synthetic contentment, and "a society, most of whose members spend a great part of their time not on the spot, not here and now and in the calculable future, but somewhere else […], will find it hard to resist the encroachments of those who would manipulate and control it."[34] In such a world, "no Big Brother is required to deprive people of their autonomy, maturity and history" for the simple reason that "people will come to love their oppression, to adore the technologies that undo their capacity to think."[35]

Like a perverse restaging of Plato's allegory of the cave for the modern age, Huxley's novel prophesied an all-too familiar future where we would come to invest in the shadows to such an extent that even if we did manage to recognize these indistinct shapes for what they truly were—and, more to the point, even if we were to come to the realization that we were, in effect, being held captive—still we would have no interest in breaking free and seeking out the sun. In this, Huxley identified arguably the single greatest threat of the modern age: the promise of a life lived in penumbral bliss, the sad and insipid fate of universal happiness.

## A New Metaphor?

While the danger of a perpetually sated and distracted public's insensibility to its own imprisonment remains as real as ever, the means by which this might take place have evolved considerably. After all, Huxley was writing during the interwar period in the early twentieth century (in 1931, to be precise), in the wake of the Second Industrial Revolution and the introduction of Fordist principles of mass production.[36] Half a century later (in 1985), Neil Postman published his own systematic account of the erosion of public discourse in the age of electronic media, in which he argued—much as we have ourselves—that it is not Orwell's world that has materialized but rather Huxley's, with the result being that "we are a people on the verge of amusing ourselves to death."[37] Unlike Huxley, however, the revolution Postman had in mind was neither industrial nor necessarily "Fordian." Rather, it was *televisual*.

In essence, Postman recognized in the move from print to television culture a seismic shift in the nature of public discourse and, accordingly, in the way that we represent, and thereby understand, the world. While we do not have the space here to do full justice to his argument, its importance to our own work is such that we should at least attempt to summarize its key ideas.

Briefly, Postman's point of departure is with Marshall McLuhan's well-known aphorism that "the medium is the message"[38] and the concomitant ideas that a medium's form largely determines the nature of its content, and that every new medium establishes a new orientation of thought, together with its own unique mode of discourse. Yet he quickly determines that the specificity of McLuhan's "message"—which necessarily takes the form of a particular statement about the world—is far too limited and insufficient to account for the broader operation of the medium in question. To this end, Postman contends that media can be better understood as functioning in the manner of *metaphors*, "working by unobtrusive but powerful implication to enforce their special definitions of reality": regardless of the particular model of mediation (be it the written word, the radio speaker, the television screen, or whatever), each and every one of our "media-metaphors" works to "classify the world around us, sequence it, frame it, enlarge it, reduce it, color it, argue a case for what the world is like."[39] In sum, "our media are our metaphors," and "our metaphors create the content of our culture."[40]

The great media-metaphor shift that took place during the twentieth century—namely, the decisive move from print to television culture—thus not only changed the very structure of discourse, but also introduced an entirely new epistemology, albeit one which, according to Postman, "not only is inferior to a print-based epistemology but is dangerous and absurdist."[41] For while a concerted engagement with the written word tends to foster a form of knowledge that is both analytic and critical (in so far as to engage in this way "means to follow a line of thought, [...] to uncover lies, confusions, and overgeneralizations, to detect abuses of logic and common sense"),[42] the epistemology attached to the "small screen" is one that, as a matter of course, produces disinformation and ignorance, promotes "incoherence and triviality," and is bit by bit "transforming our culture into one vast arena for show business."[43]

Of course, presented in this highly simplified way, Postman's argument doubtless comes off as somewhat crotchety, even curmudgeonly (or as he himself puts it, "standard-brand academic whimpering"),[44] rather like that of a disgruntled parent upset that their children are spending "too much time in front of the box." We would do well, however, to reserve our judgment, as we are yet to arrive at the core of his argument. For the real problem, as he saw it, stemmed from the following inarguable facts: first, that television had come to dictate our use of *all* media, having "achieved the status of 'meta-medium'—an instrument that directs not only our knowledge of the world, but our knowledge of *ways of knowing* as well"[45]; and second, that "television speaks in only one persistent voice—the voice of entertainment."[46] The result was that entertainment, the "supra-ideology" of all televisual discourse, not only now figured as "the natural format for the representation of all experience,"[47] but was fast becoming the paradigm for our conceptualization of *all public information*. In effect, television brought about the comprehensive "entertainmentization" of information as such.

The Huxleyan dynamics of this process are of course immediately apparent: in a televisualized world, ruled by the logic of entertainment—where news is packaged as vaudeville, and where discontinuity trumps coherence to such an extent that the very idea of logical inconsistency (or, for that matter, consistency) no longer makes sense—the public quickly finds itself in the same position as the oblivious inhabitants of Huxley's World State: "insensible to contradiction and narcoticized by technological diversions,"[48] ready and willing participants in their own agreeable subjection. (Indeed, it is worth noting here how the etymology of the word "entertain," which derives from the Old French *entretenir*, meaning to "hold together" or "maintain," itself points to this inherently static logic of entertainment, in so far as to be "entertained" equally means to be "maintained," to be, in effect, *kept in line*.)

Looking at the current state of television, more than thirty years after Postman published his study, we see that there has been little departure from this fundamentally entertaining model. While the basic technology has obviously changed considerably, the medium itself—understood in Postman's terms as "the social and intellectual environment a machine creates"[49]—remains *essentially* the same, and has arguably even doubled down on its own inherent biases. Whereas he had his sights firmly set on broadcast news, today, countries from Argentina to Ukraine run competing twenty-four-hour news networks that maintain their viewership through a combination of overblown reportage ("breaking news: dramatic police pursuit currently underway!"; "exclusive: serial killer on the loose in *your* neighborhood!"), hyperpartisan political punditry, and a veritable cavalcade of "unique, theatrical (attractive or repellent)"—which is to say, *entertaining*—"personalities."[50] Things have even come full circle to the extent that a significant proportion of viewers now opt to bypass "traditional" news channels altogether and instead turn directly to comedy shows to keep up to date with current affairs.[51]

Fears of the "death of television" in the digital age have, moreover, proven to be not only unfounded but completely wrongheaded. Far from disappearing, the medium of television (as distinct from its original technology) has only expanded, not least due to the fact that digital technology has seen the rise of a seemingly inexhaustible array of *screens*, such that almost every conceivable surface now either has been transformed into a visual screen, or is in the process of becoming one (or at the very least holds the potential to become one). Long liberated from the confines of the "living room box" of yesteryear, we now exist in "a world where every device is a television"[52]—where this entertaining medium, together with its metaphorical message, is in effect with us twenty-four seven.

It is in part for these reasons that the common idea of the internet as "disrupting" television can be understood to represent in many respects an "inversion of what's actually happening."[53] Without going so far as to say that it is in fact television which is disrupting the internet, it is nonetheless crucial that we recognize the enormous impact the former has had on the development of the latter, particularly as television's inherent epistemological biases are expanded and even perfected by this new and truly omnipresent medium.

For one thing, with advances in technology, television has been able to substantially reorder significant parts of the internet, as Internet Protocol Television and "over-the-top" streaming services effectively bring "television programming and values and behavior—like passive watching—to heretofore interactive and computing-related screens."[54] Moreover, we can see how the internet has refined so many of television's logical tics, such as its fragmented "Now ... this" grammar, or its peculiarly anticommunicatory mode of discourse that "abandons logic, reason, sequence and rules of contradiction"[55]—a perfection it accomplishes through an endless proliferation of hyperlinks, pop-ups, multiple windows, YouTube clips, blogs, news feeds, etc. Here, hierarchies of knowledge are radically rearranged (which is not necessarily to say flattened out), while the sheer excess of dis-integrated information promotes superficial modes of engagement and understanding, in the form of skimming, scanning, looking over, running through and so on. (It is, after all, not for nothing that we navigate all of this information via "browsers.")

To cut a long story short, our contention is that the journey from the brave new world of television to the digital age has been, epistemologically speaking, far smoother than we have been led to believe, in that far from challenging the former's prevailing logic, the "digital revolution" has essentially continued its metaphorical work. All of which is to say that, if digital culture is "revolutionary," it is so foremost in the sense that it brings us full circle, back to the amusing, absorbing, and anaesthetizing logic of television.

# The Real Problem

We should begin this final chapter by clarifying a key point that was made while concluding the last. For the new digital media-metaphor does not in actual fact simply entail a straightforward continuation of television's entertaining message. Rather, it represents a significant escalation or *intensification* of its logic. While television has historically formally functioned as an "entertainment machine," filtering the outside world through its enjoyable lens, the new digital media—and *social media* in particular—not only vastly amplifies and accelerates this operation but also takes it a decisive step further; it subjects our *inner* world, our otherwise "private" lives, to this same entertainmentizing process, such that its equally pacifying and satiating message comes to resonate in the deepest recesses of our being.

Our task now is accordingly that of showing how this self-satisfying (and simultaneously self-deluding) process of "entertaining ourselves" culminates in the apogee of engaging, and, crucially, *engageable* events: the social mediated scandal. If the rise of television-based epistemology and its trivializing logic of total entertainment meant that we, as a species, were only too happy to be "getting sillier by the minute,"[1] the system of thought that accompanies social media extends this same logic all the way to its controversial conclusion, ensuring that we truly *are* entertained—in the fullest sense of the word.

## A Neighborhood of Strangers

In explaining his argument that our media-metaphors bring with them whole new epistemologies, Postman turns first to the work of Northrop Frye and his principle of "resonance" (a term that we ourselves have repeatedly used in reference to the consequences of an event). While this concept nominally refers to the way in which "a particular statement in a particular context acquires a universal significance,"[2] Frye extends it to include characters, places, objects, and so on. Needless to say, the force of this resonance is wholly wrapped up with its metaphorical function. Thus Hamlet, for example, has particular resonance as a metaphor for indecisiveness, while Watergate resonates as a byword for scandal. Drawing on this elementary logic, Postman observes that "every medium of communication [...] has resonance" for the simple reason that "resonance is metaphor writ large."[3]

Given what we have already seen, we can surmise with some confidence that the extraordinary resonance of television was, in Postman's eyes, as unprecedented as it was unfortunate. Yet for all its momentous epistemological and ideological effects, the actual technology of television itself—its historical *form*—represented a distinctly isolated and intermittent experience. Subject to constraints that were both temporal (with regard to regulated programming and the rhythms of work and family life) and spatial (in terms of its physical confinement to, say, the living room or the bedroom), television, in its "classical" incarnation, could hardly live up to its own discursive hype; as a fundamentally limited technology with a comparatively enormous epistemological impact, the medium of television has always been, metaphorically speaking, punching far above its weight.

By adopting television's entertaining (and accordingly tranquilizing or "static") message, today's ubiquitous digital media have not only dramatically extended the former's reach; more importantly, they have intensified its resonance. This is never more the case than in the multiple platforms comprising social media, where this amplification is paradoxically achieved precisely by bringing about a "total inversion of how news is created, shared and distributed."[4] Indeed, considered as a whole, social media is doubtless the single most resonant medium of communication that exists today, its epistemological influence being underpinned not only by its immediacy, but also by its unique connective, collectivizing, and propagative functions.

Exemplary here is the microblogging site Twitter, where information resonates both internally, through the function of "retweeting" (being the dominant means of information propagation on the site), and externally, through a constant process of remediation in more traditional news channels.[5]

And this is to say nothing of the Twitter-introduced "hashtag," the ubiquity and influence of which is now such that it could even be said to embody the contemporary definition of resonance. Indeed, outside of its simple archiving function, a hashtag only really functions in so far as it resonates or "catches on"—and under ideal circumstances, "trends"—such that it is elevated out of its particular context and, as Frye might have said, "acquires a universal significance." (Suffice to point here to the extraordinary resonance of the hashtags, we ourselves have already had cause to mention, as well as those representing mass social movements and awareness campaigns, such as #BlackLivesMatter, or even #FakeNews.)

This logical progression from television to social media is even more apparent when we consider Postman's key assertion that, regardless of its revolutionary nature, the former did not in fact come out of nowhere, but rather integrated and extended the disruptive logics inaugurated by the nineteenth-century technologies of the telegraph and the camera. Or as he puts it, "Television gave the epistemological biases of the telegraph and the photograph their most potent expression, raising the interplay of image and instancy to an exquisite and dangerous perfection."[6] Unsurprisingly, what we dispute here—with, of course, the considerable benefit of hindsight—is the idea of television's having perfected these epistemological biases, since it is today abundantly clear that this ideal "interplay of image and instancy" has been far more convincingly attained by social media. (And even then, this "perfection" may itself only be provisional, with still purer forms waiting on the horizon.)

It is difficult, for example, not to register the logical progression from telegraph message to contemporary "tweet." After all, each and every aspect that Postman isolates as most disturbing about the overall discursive logic introduced by telegraphy—its "demons of discourse"[7]—is far better encapsulated in the word of Twitter (as well as in social media and the internet more broadly): that it functioned to "dignify irrelevance and amplify impotence"; that it "made public discourse essentially incoherent"; that "its language was the language of headlines" such that news now "took the form of slogans"; that it was designed "to be noted with excitement" and "forgotten with dispatch"; and that it ultimately instituted "a neighborhood of strangers and pointless quantity; a world of fragments and discontinuities."[8]

All of these things and more point to a logical continuity at work in the technological progression which takes us from the birth of the telegraph and the camera through the age of television up to the world of social media. Accordingly, as we have said, far from rupturing with the epistemological order established by television, the new digital media-metaphor—and principally the world of social media—takes up this decontextualized and disconnected (and now *decentralized*) mode of communication and amplifies it, giving it its "most potent expression." In fact, not only does social media represent an extraordinary intensification of its predecessors' experientially superficial, relentlessly entertaining, and fundamentally static logic; it also manages to *subjectivize* this entire process, allowing us to actively participate—thus emotionally and intellectually invest—in the world it constructs. This is, after all, the real and ostensibly "democratic"[9] revolution of digital technology: while television heralded an age where the world could speak directly *to* us, social media finally completes the circle, such that we are now able to speak directly *with* the world.

Clearly the model of social media we are presenting here is highly simplified and hardly begins to take into account the peculiarities inherent to the operations of its many constitutive platforms. That it is, all the same, perfectly adequate for our purposes, comes down to the fact that our interest lies finally not with social media *per se*, but rather with its relation to *scandal*—a relation we understand as both foundational and formational. For just as there are few things more scandalous than social media, likewise there is little that is more social mediated than scandal.

## Are You Not Entertained?

The time has finally come for us to lay our cards on the table. Bearing in mind McLuhan's basic recognition that the content of a medium is essentially determined by its form (or that "the medium *is* the message"), our contention is that, just as television formally constitutes an "entertainment machine," likewise social media such as Twitter are structurally biased to function as "scandalizing apparatuses," filtering their content and presenting it in a new, "scandalous" light. And just as the age of television saw entertainment become the metaphor for all public discourse (both on and off the screen), the contemporary rise of social media has similarly elevated controversy to the status of "universal metaphor," with the added bonus that this media's seeming "directness" (as a result of its participatory nature) encourages a deeper investment in, and even intoxication with, its "clarified" content, namely, the regulative scandal itself.

Once again, in the interest of making things as simple as possible, it is worth briefly recounting the key steps taken to arrive at this position. To begin with, we established in Part Three that real creation presents an existential threat to the state for two principal reasons: first, on account of the fact that the initial event suspends (if only temporarily) its ordinary functioning; and second, because the work of the subject ensures that the consequences of this event resonate throughout the whole of the situation, eventually destabilizing it to the point of collapse before constructing it anew (all the while operating at a remove from the state). As a process which is wholly "unaccountable" (or as Badiou puts it, "indiscernible and unclassifiable for knowledge")[10] yet has momentous effects, this act of creation will be publicly (which is to say, intra-situationally) grasped as real scandal, and only recognized by virtue of the level of controversy that it generates.

As Huxley's cautionary fiction so perfectly illustrates, the state contrives to neutralize this ever-present threat not through direct oppression but rather by maintaining the "universal happiness"—defined, of course, on its own terms— of its constituents, which it largely achieves by capitalizing on "man's almost infinite appetite for distractions."[11] Thus the state lays out a veritable cornucopia of amusements, such that they not only would "drown in a sea of irrelevance"[12] any and all form of rational dialogue, but might furthermore relieve us of the very desire for real newness and genuine change. The apotheosis of this whole process, according to Postman, is found in the twentieth-century technology of television, which swiftly rose to the level of "meta-medium" and even achieved the status of "myth" (in the Barthesian sense),[13] becoming, in effect, "the background radiation of the social and intellectual universe," so familiar and integrated that "we no longer hear its faint hissing in the background or see the flickering grey light."[14]

Thus television achieved something close to epistemological (Western) world domination, such that all information came to be filtered through the static lens of "entertainment." Although Postman was writing over three decades ago, the entertainmentizing logic he identified is still very much alive and well today, not only in the medium of television itself (which continues to thrive in the digital age), but also in a far more concentrated form in the world of social media.

Yet we cannot help but recognize here a critical gap in both Huxley's and Postman's reasoning. For while the brave new worlds they point to are only maintained by ensuring the "universal happiness" (or the "total entertainment") of their inhabitants, neither vision is able to convincingly account for the simple fact that humans are an innately accommodating species: that it is in our nature to adapt to even the most exciting stimulus and that, in doing so, we become progressively desensitized to the effect it has on us (in terms of not only its operation but also its allure), so that we might attend to other surrounding stimuli. Even the most dazzling object eventually loses its luster, leading us to desire new objects and new experiences. All of which leads us to a fundamental rule of static organization, which is that, contrary to what we might reasonably expect, familiarity is in fact antithetical to stability.

We must then be careful not to overlook how both Huxley's and Postman's worlds operate, in the end, less on a principle of perpetual excitation than one of numbing familiarity. This is explicit in Huxley's reliance on a combination of the anesthetizing effects of *soma* and an endlessly repeated cycle of distractions (the feelies, orgy-porgy, obstacle golf, centrifugal bumble-puppy, etc.) as "instruments of policy,"[15] just as it is in Postman's insistence on the homogeneous and homogenizing force of television as being ultimately responsible for "the trivialization of public information" (and thereby providing "the clearest available glimpse of the Huxleyan future").[16] In a word, both Huxley's and Postman's worlds are altogether too tranquil, too uniform, too *static*. For them to function effectively—and, crucially, enduringly—it is essential that they introduce a greater degree of dynamism.

As we saw in Part Two, the way that the state has historically accomplished this (i.e., factoring in a minimal level of agitation) has been by continually supplementing its already-entertaining environment with "safe," non-disruptive forms of novelty—what we earlier referred to as aseptic or ersatz versions of the new. (Note that this endless process of *re*newal differs from the constant distractions of Huxley's world, which never feign to be *actually new*.)[17] Yet there also appears today another way of ensuring the constant production of novel stimuli: one that takes the static idea of expropriating the new and applies this same principle not to the object itself but rather to the interferential effect it has on the situation; to the palpable, disruptive, "discordant resonance" it has in the world. We refer here, of course, to the *artificial generation of controversy by the state*.

This state-sanctioned controversy or "static interference"—which in turn gives rise to simulacral forms of scandal (in a notable inversion of the process by which its "real" model proceeds)—arguably presents an even more effective mechanism of social control than that of the endless production of aseptic novelty. That it can be seen to "upgrade" such previous measures ultimately rests on four associated ideas: first, like novel objects, such controversy is immediately entertaining; second, unlike novel objects, its dynamic, constantly shifting nature is capable of maintaining our level of excitement; third, it satisfies our desire for the new by mimicking its environmental effects; and fourth, it engages us on an intimate level by eliciting our emotional investment through participation and personal involvement.

All of which brings us back to the crucial innovation that is social media. For in intensifying television's entertaining epistemology, social media in effect distils this logic into a form that not only functions to entertain (and thereby both maintain and contain) its constituents, but at the same time offers the illusion of chaos and disruption through the proliferation of what is, in the end, a fundamentally *inconsequential form of controversy*. (Recall here that "real controversy" derives from the inexplicable and unaccountable consequences of an event.) This purified logic—the effectual synthesis of stupefying entertainment and simulated transgression—is then finally articulated in the phenomenon of scandal.

Needless to say, these social mediated scandals are not *real* scandals. Yet nor are they perforce revelatory or dissimulative: the social mediated scandal need not disclose anything that would otherwise be concealed, nor is there necessarily an expressly financial motive at play.[18] Rather, these scandals deliver us controversy for the sake of controversy—the proliferation of a literally *inconsequential* (in the "real" sense) or *empty controversy*.

## Simulacra and Stimulation

In registering this, it is impossible to overlook the case of Donald Trump, a figure who so perfectly encapsulates our overall argument that it seems almost redundant to bring him into the discussion. For not only does Trump provide the quintessence of "empty controversy"; his existence is moreover so dependent on the media—which is to say that he is so comprehensively *mediatized*—that it is arguably no longer possible to separate the two. As James Poniewozik puts it, "The 'Donald Trump' who got elected president, who has strutted and fretted across the small screen since the 1980s, is a decades-long media performance,"[19] one that has been conducted for the most part on and for the "small screen."

To be sure, it is hard not to recognize Trump as the direct personification of television and its stupefying (and indeed, stupidifying) logic. We see this in his well-documented "all-consuming obsession with TV ratings."[20] We see it in the way that he has lived his entire life chasing the media spotlight. We see it in his insatiable desire to be praised and adored; in his penchant for fantastical conspiracy theories and plot twists; and in his firm belief that by controlling the narrative, "truth" can be whatever he wants it to be. And we see it when even his harshest critics agree, time and again, that for all his faults, Trump is nonetheless an *endlessly entertaining character*.

Contrasting Trump with his presidential predecessor Ronald Reagan (who himself famously opined that "politics is just like show business"),[21] Poniewozik notes that whereas Reagan the movie star had thrived in a profession where success depends on one's ability "to believe deeply in the authenticity and interiority of people besides themselves," Trump's prior claim to fame had been as a "reality television" star[22]—an occupation where empathy presents a distinct liability—and "playing a character on reality TV means being yourself, but bigger and louder."[23] To this end, Poniewozik argues, the key to "understanding" Trump is to understand television. And what does television want? Very simply, "it wants conflict. It wants excitement. If there is something that can blow up, it should blow up. It wants a fight."[24]

Reality television, for its part, distils this conflictual logic even further by literally blowing up or *exploding the real*, in terms of both its destruction (where all sense of its "authenticity" is obliterated) and its being heightened to gargantuan, often grotesque, proportions. Accordingly, being "real" on reality TV means being "the most entertaining, provocative form of yourself. […] It is to foreground the parts of your personality (aggression, cockiness, prejudice) that will focus the red light [of the camera] on you, and unleash them like weapons." For television, as we know, wants to entertain, and the purest, most compelling form of this entertainment—the kind showcased by reality TV—is the explosion of the real found in conflict, controversy, *scandal*.

As we have argued, it is this very same controversial logic that not only applies to, but is moreover intensified by, social media. After all, what is reality TV if not the televisual prototype of social media, the permeation of the "real" (as we have just described it) into the fantastical space of the screen? That social media is the logical outcome of reality television—the extension of its epistemology of explosively real entertainment—is likewise reflected in the figure of Trump himself. Indeed, this same process of intensification takes place in Trump's own progression from reality television star to social media star—a move which of course culminated in his becoming not only the "leader of the free world," but the televisual world as well. For on Twitter, Trump has found the means to amplify his reality TV persona to such an extent that his every thought now resonates around the world, controlling even the medium whose favor he so desperately sought.[25]

Yet Trump is himself far from "free" on social media. While the common consensus is that his Twitter account provides the public—for better or worse—with an "unfiltered Presidential feed,"[26] it is in reality the opposite which is closer to the case. The irony of his Twitter handle @realDonaldTrump is not lost here: Trump's tweets are "real" precisely in as much as they are, *nolens volens*, caricatures of his "most entertaining, provocative" self.[27] Not only does this "real" Trump (i.e., his social mediated self) continue to maintain his "decades-long media performance" by playing a part—specifically, that of controversial-reality-television-star-turned-even-more-controversial-president. More to the point, he is also very much *a part being played*. For Twitter is, after all, a medium which not only rewards but in effect *determines* conflict. (Here we inevitably circle back to McLuhan's fundamental point that the form of a medium determines its content, the primary determining factors of Twitter being its instancy and its limited character count, each of which promotes epigrammatic commentary over nuanced argumentation, leading to misrepresentation, decontextualization, and ultimately, polarization and polemy.)[28]

In the end, Trump's "success" has been contingent not on his mastery over, but rather on his *reduction to* media, his reducing himself to its most elementary logic—that of scandal and controversy. And even while this logic may serve him well, it is by no means of his own making.

All the same, we can immediately identify three key interrelated ways that the "real" Trump, which is to say, the Trump manufactured by and through social media, exploits controversy for his own political ends. While the mechanics of each of these forms of (both literal and metaphorical) state-sanctioned controversy differ, all three share the same ultimate goal: to foment a sense of chaos that masks a fundamental continuity, ensuring that, for all the sound and fury they generate, things remain exactly the same.

First, as "a showman with a brilliant gift for misdirection,"[29] Trump has long understood how to use controversy as a means not simply of attracting attention, but also of repulsing it, invoking polemos (in its "confronting" sense)[30] as both a diversionary and a blinding tactic. This much is immediately apparent to all but the most insensible of observers: on the one hand, a well-timed incendiary pronouncement serves to divert focus away from more substantial matters; on the other, the constant barrage of fresh crises and provocations— the fact that, regardless of their rapid response rate, "by the time the 24-hour networks have picked up on a particular tweet, it's already disappeared down the page"[31]—achieves the effect of overstimulation, such that each offsets the other, with as earlier instances being either forgotten or overlooked in the race to keep up with the cycle.[32] As a means of simultaneously distracting and overwhelming the public, we can say that controversy functions here to *inundate* the situation.

Second, controversy is used to generate the false appearance or the *simulacrum of eventness*. Critical here is the way that key episodes of Trump's presidential campaign assume the disruptive quality of real controversy, which we know only arises in the wake of an authentic event. These contentious episodes are then endlessly recycled (in rallies, for example) to promote and reinforce among his "base" the idea that his electoral success represented a resoundingly real event, and even that his particular brand of "undiplomacy" constitutes a new political truth. This form of controversy accordingly serves to *innervate* parts of the situation—specifically, those parts which are aligned with the fundamental ideals of Trumpian politics.

Third, controversy is utilized to ensure that no real event might take place, and in this way simultaneously secure the state's power over the situation as well as its monopoly over what *can* and *cannot be* (or "what is possible and impossible").[33] Here the continuous production of an ultimately *in*consequential (with regard to the real) form of controversy coalesces in simulacral scandal, giving the overall impression of an actual state of chaos and disorder precisely in order to render the possibility of real disruptive creation null and void. Thus, in a move that could almost have been lifted directly out of the contemporary Hollywood playbook, the scandal itself is appropriated and "remade" by state actors, heightening its appearance while at the same time ensuring that nothing of actual consequence remains. No longer the stumbling block *of* the real, the scandal now becomes a stumbling block *to* the real. Of this crucial third form of controversy, we will say that its role is to *enervate* the situation.

As we have already indicated, in all of these cases—overstimulation (or "inundation"), simulacrum of the event (or "innervation"), and scandalous obstruction (or "enervation")—the overall desired outcome is ultimately the same: a single and same result that is itself *the perpetuation of the same*. While there is everywhere the appearance of radical disruption, at the crucial level of structure or of the *state*, nothing has changed: the exact same order remains in place, namely, that of wealth and vastly unequal power relations authorized by the overarching system of capitalist-parliamentarianism (or simply the capitalist state). Indeed, if anything, this order has only grown stronger for all the disturbance. Thus, the more "disruptive" Trump is, the more we find ourselves naively extolling the "previous" political order—an order which is equally beholden to power and capital and hence *essentially* the same, but which at least had the common decency to keep its corruption (mostly) out of sight.

Hence the futility of expecting Trump or any of his enablers to finally receive their "just" deserts. Because even if he were eventually convicted of a crime—an outcome that, at the time of writing at least, appears highly doubtful—far from qualifying as real "justice," this would in all likelihood simply represent just another false scandal whereby the rule itself would be recast in the role of the "exception." For the fact of the matter is that, regardless of what actually happens, the only real crimes Trump is guilty of in the eyes of the state are, as usual, those of indiscretion, ostentation, and vulgarity.

## Matters of Consequence

Having taken stock of the careful utilization and, in effect, weaponization of controversy by the state, we at last find ourselves confronted with one final difficult but nonetheless crucial question, which is, what exactly an "ethics of scandal" might look like? Indeed, it should by now be abundantly clear that different forms of scandal can be classified as either "good" or "bad." We have even referred on numerous occasions to real or original scandal as constituting its "good" form, and have similarly observed how the progenitor of real scandal—i.e., the scandalous subject itself—is "good" in so far as it remains firmly committed to drawing forth the consequences of an event and, in this way, functions to create something truly new.

Likewise, the forms of controversy employed by Trump and similar state actors clearly fall well short of this basic standard. And yet, as we said at the very beginning of this book, these latter forms are constructed in such a way as to *appear* to be good. This is, after all, the elementary logic of simulacral scandal: by taking on the form of the real, divorcing it of all consequence, and then multiplying this synthetic real over and over again, the *real* real is effectively incapacitated to the point where it becomes indistinguishable from the established order. Subdued by the state, the exceptional real finds itself reduced to the rank of the ordinary. Given this simulacral state of affairs, how can we expect to be able to judiciously differentiate between the two?

This is, in truth, a decidedly subjective question—both in the sense that it obviously involves questions of judgment and discernment and in so far as it concerns the figure of the subject as we have defined it. We can, however, at least begin to formulate an answer by turning one last time to the work of Badiou, who supplements his own demanding philosophy with an equally uncompromising "ethics of the subject"—one that is unsurprisingly entirely conditional on the event and its concomitant process of real creation.

That there is for Badiou no such thing as a "general" ethics, but "only—eventually—ethics of processes by which we treat the possibilities of a situation,"[34] in effect stems from his equation of ethicality with subjectivity. To act ethically is then to be a *good* subject, a subject resolutely faithful to the consequences of an event; it is to adhere to what Lacan earlier put forward as our sole imperative and hold true to the process that animates us.[35] (Or as Badiou puts it in his most recent work: to follow "three interrelated imperatives: to take up an Idea; to take part in its uncovering; to extricate oneself from finitude by opening thought onto the real infinite.")[36] It is, after all, this absolute fidelity of a subject to an event that Badiou calls (after Plato) the Good. Or more precisely, the Good designates the truth of real creation itself, "the point of radical alterity at which all referrals and all relations come to be suspended," and which "is consequently subtracted from both the Idea and exposition."[37] To this end, the ethical imperative of the subject is not so much that of "being good" as of *remaining faithful to the Good.*

Yet if there exists such a thing as an ethical or a "good subject," clearly there must also exist a correlative *unethical* subject: a subject that sharply deviates from this logic that abandons or in some way opposes the event and the new possibilities it implies. To turn one's back on an event—to "give ground" on it (as Lacan would say) and thereby "rupture with the rupture"—is then to adopt a determinedly unethical position. For in renouncing an event we necessarily "become the enemy of that truth,"[38] in so far as in doing so we affirm the *continuity* of the situation (which is, of course, precisely what the process of real creation disqualifies). To this end, Badiou recognizes the existence of a kind of perverse countersubject, a "reactive" subject which, disenchanted or even appalled by the event's more controversial consequences, proposes instead a mild situational corrective in the form of a marginally modified regime—one that is "'a little less worse' than the past, if only because it resisted the catastrophic temptation [...] contained in the event."[39]

In addition to this reactive countersubject, however, there can also exist an "obscure" subject—a subject which goes further than its faithless counterpart by seeking to destroy all trace of the scandalous event, invoking in its place a "full and pure transcendent Body, an ahistorical or anti-evental body (City, God, Race)."[40] While Badiou does not do so himself, we can draw a connection between this obscure subject and his earlier concept of "terror" (even if this last phenomenon cannot be truly classified as "subjective" since it only presents the illusion of subjectivity).[41] Indeed, the sole objective of terror, as Badiou conceives it, is the gross imitation or "the simulacrum of an event," the fidelity to which establishes "a simulacrum of the subject," which inevitably leads to the "simulacrum of a truth."[42] Here, the supposed event invokes "not the void of the earlier situation, but its plenitude—not the universality of that which is sustained, precisely, by no particular characteristic (no particular multiple), but the absolute particularity of a community, itself rooted in the characteristics of its soil, its blood, and its race."[43] In short, the roots of terror always lie in a false event that grounds itself in an already-represented part of the situation: a part which imagines its status as being simultaneously unquestionable and under real threat.

While the key historical example of such terror remains the rise of Nazism following the 1933 National Socialist Revolution, we can easily recognize the same logic at work in, for example, contemporary right-wing populism: in its obsession with the prospect of being "replaced" by *x* other, and its attendant focus on questions of "belonging" organized along identitarian, national, and racial lines.[44] (In point of fact, populism in general exhibits an intrinsically controversial political logic: one that is foremost characterized by the way in which "it divides the world into two opposing 'camps'—'us' and 'them.'")[45] We see this the world over today, from Erdoğan's Turkey to Bolsonaro's Brazil, from Orbán's Hungary to Duterte's Philippines. We see it in the considerable support for political parties like the *Front National* in France or the *Alternative für Deutschland* in Germany, and in the recent influence of social movements like the Tea Party, The English Defence League, *Pegida*, and *Les Identitaires*. We see it in Brexit and the maneuverings of that other "great entertainer,"[46] Boris Johnson. And, of course, we see it in Donald Trump's America.

Indeed, it is precisely Trump's programmatic use of controversy and scandal to inundate, enervate, and innervate different parts of the situation that makes him—together with his entire administration, his eunuchized republican guard, his devoted "base," and of course the media channels most sympathetic to his political polemos, be this ideologically (Fox News, One America News Network ...) or formally (Twitter, Facebook ...)—a grotesque conflation of obscure subjectivity and terror. That the emphatically unethical subject that emerges out of all of this is, quite literally, *terrifyingly obscure*, should then come as little surprise.

Yet it is at the same time for this very reason that, for all the noise he makes, Trump nonetheless remains, in the final analysis, essentially *inconsequential*. Needless to say, this is not at all to suggest that he has had no effect on the situation—far from it![47] Rather, that Trump and the politics he represents remain truly inconsequential stems from the fact that, as an unethical purveyor of simulacral scandal, he has no relation whatsoever to the real consequences of an actual event. Or again, in steadfastly "avoiding the void" and instead grounding his politics in those parts of the situation that perceive their own representation as being under threat—hence the infamous rally cries: "Build the Wall!"; "Lock Her Up!"; "Send Them Back!"—Trump is not only utterly incapable of presenting any new possibilities; he is equally powerless to have any real effect on the ultimate structure underlying the situation itself. Regardless of the damage he inflicts on the world as a whole, the system that empowered him in the first place—what we accurately refer to as capitalist-parliamentarianism, "the mandatory form for the administration of phenomena in our 'West'"[48]—remains unscathed and firmly in place.

It is finally this question of "consequence" which provides us with a rudimentary means of differentiating between both scandals and events, and accordingly, a way of positioning ourselves ethically in relation to these phenomena. For while we cannot strictly speaking *know*, from a position inside the situation, when the scandal we are confronted with is real and when it is simulacral—just as we will not necessarily be able to tell the difference between its revelatory and dissimulatory counterparts (without being in possession of some kind of additional information)—we can nevertheless begin to evaluate it according to certain recognizable criteria.

After all, we do know that real scandal is truly consequential, since it arises out of the good subject's experimentations with the new possibilities implied by a vanished event, and in particular its prescription of strict measures and ideas that shake the very foundations of the situation. Correspondingly, we know that simulacral scandal is ultimately *in*consequential, on account of the fact that it derives from appeals made by a false subject to an equally false event—appeals which (in the absence of any relation to the new) only serve to reinforce existing impossibilities by proscribing all but the most retrogressive measures and ideas, effectively fortifying the prevailing situation against assault.

So even while these antithetical forms of scandal remain broadly indistinguishable from one another, a list of narrowly discernible yet no less *absolute* differences nonetheless begins to take form, allowing us to oppose, for example, the real consequences of original scandal with the essentially inconsequential nature of its simulacral counterpart. By the same token, we can contrast the invocation of what had previously failed to appear (or had been "voided") in the situation, with the simulacrum's preoccupation with certain of its already-established elements, just as we can distinguish between the introduction of radically new possibilities and the reiteration of extant probabilities and presumptions. Likewise, we know that the universal address of real creation derives from the fact that its core content is scandalously unaccountable in the situation, whereas its simulacral foil speaks only to (and for) the particular, and its attempts to raise this to the level of the universal are less unaccountable than they are unjustifiable. Lastly, we know that while real scandal generates controversy, it is contrariwise state-sanctioned controversy that generates simulacral scandal.

If we have a minimal ethical responsibility today, it is accordingly that of familiarizing ourselves as best we can with these crucial resources of discernment, so that we are able to distinguish the consequential from the inconsequential, the unrepresented from the represented, new possibility from tired predictability, the universal from the particular, the unaccountable from the unjustifiable, and, ultimately, real scandal from static controversy. For in the end, it is only through arming ourselves with these critical intellectual resources—together with no small amount of courage and conviction—that we may be able to navigate our way through these scandalous times.

It is, moreover, precisely in taking on this ethical mantle that we might rise above the static pleasures that otherwise determine and delimit our existence and in doing so come to experience a form of real happiness far removed from the debilitating kind envisioned by Huxley. Not happiness in the sense of "satiation," that anesthetic state of ersatz happiness induced by constant amusement, where the static law of absolute entertainment ensures that "people are happy; they get what they want, and they never want what they can't get."⁴⁹ To the contrary, the happiness we have in mind here is the properly subjective *happiness of the universal*, the joy that comes with "discovering, beneath the dull and dreary existence of our world, the luminous possibilities offered by the affirmative real" and, accordingly, of being able "to enjoy the powerful and creative existence of something which had been, from the world's perspective, impossible."⁵⁰

This, finally, is where real happiness lies, beyond the palliative comforts offered by the state and the constraints of scandalous satisfaction: in our subjective engagement with *real creative existence*, in the experience of something heretofore impossible that cuts through the static interference and entertaining diversions which otherwise keep us in check, in rising above the moralizing machinery of ordinary everyday scandal to establish an ethical absolute, in transforming the initial trauma of disruption into the exhilaration of the new and introducing an element of truth into our allegedly "post-truth" times.

Such is the affective recompense for *not* being amused: for recognizing in an authentically scandalous event something of real consequence, and resolving then and there to take up its controversial cause. It is the reward of real joy which is nothing less than the joy of the real itself: the true happiness we find in a good scandal.

# Notes

## Introduction

1    Note that we are concerned here with the philosophical study of scandal *sui generis*, as opposed to, say, the study of philosophical controversies, on which copious scholarship already exists. On the latter, we might consult, for example, edited collections such as *Scientific and Philosophical Controversies* (Lisbon: Fragmentos, 1990) or Pierluigi Barrotta and Marcelo Dascal's *Controversies and Subjectivity* (Amsterdam: John Benjamins Publishing Company, 2005), not to mention historically "scandalous" works such as Victor Farías's *Heidegger and Nazism* (Philadelphia: Temple University Press, 1989) or Alan Sokal and Jean Bricmont's *Fashionable Nonsense: Postmodern Intellectuals' Abuse of Science* (New York: Picador, 1998). Outside of this, we should also note how the history of philosophy is in many ways the history of controversy, from Socrates—who was of course put to death for scandalously "corrupting the young" and "not believing in the gods in whom the city believes, but in other new spiritual things," Plato, "Apology," in *Complete Works*, ed. John M. Cooper, trans. G. M. A. Grube (Cambridge: Hackett Publishing Company, 1997)—up to the present day. We can equally register this controversial connection on a theoretical level. To take an obvious example, one way of conceiving of the famous *dialectic*, from Plato to Hegel, is precisely in terms of controversy, that is, as the process by which apparent controversies are resolved or "sublated." Arthur Schopenhauer even develops his own "controversial dialectic" as "the branch of knowledge which treats of the obstinacy natural to man," *The Art of Controversy and Other Posthumous Papers*, ed. and trans. T. Bailey Saunders (New York: Macmillan, 1896), 3–4. This connection is equally recognized in the sciences, Gideon Freudenthal for example observing how "a resolution of a controversy is best exemplified by conceptual development, as a result e.g. of the differentiation or the integration of concepts. The concept of *Aufhebung* refers to such processes," "Controversy," *Science in Context* 11, no. 2 (1998): 159. Finally, it is worth noting how one of the peculiarities of philosophy is that once its claims altogether cease to be controversial—i.e., when a philosophical proposition is considered to have been definitively *proven*—it

no longer counts as philosophy *per se*, but is rather understood to be something altogether different: it becomes, in effect, *science*. (Hence the historical progression from natural philosophy to modern science.)

2   John Thompson, *Political Scandals: Power and Visibility in the Media Age* (London: Polity Press, 2000), 5.

3   Thompson, *Political Scandals*, 5.

4   Steffen Burkhardt, "Scandals in the Network Society," in *Scandalogy: An Interdisciplinary Field*, ed. André Haller, Hendrick Michael, and Martin Krauss (Köln: Herbert von Halem Verlag, 2018), 21.

5   Max Gluckman, "Gossip and Scandal," *Current Anthropology* 4, no. 3 (1963): 308.

6   Gluckman, "Gossip and Scandal," 311.

7   Ari Adut, "A Theory of Scandal: Victorians, Homosexuality, and the Fall of Oscar Wilde," *American Journal of Sociology* 111, no. 1 (2005): 213.

8   Ari Adut, *On Scandal: Moral Disturbances in Society, Politics and Art* (New York: Cambridge University Press, 2008), 287.

9   Burkhardt, "Scandals in the Network Society," 21.

10  Sigurd Allern and Ester Pollack, "Nordic Politics Scandals—Frequency, Types and Consequences," in *Mediated Scandals: Gründe, Genese und Folgeeffekte von medialer Skandalberichterstattung*, ed. Mark Ludwig, Thomas Schierl, and Christian von Sikorski (Köln: Herbert von Halem Verlag, 2016), 160.

11  Pierre Schlag, "The Problem of the Subject," *Texas Law Review* 69, no. 1627 (1991): 1730.

12  Antoine Arnauld in René Descartes, *Meditations on First Philosophy with Selections from the Objections and Replies*, ed. and trans. John Cottingham (Cambridge: Cambridge University Press, 1996), 74.

13  Sigmund Freud, *The Standard Edition of the Complete Psychological Works of Sigmund Freud, Volume XIX (1923–1925): The Ego and the Id and Other Works*, ed. and trans. James Stratchey (London: Vintage, 2001), 23. Freud is of course drawing here on the work of Georg Groddeck (who himself drew on the work of Nietzsche), who held that "the affirmation 'I live' is only conditionally correct, it expresses only a small and superficial part of the fundamental principle 'Man is lived by the Es,'" *The Book of the It: Psychoanalytic Letters to a Friend* (New York: Nervous and Mental Disease Publishing Company, 1928), 9.

14  Jacques Lacan, *My Teaching*, trans. David Macey (London: Verso, 2008), 89. As Lacan points out, "the dissymmetry between Freud and Descartes is revealed […] not in the initial method of certainty grounded on the subject. It stems from the fact that the subject is 'at home' in this field of the unconscious"; Jacques

Lacan, *The Seminar of Jacques Lacan, Book XI: The Four Fundamental Concepts of Psychoanalysis*, ed. Jacques-Alain Miller, trans. Alan Sheridan (New York: Norton, 1998), 36.

15  Edmund Husserl, *Cartesian Meditations: An Introduction to Phenomenology*, trans. Dorian Cairns (The Hague: Martinus Nijhoff Publishers, 1982), 1, 150.

16  Jean-Paul Sartre, *Existentialism Is a Humanism*, trans. Carol Macomber (New Haven: Yale University Press, 2007), 22.

17  Martin Heidegger, *Being and Time*, trans. John Macquarrie and Edward Robinson (New York: HarperCollins, 1962), 46.

18  See for example Louis Althusser, "Ideology and Ideological State Apparatuses (Notes towards an Investigation)," in *On Ideology* (London: Verso, 2008), 1–60; Maurice Merleau-Ponty, *Phenomenology of Perception*, trans. Donald A. Landes (London: Routledge, 2012); Michel Foucault, "The Subject and Power," *Critical Inquiry* 8, no. 4 (1982): 777–95; Emmanuel Levinas, *Totality and Infinity: An Essay on Exteriority*, trans. Alphonso Lingis (The Hague: Martinus Nijhoff Publishers, 1979).

19  Alain Badiou, *Being and Event*, trans. Oliver Feltham (London: Continuum, 2005), 392 (emphasis added).

20  Quentin Meillassoux, *After Finitude*, trans. Ray Brassier (London: Continuum, 2008), 63. By "correlationism," Meillassoux refers to the dominant philosophical mode of thought, inherited from Kant (and subsisting through Husserl, Heidegger, Sartre et al.), that "we can only ever have access to the correlation between thinking and being, and never to either term considered apart from the other" (5), and which has accordingly led us to lose access to "the great outdoors, the eternal in-itself, whose being is indifferent to whether or not it is being thought" (63), namely, the *absolute* as such.

21  Note that this is not to dismiss the Cartesian model of subjectivity altogether, since it remains the template on which the contemporary subject is constructed. Hence Lacan, for example, supplements his important "return to Freud" with an equally vital "return to Descartes," Jacques Lacan, *Écrits: The First Complete Edition in English*, trans. Bruce Fink (New York: Norton, 2006), 133. Likewise, the model of subjectivation we will be employing here is wholly indebted to the figure of Descartes, who, together with Lacan, "paved the way for a formal theory of the subject whose basis is materialist." Alain Badiou, *Logics of Worlds: Being and Event, 2*, trans. Alberto Toscano (London: Continuum, 2009), 48. See also Badiou, *Being and Event*, 431–5.

22  Robert M. Entman, *Scandal and Silence: Media Reponses to Presidential Misconduct* (London: Polity Press, 2012), 5. To be clear, Entman qualifies this

statement in his own work exploring how and why certain (political) misconduct becomes "scandal" while other comparable acts of malfeasance do not. Indeed, according to Entman, a key problem of much of the scholarship is precisely its "[reliance] on public outrage as a condition for scandal," in so far as this "means omitting the instances where substantively serious misbehavior never receives sufficient publicity to stimulate a scandalized response" (Entman, *Scandal and Silence*, 5). Note that this does not, however, negate the fact that scandalous behavior only qualifies as *a* scandal to the extent that it is made public (regardless of the level of indignation attached to this publicity).

23  Molière, *Tartuffe*, in *The Broadway Anthology of Drama: Plays from the Western Theatre Volume 1: From Antiquity through the Eighteenth Century*, ed. Jennifer Wise and Craig S. Walker, trans. Richard Wilbur (Ontario: Broadway Press, 2003), 461.

24  We understand "mediatization" here not only in its "immediate" sense—i.e., as straightforwardly referring to "communication processes induced by mass media" (Burkhardt, "Scandals in the Network Society," 22)—but also in the more active or "constructive" sense given to it in media and communication studies, as capturing "long-term interrelation processes between media change on the one hand and social and cultural change on the other." Andreas Hepp, Stig Hjarvard, and Knut Lundby, "Mediatization—Empirical Perspectives: An Introduction to a Special Issue," *Communication* 35, no. 3 (2010): 223.

25  Thompson, *Political Scandals*, 13. Thompson goes on to outline four alternative and often-conflicting theories of scandal—a "no-consequence theory" (where scandals are essentially conceived as media beat-ups that have little purchase on real social and political life), a "functionalist theory" (in which scandals figure as "rituals of collective absolution" (235) that ultimately function to reaffirm the status quo), a "trivialization theory" (whereby the media's obsession with scandals lowers the tone of public discourse while marginalizing important issues), and a "subversion theory" (which contrarily holds that scandal enriches public discourse precisely by calling the status quo into question)—before advancing his own "social theory" which holds that "scandals are struggles over symbolic power in which reputation and trust are at stake" (245).

26  Thompson, *Political Scandals*, 13–14.

27  Adut, "A Theory of Scandal," 213–4.

28  Burkhardt, "Scandals in the Network Society," 20.

29  Frank Esser and Uwe Hartung, "Nazis, Pollution and No Sex: Political Scandals as a Reflection of Political Culture in Germany," *American Behavioral Scientist* 47, no. 8 (2004): 1041.

30  James Lull and Stephen Hinerman, for example, hold that scandals occur when "private acts that disgrace or offend the idealized, dominant morality of a social community are made public and narrativized by the media, producing a range of effects from ideological and cultural retrenchment to disruption and change," "The Search for Scandal," in *Media Scandals: Morality and Desire in the Popular Culture Marketplace*, ed. James Lull and Stephen Hinerman (New York: Columbia University Press, 1997), 3. For further (similar) examples, see Adut, *On Scandal*; Paul Apostolidis and Juliet A. Williams, "Introduction: Sex Scandals and Discourses of Power," in *Public Affairs: Politics in the Age of Sex Scandals*, ed. Paul Apostolidis and Juliet A. Williams (Durham, NC: Duke University Press, 2004), 1–35; Scott Basinger et al. "Preface: Counting and Classifying Congressional Scandals," in *Scandal! An Interdisciplinary Approach to the Consequences, Outcomes and Significance of Political Scandals*, ed. Alison Dagnes and Mark Sachleben (London: Bloomsbury, 2014), 3–28; Maria Jose Canel and Karen Sanders, *Morality Tales: Political Scandals and Journalism in Britain and Spain in the 1990s* (Creskill, NJ: Hampton Press, 2006); Entman, *Scandal and Silence*; John Garrard, "Scandals: An Overview," in *Scandals in Past and Contemporary Politics*, ed. John Garrard and James L. Newell (Manchester: Manchester University Press, 2006), 12–29; Hinda Mandell and Gina Masullo Chen, "Introduction: Scandal in an Age of Likes, Selfies, Retweets and Sexts," in *Scandal in a Digital Age*, ed. Hinda Mandell and Gina Masullo Chen (New York: Palgrave Macmillan, 2016), 3–14; and Howard Tumber and Silvio R. Waisbord, "Introduction: Political Scandals and Media across Democracies, Volume II," *American Behavioral Scientist* 47, no. 9 (2004): 1043–52. Note that none of these characterizations of scandal are far removed from its "legal" definition as "disgraceful, shameful, or degrading acts or conduct that brings about disgrace or offends the moral sensibilities of society" ("Scandal Law and Legal Definition," *USLegal*, https://definitions.uslegal.com/s/scandal/, accessed 27 November 2018).

31  It is, of course, this notion of sufficient causation that allows us to conclude that actual transgression lies in irremediable excess over scandal. Or as Theodore J. Lowi puts it (with regard to specifically *political* scandals): "Corruption is a constant and scandal is a variable," "Power and Corruption: Political Competition and the Scandal Market," in *Public Affairs: Politics in the Age of Sex Scandals*, ed. Paul Apostolidis and Juliet A. Williams (Durham, NC: Duke University Press, 2004), 70.

32  Indeed, according to Badiou, the subject essentially constitutes a "forced exception," Alain Badiou, *Theory of the Subject*, trans. Bruno Bosteels (London: Continuum, 2009), 88.

33  As suggested above, Badiou's subject represents the logical continuation of the great twentieth-century/early twenty-first-century process of desubjectivization, not least concerning Sartre's famous contention that "existence precedes essence" and Lacan's equation of the subject with a "lack-of-being." See for example Alain Badiou, *The Century*, trans. Alberto Toscano (Cambridge: Polity Press, 2007), 100.

34  "The Good" of course constitutes one of the central ideas of classical philosophy after Plato, who recognized that "what provides the truth to the things known and gives the power to the one who knows, is the *idea of the good*," Plato, *The Republic of Plato*, trans. Alan Bloom (New York: HarperCollins), 189 (508e). Badiou himself explicitly aligns his own key concept of "truth"—toward which the subject aims, and around which the entirety of his philosophy is constructed—with "the Good," even going so far as to substitute the latter with the former in his "hyper-translation" of Plato's work. See Alain Badiou, *Plato's Republic: A Dialogue in 16 Chapters*, trans. Suzan Spitzer (New York: Columbia University Press, 2012), xxxiv; and Alain Badiou, *Second Manifesto for Philosophy*, trans. Louise Burchill (Cambridge: Polity Press, 2011), 105–6.

35  Needless to say, exactly how "dramatically realized" this chaotic state will be is going to vary considerably: while a real political invention may well lead to sensational scenes of public tumult, a new scientific theory is likely to introduce a far more measured—though no less absolute—form of (predominantly "intellectual") chaos.

36  Cf. Robert Hughes, *The Shock of the New: Art and the Century of Change* (London: Thames & Hudson, 1980), 6. The scandal's historical relation to radical creation is, for obvious reasons, most immediately recognizable in the field of art where, as Guy Debord observes, "True artistic activity […] appears in the form of scandal," "Situationist Manifesto," in *100 Artists' Manifestos: From the Futurists to the Stuckists*, ed. Alex Danchev (London: Penguin, 2011): 349.

37  Cf. Edward Herman and Noam Chomsky, *Manufacturing Consent: The Political Economy of the Mass Media* (New York: Pantheon Books, 2002). As Herman and Chomsky (lix) point out, this phrase—which the authors do not actually employ themselves—has its origins in the work of Walter Lippmann, who described the operation of propaganda in terms of "the manufacture of consent," *Public Opinion* (New Brunswick: Transaction Publishers, 1992), 248.

38  Kerry Sanders, "Donald Trump: The King of Twitter?" *NBC News*, March 15, 2016, https://www.nbcnews.com/politics/2016-election/donald-trump-king-twitter-n539131 (accessed 27 November 2018).

# Chapter 1

1  On this point it is worth bearing in mind that, outside of the Greek *skandalon* or "stumbling block," one of the etymological roots of the word "scandal" is the French *scander*, meaning "to chant" (as in, for example, the public chanting of slogans).

2  Note that by "celebrity" we refer to anyone who has been thrust, intentionally or not, into the public eye.

3  While we can point to numerous psychological studies in support of this claim, arguably the most immediately applicable (and certainly the most widely known) relates to the concept of "bounded rationality" and the fact that, in situations of uncertainty, we tend to form judgments through recourse to common biases and heuristics. This "intuitive" (as opposed to "rational") process is "fast, automatic, effortless, associative, and often emotionally charged" and "governed by habit, and […] therefore difficult to control or modify," Daniel Kahneman, "Maps of Bounded Rationality: Psychology for Behavioral Economics," *The American Economic Review* 93, no. 5 (2003): 1451. Kahneman further argues that "the central characteristic of agents is not that they reason poorly but that they often act intuitively. And the behavior of these agents is not guided by what they are able to compute, but by what they happen to see at a given moment" (1469). See also Herbert A. Simon, *Models of Man: Social and Rational; Mathematical Essays on Rational Human Behavior in a Social Setting* (New York: Wiley, 1957).

4  In addition to models of "bounded rationality" discussed above (see previous footnote), this reflexive/considered approach can be roughly mapped onto standard dualistic models of information processing, such as the popular "fast" and "slow thinking" system recently put forward by Kahneman (where "fast thinking" operates on an automatic, instinctual or emotional level, while "slow thinking" designates the more controlled and deliberative logical processes that supplement our initial "fast" judgment). See Daniel Kahneman, *Thinking, Fast and Slow* (New York: Farrar, Straus and Giroux, 2011).

5  Alain Badiou, *À la recherche du réel perdu* (Paris: Fayard, 2015), 15.

6  Howard Tumber and Silvio R. Waisbord, "Introduction: Political Scandals and Media across Democracies, Volume I," *American Behavioral Scientist* 47, no. 8 (2004): 1036–7.

7  In his analysis of the structure of tragic theatre that constitutes the bulk of his *Poetics*, Aristotle outlines two forms of dramatic "revelation": *anagnorisis* or "recognition," which refers to a character's sudden awareness of the "true nature" of a situation (thus marking "a change from ignorance to knowledge"); and

*peripeteia* or "reversal," which designates a radical "turning point" concerning a character's fate, or what Aristotle describes in terms of "a change to the opposite in the actions being performed," Aristotle, *Poetics*, trans. Malcolm Heath (London: Penguin Books, 1996), 18.

8  Thompson, *Political Scandals*, 18.

9  Just as in anagnorisis, where it is the *character* who experiences the revelation, a key feature of such scandals—at least, so far as they are played out in the media—is the idea that the protagonists come to realize the error of their ways. This personal admission of guilt leads directly to a cathartic spectacle of repentance: the "Hollywood elite" recognize their hypocrisy and seek forgiveness for their actions, which they now understand to have been "misguided and profoundly wrong" (Felicity Huffman cited in Mark Morales, "Felicity Huffman Issues Apology over College Admissions Case," *CNN*, April 8, 2019, https://edition.cnn.com/2019/04/08/entertainment/felicity-huffman-statement/index.html, accessed 12 April 2019); the corrupt political operator throws himself upon the judge's mercy after claiming in court to be "a different person than the one who came before you in October 2017" (Paul Manafort cited in Sharon LaFraniere, "Paul Manafort's Prison Sentence Is Nearly Doubled to 7½ Years," *The New York Times*, March 13, 2019, https://www.nytimes.com/2019/03/13/us/politics/paul-manafort-sentencing.html, accessed 12 April 2019). Needless to say, the "genuineness" of this repentance is always up for debate.

10  Interviewed in the immediate wake of the college bribery scandal, Daniel Golden—whose 2006 book *The Price of Admission* (New York: Broadway Books) had detailed the pervasiveness of this problem—wastes no time pointing out how the whole affair is little more than a "logical outgrowth" of an already firmly entrenched practice, and that by pushing "to the fullest extent, an unfair system that has been in place for a long time," these parents simply present "the fantasy, extreme version of an endemic problem," Isaac Chotiner and Daniel Golden, "An Investigative Journalist on How Parents Buy College Admissions," *The New Yorker*, March 12, 2019, https://www.newyorker.com/news/q-and-a/an-investigative-journalist-on-how-parents-buy-college-admissions (accessed 13 March 2019).

11  Naomi Fry, "The College-Admissions Scandal and the Banality of Scamming," *The New Yorker*, March 13, 2019, https://www.newyorker.com/culture/cultural-comment/the-college-admissions-scandal-and-the-banality-of-scamming (accessed 13 March 2019).

12  See Jo Becker, Adam Goldman, and Matt Apuzzo, "Russian Dirt on Clinton? 'I Love It', Donald Trump Jr. Said," *The New York Times*, July 11, 2017, https://www.nytimes.com/2017/07/11/us/politics/trump-russia-email-clinton.html (accessed 12 April 2019).

13  Michael Wolff, *Television Is the New Television: The Unexpected Triumph of Old Media in the Digital Age* (New York: Penguin, 2015), 56.

14  Andres Serrano and Ben Beaumont-Thomas, "Andres Serrano's Best Photograph: A White Man with Black Skin," *The Guardian*, April 6, 2017, https://www.theguardian.com/artanddesign/2017/apr/06/andres-serrano-best-photograph-interview (accessed 3 March 2018).

15  Andres Serrano cited in Angelique Chrisafis, "Attack on 'Blasphemous' Art Work Fires Debate of Role of Religion in France," *The Guardian*, April 18, 2011, https://www.theguardian.com/world/2011/apr/18/andres-serrano-piss-christ-destroyed-christian-protesters (accessed 3 March 2018).

16  This is especially clear in Joseph Nye's now standard definition of corruption as "behavior which deviates from the formal duties of a public role because of private-regarding (personal, close family, private clique), pecuniary, or status gains; or violates rules against the exercise of certain types of private-regarding influence," "Corruption and Political Development: A Cost-Benefits Analysis," *American Political Science Review* 85 (1991): 419.

17  Marcel Duchamp and Pierre Cabanne, *Dialogues with Marcel Duchamp*, trans. Ron Padgett (New York: Da Capo Press, 1987), 30.

18  See Milton Brown, *The Story of the Armory Show* (New York: Joseph Hirshhorn Foundation, 1963), 110.

19  Michael Leva, *Looking Askance: Skepticism and American Art from Deakins to Duchamp* (California: University of California Press, 2007), 233.

20  Theodor Roosevelt, "Mr. Roosevelt on the Cubists," *The Literary Digest*, April 5, 1913: 772–3.

21  We should also bear in mind that cubism was not in fact altogether unknown to American audiences. The front page of the October 8, 1911, edition of *The New York Times* featured a full-page article discussing the influence of the cubist movement and describing cubist works as "pictures before which descriptive adjectives retreat in disorder," "The 'Cubists' Dominate Paris' Fall Salon," *The New York Times*, October 8, 1911, 1. Furthermore, the May 19, 1912, edition of the same newspaper ran a review of a British exhibition of Picasso's works which deemed the show a "deplorable display," labeling the exhibited works "a series of childish, not to say imbecile, scribbles that are of no interest either as independent works of art or as steps toward achieving the complete work." See Mark Bulik, "Picasso and the 'Eccentric' Cubists," *The New York Times*, February 2, 2015, https://www.nytimes.com/times-insider/2015/02/02/1911-picasso-and-the-eccentric-cubists/ (accessed 5 March 2018).

22 Stelios Phili, "Robin Thicke on That Banned Video, Collaborating with 2 Chainz and Kendrick Lamar, and His New Film," *GQ Magazine*, May 6, 2013, https://www.gq.com/story/robin-thicke-interview-blurred-lines-music-video-collaborating-with-2-chainz-and-kendrick-lamar-mercy (accessed 9 March 2018).

23 MTV News Staff, "Thanks Miley! 2013 VMAs Shatter Twitter Records," *MTV News*, August 26, 2013, http://www.mtv.com/news/1713119/vma-ratings-record/ (accessed 9 March 2018).

24 Stuart Dredge, "Global Music Sales Fell in 2013 despite Strong Growth for Streaming Services," *The Guardian*, March 18, 2014, https://www.theguardian.com/technology/2014/mar/18/music-sales-ifpi-2013-spotify-streaming (accessed 9 March 2018).

25 Jan Blumentrath, "Interview with Jordan Feldstein," *HitQuarters*, October 30, 2013, https://web.archive.org/web/20140209042751/http://www.hitquarters.com/index.php3?page=intrview/2013/October30_17_1_48.html (accessed 9 March 2018).

26 Responding to a question regarding the video's genesis, Martel stated "I've been thinking about music videos, marketing and the Internet for a while. I want to make videos that sell records. That is my main focus right now, not to make videos that express my own obsessions, but to make videos that move units," Diane Martel and Eric Ducker, "Q&A: Veteran Music Director Diane Martel on Her Controversial Videos for Robin Thicke and Miley Cyrus," *Grantland*, June 26, 2013, http://grantland.com/hollywood-prospectus/qa-veteran-music-video-director-diane-martel-on-her-controversial-videos-for-robin-thicke-and-miley-cyrus/ (accessed 9 March 2018).

27 NPR Staff, "Pharrell Williams on Juxtaposition and Seeing Sounds," *NPR*, December 31, 2013, http://www.npr.org/sections/therecord/2013/12/31/258406317/pharrell-williams-on-juxtaposition-and-seeing-sounds (accessed 9 March 2018). Martel, for her part, insisted that the models' exaggerated performances indicated they were "subtly ridiculing" the men, and that by looking directly into the camera "they are in the power position," Martel and Ducker, "Q&A."

28 This idea of the scandal as "throwing open the gates" is of course reflected in our insistence on applying the suffix "gate" to anything even remotely scandalous. While nominally referring back to the Watergate scandal, the use of this suffix is arguably more commonly understood today to indicate any instance in which an ordinarily confidential activity—which may or may not be "real," and which can range from the merely private to the sinister or conspiratorial—is revealed to the public. Recent prominent examples include 2009's "climategate," 2014's "celebgate," 2016's "pizzagate," and 2018's "spygate."

29 See for example Max Horkheimer and Theodore Adorno, *Dialectic of Enlightenment: Philosophical Fragments*, ed. Gunzelin Schmid Noerr, trans. Edmund Jephcott (Stanford, CA: Stanford University Press, 2002); Jean Baudrillard, *Simulacra and Simulation*, trans. Sheila Faria Glaser (Ann Arbour, MI: University of Michigan Press, 1994); Fredric Jameson, *Postmodernism, or, the Cultural Logic of Late Capitalism* (London: Verso, 1991); Slavoj Žižek, *Absolute Recoil: Towards a New Foundation of Dialectical Materialism* (London: Verso, 2014).

30 Monika Verbalyte, "Deconstruction of the Emotional Logic of Political Scandal," in *Scandalogy: An Interdisciplinary Field*, ed. André Haller, Hendrick Michael and Martin Krauss (Köln: Herbert von Halem Verlag, 2018), 62.

31 Adut, *On Scandal*, 8.

32 Adut, *On Scandal*, 9. Further variations on this dualistic theme can easily be found. To cite only one such example, Monika Verbalyte presents a similar division in terms of "functionalist" and "discursive-communicative" perspectives, where "the functionalist perspective represents the ideal type of theories which describe the normative and societal functionality of the scandal," whereas the discursive-communicative position concerns "theories which analyze how scandals are symbolically constructed and performed," Verbalyte, "Emotional Logic of Political Scandal," 63.

33 If there is a single point of disagreement between these "simple" models of scandal and the more nuanced ones proposed in orthodox scandal research (such as those discussed in the previous chapter), it is with the latter's occasional insistence that the scandalous party incurs some form of reputational damage (a qualification which is almost exclusively reserved for "political" models of scandal). To take only one such example, writing in *The Encyclopedia of Political Science*, Tereza Capelos defines scandal as "the information about an act that is considered immoral or shocking, made available to a large audience, which results in a loss or injury to the reputation of the actor(s) involved," "Scandals and Blame Management, Political," in *The Encyclopedia of Political Science*, ed. George Thomas Kurian et al. (Washington: CQ Press, 2011), 1511. The insistence on this "injurious" clause is, however, rare, or at the very least, subject to qualification. Thus, while Thompson, for example, similarly includes "reputational damage" as one of the key features of scandal, he nonetheless recognizes that "the damage or loss of reputation is neither a necessary feature nor an inevitable consequence of scandal," but rather "a *risk* which is always present when a scandal erupts and unfolds," Thompson, *Political Scandals*, 22.

# Chapter 2

1  While we will of course approach this question from our own unique angle, it
   is worth noting how a number of major twentieth-century philosophers turned
   to literature to draw an explicitly *productive* connection between transgression,
   chaos, and scandal. Merleau-Ponty, for example, mounts a rousing defense of
   "Sartre's obsession with the chaotic and disgusting as an attempt to dig beneath
   the perceptual and social order to discover its roots in a more savage experience,"
   Hubert L. Dreyfus and Patricia Allen Dreyfus, in Maurice Merleau-Ponty, *Sense
   and Non-Sense*, trans. Hubert L. Dreyfus and Patricia Allen Dreyfus (Evanston, IL:
   Northwestern University Press, 1964), xiv. Elsewhere, Michel Foucault observes
   how the principal task of modern literature has been to "seek out the quotidian
   beneath the quotidian itself, to cross boundaries, to ruthlessly or insidiously
   bring our secrets out in the open, to displace rules and codes, to compel the
   unmentionable to be told," and for this reason holds that great literature tends
   "to place itself outside the law, or at least to take on the burden of scandal,
   transgression, or revolt," *Power: Essential Works of Foucault 1954–1984*, ed. James
   D. Faubion, trans. Robert Hurley (New York: The New Press, 2001), 174.
2  Gilles Deleuze and Felix Guattari, *What Is Philosophy*, trans. Hugh Tomlinson and
   Graham Burchill (New York: Columbia University Press, 1994), 202.
3  The axis on which Badiou's entire philosophy turns, the "event" is itself entirely
   dependent on his concept of the "void," which is itself etymologically linked
   to both the Latin *chaos* and the Greek χάος (*khaos*), meaning "gaping void" or
   "empty, immeasurable space."
4  On this "vertiginous" note, it is worth recalling Jean-Paul Sartre's famous
   contention that "the affective apprehension of an absolute contingency […] is
   a particular type of *nausea*" (*Being and Nothingness*, 367). Sartre hammers this
   point home in his novel of the same title, when the protagonist Antoine details
   his experience of existential clarity, as all of a sudden "I understood the Nausea,
   I possessed it. […] The essential thing is contingency. I mean that one cannot
   define existence as necessity. […] When you realise that, it turns your heart upside
   down and everything begins to float […]: here is Nausea," *Nausea*, trans. Lloyd
   Alexander (New York: New Directions, 2007), 131.
5  This logical principal is found repeatedly throughout the history of philosophy,
   from the ancient Greeks (first in Parmenides then taken up by Plato and Aristotle)
   and through the celebrated poetry of Lucretius, who declares as a "first law" that
   "nothing is ever begotten of nothing," *On the Nature of Things*, trans. Cyril Bailey

(London: Oxford University Press, 1910), 32. The phrase remains a mainstay of popular culture, appearing equally at home in the canonical works of Shakespeare (the eponymous *King Lear* admonishing his daughter Cordelia with the phrase) as in treacly cinematic dramas like Robert Wise's *The Sound of Music* (1965) and Marc Forster's more recent *Christopher Robin* (2018).

6  It is, for example, precisely this paradox that establishes the elementary form of the dialectic in *The Science of Logic* (which we have already noted also establishes the philosophical basis for "controversy"), Hegel beginning his masterwork by noting that, in so far as "*pure being* and *pure nothing* are […] the same," "their truth is, therefore, this movement of the immediate vanishing of the one into the other: *becoming*," *The Science of Logic*, trans. A. V. Miller (New York: Humanity Books, 1969), 82–3. Hegel makes the same point in a slightly clearer way in his *Encyclopaedia Logic*: "If we speak of the concept of being, this can only consist in becoming, for as being it is the empty nothing, but as the latter it is empty being. So, in being we have nothing, and in nothing being; but this being which abides with itself in nothing is becoming," *The Encyclopedia Logic*, trans. T. F. Geraets, W. A. Suchting, and H. S. Harris (Albany, NY: State University of New York Press, 1991), 144.

7  Jacques Lacan defines his key concept of the "real" in terms of a radical "absence of sense" or an "ab-sense," *Autres Écrits* (Paris: Éditions du Seuil, 2001), 452. As Badiou explains, Lacan's essential point is that "an access to the real can be opened only if it is assumed that the real is like an absence in sense, an ab-sense, or a subtraction of, or from, sense," Alain Badiou and Barbara Cassin, *There's No Such Thing as a Sexual Relationship: Two Lessons on Lacan*, trans. Susan Spitzer and Kenneth Reinhard (New York: Columbia University Press, 2017), 50.

8  As Badiou puts it, with regard to the event, "this rupture is not the passage from an inferior to a superior world. We are always in the same world," Alain Badiou, *Métaphysique du Bonheur Réel* (Paris: Presses Universitaires de France, 2015), 80.

9  Jacques Lacan, *Le Séminaire de Jacques Lacan, Livre XXII: R.S.I.* (1974–5), unpublished manuscript, seminar of 11 March 1975, http://staferla.free.fr/S22/S22.htm (accessed 3 March 2019).

10 Jacques Lacan, *The Seminar of Jacques Lacan, Book I: Freud's Papers on Technique*, ed. Jacques-Alain Miller, trans. John Forrester (New York: Norton, 1991), 66.

11 Lacan, *The Four Fundamental Concepts of Psychoanalysis*, 167 (emphasis added). Obviously our critical invocation of the "real" here should not be confused with our earlier "revelatory" assessment of the scandal, where the "real" better approximated "naked" or "transparent" reality, that is, the elementary of the situation which is generally kept under wraps.

12 Plato speaks of two types of image-making in the "Sophist": those concerning εἰκόν (*likeness*) and those concerning φάντασμα (*phantasma* or *simulacra*). While the former constitutes a "faithful" reproduction, in so far as the artist "produces an imitation by keeping to the length, breadth and depth of his model," the latter involve a perversion or a deviation away from the "Idea," in that they figure representations that have been intentionally distorted in order to make them appear more "real," and in this sense "say goodbye to truth," Plato, "Sophist," in *Complete Works*, ed. John M. Cooper, trans. Nicholas P. White (Cambridge: Hackett Publishing Company, 1997), 256 (235e–236a). Baudrillard, for his part, reinterprets simulacra as quintessentially (post)modern phenomena, as having masked and replaced reality to such an extent that they no longer bear any relation to any "true" reality whatsoever, thereby establishing a "hyperreal," or "the generation by models of a real without origin or reality" (*Simulacra and Simulation*, 1): "it is the simulacrum which ensures the continuity of the real today, the simulacrum which now conceals not the truth, but the fact that there isn't any—that is to say, the continuity of the nothing," Jean Baudrillard, *The Perfect Crime*, trans. Chris Turner (London: Verso, 1996), 101.

13 Marcel Duchamp cited in Thierry De Duve, *Pictorial Nominalism: On Marcel Duchamp's Passage from Painting to the Readymade*, trans. Dana Polen (Minneapolis: University of Minnesota Press, 1991), 172.

14 Marcel Duchamp, "Apropos of 'Readymades,'" *Art and Artists* 1, no. 4 (1966): 47.

15 In a 2004 poll of five hundred British art experts, *Fountain* was found to be "the single most influential artwork of the twentieth century," Sophie Howarth and Jennifer Mundy, "Marcel Duchamp: Fountain 1917, Replica 1964," *The Tate*, revised August, 2015, https://www.tate.org.uk/art/artworks/duchamp-fountain-t07573 (accessed 1 May 2018).

16 Duchamp and Cabanne, *Dialogues with Marcel Duchamp*, 55.

17 Unattributed, "The Richard Mutt Case," *The Blind Man* 2 (1917): 3–4.

18 In response to the affair, the board issued a statement saying that "The *Fountain* may be a very useful object in its place, but its place is not an art exhibition and it is, by no definition, a work of art," cited in Francis Naumann, *The Recurrent, Haunting Ghost: Essays on the Art, Life and Legacy of Marcel Duchamp* (New York: Readymade Press, 2012), 72.

19 As Duchamp explains with regard to painting, "let's say that you use a tube of paint; you didn't make it. You bought it and used it as a readymade. Even if you mixed two vermilions together, it's still a mixing of two readymades. So man can never expect to start from scratch; he must start from ready-made things like

even his own mother and father," Duchamp cited in Thierry De Duve, *Kant after Duchamp* (Cambridge, MA: MIT Press, 1996), 162.

20 Obviously we are conceiving of "real art" here in the strictest of terms: as giving form to something *real* (in the sense that we have come to know it); hence as presenting something radically *new*.

21 This "at first" is crucial: as Duchamp himself points out, "an abstract painting might not look at all 'abstract' in 50 years," "The Great Trouble with Art in This Country," *The Writings of Marcel Duchamp*, ed. Michel Sanouillet and Elmer Peterson (New York: Da Capo Press, 1973): 123.

22 "The 'Cubists' Dominate Paris' Fall Salon," 1.

23 Debord, "Situationist Manifesto," 349 (emphasis added). Debord is hardly alone in this sentiment, Kasimir Malevich similarly (and memorably) pointing out how "art and its new have always been a spittoon," "Suprematist Manifesto," in *100 Artists' Manifestos: From the Futurists to the Stuckists*, ed. Alex Danchev (London: Penguin, 2011), 123.

24 Unattributed, "2016 Academy Award Nominations and Winner for Best Picture," *Box Office Mojo*, February 16, 2017, http://www.boxofficemojo.com/oscar/chart/?yr=2016&view=fulldetail&p=.htm (accessed 5 May 2019).

25 The same year would see one of the most divisive moments of Trump's presidency when, following the terrible events surrounding a white supremacist rally in Charlottesville, the president infamously declared there to have been "very fine people, on both sides," Donald Trump cited in Angie Drobnic Holan, "In Context: Donald Trump's 'Very Fine People on Both Sides' Remarks (Transcript)," *Politifact*, April 26, 2019, https://www.politifact.com/truth-o-meter/article/2019/apr/26/context-trumps-very-fine-people-both-sides-remarks/ (accessed 5 May 2019).

# Chapter 3

1  As Verbalyte points out, "Scandal is a staging process which directs the resentment of the people against the political system to the singular event or one political personality, canalizes this resentment, and therewith stabilizes the system instead of really challenging and changing it," "Emotional Logic of Political Scandal," 62.

2  Alain Badiou, "In Search of the Lost Real," in *Badiou and His Interlocutors: Lectures, Interviews and Responses*, ed. A. J. Bartlett and Justin Clemens (London: Bloomsbury, 2018), 9.

3  Badiou, *À la recherche du réel perdu*, 17.

4   As noted above, the term "scandal" is etymologically derived from the Greek "skandalon" (σκανδαλον), meaning "stumbling block," in the sense of a trap or a snare laid out for an enemy. Technically, the skandalon refers to the piece of wood or other material that, when touched, causes the trap to shut tight. For a more in-depth consideration of the term's etymology, see Thompson, *Political Scandal*, 11–13.

5   See Herbert Marcuse, *One-Dimensional Man: Studies in the Ideology of Advanced Industrial Society* (Boston: Beacon Press, 1964); Jean-François Lyotard, *The Postmodern Condition: A Report on Knowledge*, trans. Geoff Bennington and Brian Massumi (Manchester: Manchester University Press, 1984); and Jean Baudrillard, *The Gulf War Did Not Take Place*, trans. Paul Patton (Bloomington: Indiana University Press, 1995).

6   Needless to say, Badiou (whose philosophy we have already pointed out largely underpins the current work) is himself well aware of the conservative function of endless novelty, holding that one of the key failures of contemporary political opposition comes down to "the commercial cult of the 'novelty' of products" which "simultaneously prevents people from learning about the past, from understanding how structural repetitions work, and from not falling for fake 'modernities,'" Alain Badiou, *I Know There Are So Many of You*, trans. Susan Spitzer (Cambridge: Polity Press, 2019), 46.

7   Lacan, *Freud's Papers on Technique*, 66.

8   This does not, however, negate the fact that it is "the capitalist machine which constitutes the real of naked power," Alain Badiou, *Pornographie du Temps Présent* (Paris: Fayard, 2013), 40.

9   The reference here is of course to the Wachowskis's film *The Matrix* (1999) and Baudrillard's *Simulacra and Simulation* (1).

10  Edward Bernays, "The Engineering of Consent," *The Annals of the American Academy of Political and Social Science* 250, no. 1 (1947): 114. It is worth noting that Bernays, the purported "father of public relations," himself draws an explicit connection between these two offices—i.e., the shadowy "real" state and the art of propagandistic manipulation in the very first lines of his influential handbook on *Propaganda*, observing that "the conscious and intelligent manipulation of the organized habits and opinions of the masses is an important element in democratic society. Those who manipulate this unseen mechanism of society constitute an invisible government which is the true ruling power of our country," Edward Bernays, *Propaganda* (New York: Ig Publishing, 2005), 37.

11  See Lacan, *Écrits*, 58–74; and Albert Einstein, "A propos de 'La déduction relativiste' de M. Emile Meyerson," *Revue Philosophique* 105 (1928): 161–6.

12 Émile Meyerson, *La déduction relativiste* (Paris: Payot, 1925), 79.

13 As Martin Heidegger notes, "The many and all too many pursue only the beings that are current; for them, these are real, if not precisely 'the' reality. But in mentioning 'reality', the throng attests that, besides what is currently real, it has something else in view, which, to be sure, it does not clearly see [...]. But where, on the contrary, Being comes into focus, there the extraordinary announces itself, the excessive that strays 'beyond' the ordinary, that which is not to be explained by explanations on the basis of beings," *Parmenides*, trans. André Schuwer and Richard Rojcewicz (Indianapolis: Indiana University Press, 1992), 100.

14 Cf. "There is a kind of science whose remit is being *qua* being and the things pertaining to that which it is *per se,*" Aristotle, *The Metaphysics*, trans. Hugh Lawson-Tancred (London: Penguin, 1998): 79. Moreover, given that the substance of being "is prior to all others [then] the science of it is First Philosophy—*and such a science is universal just because it is first*" (156).

15 Hegel, *The Science of Logic*, 82.

16 Hegel, *The Science of Logic*, 82.

17 See Lacan, *Autres Écrits*, 314; and Jacques Lacan, "Monsieur A," *Ornicar?* 21–2 (1980): 17. Note that "antiphilosophy" is not directly opposed to philosophy, with which it in fact shares many common characteristics. As Justin Clemens explains, "Antiphilosophy is not antiphilosophical in the sense of being 'non-philosophical'; on the contrary, the antiphilosopher is not out to evade or destroy philosophy, but rather to draw attention to forms of knowledge that philosophy cannot know, by affronting philosophy and subverting its claims," Justin Clemens, *Psychoanalysis in as Antiphilosophy* (Edinburgh: Edinburgh University Press, 2013), 2. Antiphilosophy is then an inescapably controversial activity, being, quite literally, a "turning against" philosophy (the term "controversy" deriving from the Latin *controversus*, meaning "turned against").

18 Jacques Lacan, *On the Names-of-the-Father*, trans. Bruce Fink (Cambridge: Polity Press, 2013), 52.

19 Jacques Lacan, *The Seminar of Jacques Lacan, Book XVII: The Other Side of Psychoanalysis*, ed. Jacques-Alain Miller, trans. Russell Grigg (New York: Norton, 2007), 123.

20 Jacques Lacan, *Le Séminaire de Jacques Lacan, Livre XII: Problèmes Cruciaux pour la Psychanalyse*, unpublished manuscript, seminar of 2 June 1965, http://staferla. free.fr/S12/S12.htm (accessed 3 March 2019).

21 Lacan, *R.S.I.* (seminar of March 11, 1975).

22 Lacan, *Écrits*, 676.

23 Lacan, *The Four Fundamental Concepts of Psychoanalysis*, 167 (translation modified).

24 It is worth noting how, in his seminar on *The Four Fundamental Concepts of Psychoanalysis*, Lacan arrives at his conception of the "encounter" by rethinking the Aristotelian categories of *tuché* and *automaton*. Here, *tuché* comes to designate the traumatic "encounter with the real" (53); the chance event that functions as the absent "cause" of the *automaton*, which itself figures the repetitive or "automatic" unfolding of signification qua "insistence of signs" (54). In this sense, *automaton* is clearly aligned with the order of the symbolic—being, as he puts it, nothing other than "the network of signifiers" (52)—while *tuché*, as both exceeding and preceding the *automaton*, points firmly to the real.

25 Lacan, *The Four Fundamental Concepts of Psychoanalysis*, 167.

26 As Lacan explains, "repetition," which is the hallmark of the symbolic, "is unique in being necessary" (*Écrits*, 307), while "the regime of the encounter is tantamount to contingency," Jacques Lacan, *The Seminar of Jacques Lacan, Book XX: On Feminine Sexuality, the Limits of Love and Knowledge*, ed. Jacques-Alain Miller, trans. Bruce Fink (New York: Norton, 1999), 94.

27 Lacan, *Autres Écrits*, 452.

28 Lacan, *The Four Fundamental Concepts of Psychoanalysis*, 55.

29 Lacan, *On Feminine Sexuality*, 94 (emphasis added).

30 Heidegger, *Being and Time*, 21.

31 Heidegger, *Being and Time*, 24.

32 Heidegger, *Being and Time*, 24.

33 Lacan, *The Four Fundamental Concepts of Psychoanalysis*, 30.

34 Jacques Lacan, *The Seminar of Jacques Lacan, Book XIX: … or Worse*, ed. Jacques-Alain Miller, trans. A. R. Price (Cambridge: Polity Press, 2018), 119 (translation modified).

35 Lacan, *Problème Cruciaux pour la Psychanalyse* (seminar of June 9, 1965).

36 Lacan, *… or Worse*, 126.

37 Alain Badiou and Jean-Luc Nancy, *German Philosophy: A Dialogue*, ed. Jan Völker (Cambridge, MA: MIT Press, 2018), 53. Badiou freely acknowledges here that "it was only in a space opened by the Heideggerian question that I was able to arrive at a mathematical vision of the indifference of being" (59).

38 Lacan, *Freud's Papers on Technique*, 229. Lacan in fact goes so far as to argue—in true antiphilosophical style—that "the gap of the unconscious may be said to be *pre-ontological*" in as much as "it does not lend itself to ontology"; rather, "what truly belongs to the unconscious, is that it is neither being, nor non-being, but the unrealized," *The Four Fundamental Concepts of Psychoanalysis*, 29–30.

39 Badiou, *Being and Event*, 4.

40 Lacan, *On Feminine Sexuality*, 131.

41 In this sense, both Badiou and Lacan can be shown to subscribe—each by appealing to the quintessence of pure rationality and apodicticity that is mathematical thought—to Hegel's core belief that "what is rational is real; and what is real is rational," Georg Wilhelm Friedrich Hegel, *Elements of the Philosophy of Right*, ed. Allen W. Wood, trans. H. B. Nisbet (Cambridge: Cambridge University Press, 1991), 20.

42 As Parmenides put it, "There are signs aplenty that, being, it is ungenerated and indestructible, whole, of one kind and unwavering, and complete. Nor was it ever, nor will it be, since now it is, all together, one, continuous," cited in Jonathan Barnes, *Early Greek Philosophy* (London: Penguin Books, 1987), 82.

43 Cf. Plato, "Parmenides," in *Complete Works*, ed. John M. Cooper, trans. Mary Louise Gill and Paul Ryan (Cambridge: Hackett Publishing Company, 1997), 362–3 (129a).

44 Badiou, *Being and Event*, 28.

45 Badiou, *Logics of Worlds*, 243.

46 Badiou's core philosophy is contained in the three volumes of "Being and Event," published over a period of thirty years: *Being and Event* (originally published as *L'être et l'événement*, Paris: Seuil, 1988); *Logics of Worlds: Being and Event, 2* (first appearing as *Logiques des Mondes: L'être et l'événement, 2*, Paris: Seuil, 2006); and *L'Immanence des vérités: L'être et l'événement, 3* (Paris: Fayard, 2018). The first of these works details his mathematical ontology. The second, *Logics of Worlds*, develops his logical phenomenology, while the third offers, in true Hegelian style, a final synthesis by addressing the question of the absolute.

# Chapter 4

1 An abridged version of the first part of this work, originally delivered as a public address, has been published as "In Search of the Lost Real" in the collection *Badiou and His Interlocuters*.

2 Badiou, *À la recherche du réel perdu*, 15.

3 Cf. "The scandal is precisely what, in terms of opinion, opens the door to a kind of unveiling of a piece of the real, but at the price of this fragment being immediately treated as an exception," Badiou, *À la recherche du réel perdu*, 15.

4 Badiou, *À la recherche du réel perdu*, 17.

5  Cf. "An interesting symptom of our society is that the scandal is, in general, a scandal of corruption. This is its essential name," Badiou, *À la recherche du réel perdu*, 16.

6  Badiou, "In Search of the Lost Real," 10. Cf. "We could even argue that corruption is an intimate law of society, and that it is in order to conceal this systematic and only too real corruption that the scandal represents what is, in the end, a kind of scapegoat," Badiou, *À la recherche du réel perdu*, 16.

7  Alain Badiou, *Lacan: Antiphilosophie 3: 1994–1995* (Paris: Fayard, 2014), 7.

8  Badiou, *Lacan: Antiphilosophie*, 8.

9  Badiou and Nancy, *German Philosophy*, 18. More precisely, Badiou holds that "the axiom of knowledge as such is that we can know everything. There is the not known and the unknown, but strictly speaking there's nothing unknowable" (18).

10  Badiou, *Lacan: Antiphilosophie*, 9.

11  As Badiou says: "What does *jouissance* have to do with anything? A differential equation doesn't really enjoy anything," Badiou and Nancy, *German Philosophy*, 60.

12  In Lacan's words, "The real is either totality or the vanished instant," *The Names-of-the-Father*, 42.

13  Badiou, *Being and Event*, 53.

14  Alain Badiou, *Pocket Pantheon: Figures of Postwar Philosophy*, trans. David Macey (London: Verso, 2009), 141. See also Badiou, *Being and Event*, 53.

15  Badiou, *Being and Event*, 53.

16  Hence it is structure itself which constitutes, according to Badiou, "the place of risk due to its pure operational transparency and due to the doubt occasioned, as for the one, by its having to operate on the multiple," *Being and Event*, 95.

17  Badiou, *Being and Event*, 56.

18  Badiou, *Being and Event*, 55.

19  Lacan, *Freud's Papers on Technique*, 65, 58.

20  Badiou, *Being and Event*, 447. Cf. "The void is […] the first multiple, the very being from which any multiple presentation, when presented, is woven and numbered" (59).

21  In axiomatic set theory (the most commonly employed foundational system for mathematics), the empty or "void" (or "null") set constitutes the sole *existential* axiom, meaning "this is the only set whose existence is directly asserted. Every other set is constructed in some way or other from this set," Mary Tiles, *The Philosophy of Set Theory: An Philosophical Introduction to Cantor's Paradise* (New York: Dover Publications, 1989), 124.

22  Badiou, *Being and Event*, 57.

23 Badiou, *Being and Event*, 57.

24 Badiou, *Being and Event*, 93.

25 Badiou, *Being and Event*, 95.

26 Alain Badiou and Fabien Tarby, *Philosophy and the Event*, trans. Louise Burchill (Cambridge: Polity Press, 2013), 11 (translation modified). We can thus detect a certain limited homology between Badiou's state and Foucault's concept of *episteme* as referring to "the strategic apparatus which permits of separating out from among all the statements which are possible those that will be acceptable within [...] a field of scientificity, and, which it is possible to say are true or false," Michel Foucault, *Power/Knowledge: Selected Interviews and Other Writings 1972–1977*, ed. Colin Gordon, trans. Colin Gordon et al. (New York: Pantheon Books, 1980), 197. See also Michel Foucault, *The Archaeology of Knowledge and the Discourse on Language*, trans. A. M. Sheridan Smith (New York: Pantheon Books, 1972), 191–2.

27 Lacan, *Freud's Papers on Technique*, 79.

28 Alain Badiou, *Metapolitics*, trans. Jason Barker (London: Verso, 2005), 73.

29 On this account we also might register certain correspondences between the ontological state and Claude Lévi-Strauss's own "structural unconscious," which refers "only to a form (or aggregate of forms) empty of any content [whose] function is to impose structural laws upon psychic content, which by itself is inarticulate and originates elsewhere," Ino Rossi, "The Unconscious in the Anthropology of Claude Lévi-Strauss," *American Anthropologist* 75, no. 1 (1973): 29. Or as Lévi-Strauss himself puts it, the "truly atemporal" unconscious is "reducible to [...] the symbolic function," meaning it is "always empty—or, more accurately, it is as alien to mental images as is the stomach to the foods which pass through it. As the organ of a specific function, the unconscious merely imposes structural laws upon inarticulated elements which originate elsewhere," *Structural Anthropology*, trans. Claire Jacobson and Brooke Grundfest Schoepf (New York: Basic Books, 1963), 202–3.

30 Alain Badiou and Marcel Gauchet, *What Is to Be Done?: A Dialogue on Communism, Capitalism, and the Future of Democracy*, trans. Susan Spitzer (Cambridge: Polity Press, 2016), 40.

31 The specific model of set theory Badiou employs is ZFC, which stands for Zermelo-Fraenkel set theory with the Axiom of Choice, and which is far and away the most frequently employed foundational system of mathematics.

32 Felix Hausdorff, *Set Theory* (New York: Chelsea Publications, 1962), 11.

33 Robert Goldblatt, *Topoi: The Categorial Analysis of Logic* (New York: Dover Publications, 2006), 308.

34 Tiles, *The Philosophy of Set Theory*, 124. This mathematical absolute should finally put paid to our previous discussion of the ancient principle that "nothing comes from nothing."

35 Lacan, *On Feminine Sexuality*, 131.

36 Lacan, *Autres Écrits*, 479.

37 Lacan, *On Feminine Sexuality*, 93.

38 Alain Badiou and Élizabeth Roudinesco, *Jacques Lacan: Past and Present*, trans. Jason E. Smith (New York: Columbia University Press, 2014), 50.

39 Badiou and Roudinesco, *Jacques Lacan: Past and Present*, 50.

40 Badiou, *Being and Event*, 5.

41 Boris Groys, *On the New*, trans. G. M. Goshgarian (London: Verso, 2014), 1 (emphasis added).

42 Lacan, *Écrits*, 676.

43 Groys, *On the New*, 34.

44 Joseph Schumpeter, *Capitalism, Socialism and Democracy* (New York: Harper Perennial, 2008), 83.

45 See for example Davide Valenti, Giorgio Fazio, and Bernardo Spagnolo, "Stabilizing Effect of Volatility in Financial Markets," *Physical Review E* 97, no. 6 (2018): 1–9; Yuriy Stepanov et al., "Stability and Hierarchy of Quasi-Stationary States: Financial Markets as an Example," *Journal of Statistical Mechanics: Theory and Experiment* August (2015): 1–19; and Tobias Preis, Johannes J. Schneider and H. Eugene Stanley, "Switching Processes in Financial Markets," *Proceedings of the National Academy of Sciences of the United States of America* 108, no. 19 (2011): 7674–8.

46 Schumpeter, *Capitalism, Socialism and Democracy*, 83. Schumpeter defines "creative destruction" in this work as the "process of industrial mutation [...] that incessantly revolutionizes the economic structure *from within*, incessantly destroying the old one, incessantly creating a new one" (83).

47 Giuseppe di Lampedusa, *The Leopard*, trans. Archibald Colquhoun (New York: Pantheon Books, 1960), 40.

48 Theodore Adorno, *The Culture Industry: Selected Essays on Mass Culture*, ed. J. M. Bernstein (London: Routledge, 1991), 100.

49 Guy Debord, *Situationist International Anthology*, ed. Ken Knabb (Berkeley, CA: Bureau of Public Secrets, 2006), 26–7. A decade later, Debord would observe how "waves of enthusiasm for particular products, fueled and boosted by the communications media, are propagated with lightning speed. A film sparks a

fashion craze, or a magazine launches a chain of clubs that in turn spins off a line of products. The sheer fad item perfectly expresses the fact that, as the mass of commodities become more and more absurd, absurdity becomes a commodity in its own right […]. The only use still in evidence here, meanwhile, is the basic use of submission," Guy Debord, *The Society of the Spectacle*, trans. Donald Nicholson-Smith (London: Zone Books, 1995), 44.

50 John Howkins, *The Creative Economy: How People Make Money from Ideas* (London: Penguin Books, 2013), ix.

51 Howkins, *The Creative Economy*, vii.

52 "Creative ecologies" represent "energy-expressive relationships" in which "diverse individuals express themselves in a systematic way, using ideas to produce new ideas; and where others support this endeavor even if they don't understand it," John Howkins, *Creative Ecologies: Where Thinking Is a Proper Job* (St Lucia: University of Queensland Press, 2009), 11.

53 Richard Florida, *The Rise of the Creative Class, Revisited* (New York: Basic Books, 2012), 38.

54 Deleuze and Guattari, *What Is Philosophy*, 10.

55 Badiou and Tarby, *Philosophy and the Event*, 11.


# Chapter 5

1 Badiou, *Being and Event*, 181.

2 Badiou, *Metapolitics*, 143. See also Alain Badiou, *Conditions*, trans. Steve Corcoran (London: Continuum, 2008), 225; and Badiou, *Ethics*, 25.

3 Alain Badiou, *Theoretical Writings*, ed. and trans. Ray Brassier and Alberto Toscano (London: Continuum, 2004), 45.

4 Paul Cohen, *Set Theory and the Continuum Hypothesis* (New York: W. A. Benjamin, 1966), 151. Although the continuum hypothesis—which states that there is no cardinal $\delta$ such that $\aleph0 < \delta < 2^{\aleph0}$ (where $\aleph0$ is the smallest cardinality, being the set of natural numbers)—has not been proven, its *independence* of the laws of standard (axiomatic) set theory has: in the late 1930s, Kurt Gödel demonstrated that it is impossible to disprove in ZFC—although he too believed that the subsequent "discovery of new axioms will make it possible to disprove Cantor's conjecture" (Kurt Gödel, "What Is Cantor's Continuum Problem?" *The American Mathematical Monthly* 54, no. 9, 1947: 524)—while in 1963 Paul Cohen showed that it likewise cannot be proved in ZFC.

5   Eugenia Chung, *Beyond Infinity: An Expedition to the Outer Limits of the Mathematical Universe* (London: Profile Books, 2017), 116.

6   As Sy-David Friedman and Radel Honzik put it (in the typically understated language of mathematics), Easton's theorem shows that "the function $\alpha \to 2^{\alpha}$ [...] on regular cardinals has *great freedom*," "Easton's Theorem and Large Cardinals," *Annals of Pure and Applied Logic* 154 (2008): 191(emphasis added). See also William B. Easton, "Powers of Regular Cardinals," *Annals of Mathematical Logic* 1, no. 2 (1970): 139–78; and Badiou, *Being and Event*, 279–80.

7   Badiou, *Theory of the Subject*, 273.

8   Badiou, *Being and Event*, 278.

9   Badiou, *Being and Event*, 429.

10  Badiou, *Being and Event*, 429.

11  Alain Badiou, *Second Manifesto for Philosophy*, trans. Louise Burchill (Cambridge: Polity Press, 2011), 91.

12  Cf. Gilles Deleuze, *Difference and Repetition*, trans. Paul Patton (London: Continuum, 2004), 44. Badiou of course uses this expression as the title of his book on Deleuze, *Deleuze: The Clamor of Being*, trans. Louise Burchill (Minneapolis: University of Minnesota Press, 2000).

13  Oliver Feltham, *Alain Badiou: Live Theory* (London: Continuum, 2008), 101.

14  Badiou and Nancy, *German Philosophy*, 55 (emphasis added).

15  Badiou, *L'Immanence des vérités*, 18.

16  Badiou, *Being and Event*, 184.

17  Badiou, *Being and Event*, 175.

18  Badiou, *Logics of Worlds*, 452, 363.

19  Badiou, *Logics of Worlds*, 369.

20  Badiou, *L'Immanence des vérités*, 514.

21  Alain Badiou, *Ethics: An Essay on the Understanding of Evil*, trans. Peter Hallward (London: Verso, 2001), 73.

22  Alain Badiou, *Briefings on Existence: A Short Treatise on Transitory Ontology*, trans. Norman Maderasz (New York: State University of New York Press, 2006), 60 (translation modified).

23  Badiou, *Briefings on Existence*, 60 (translation modified).

24  Badiou, *À la recherche du réel perdu*, 30.

25  Technically, Gödel shows that "since, for every consistent class $c$, $w$ is not $c$-provable, there will always be propositions which are undecidable (from $c$), namely, $w$, so long as Neg($w$) is not $c$-provable," Kurt Gödel, *On Formally Undecidable Propositions of Principia Mathematica and Related Systems*, trans. Bernard Meltzer (New York: Basic Books, 1962), 71–2.

26 Lacan, *... or Worse*, 29 (emphasis added).

27 Lacan, *The Four Fundamental Concepts of Psychoanalysis*, 29.

28 Lacan, *... or Worse*, 29 (emphasis added).

# Chapter 6

1 Badiou, *L'Immanence des vérités*, 512.

2 Badiou, *L'Immanence des vérités*, 516.

3 Cf. Georg Cantor, *Contributions to the Founding of the Theory of Transfinite Numbers*, trans. Philip E. B. Jourdain (New York: Dover Publications, 1955).

4 Badiou, *L'Immanence des vérités*, 512. In general terms, the generic set "avoids" every recognizable property in the situation by ensuring that, for each and every property, it contains at least one element that negates this property and one that affirms the same property.

5 Badiou, *Second Manifesto for Philosophy*, 125.

6 Badiou, *Logics of Worlds*, 36 (translation modified).

7 Badiou, *Logics of Worlds*, 36 (translation modified).

8 Badiou, *Being and Event*, 338.

9 Badiou, *Métaphysique du Bonheur Réel*, 69.

10 Peter Hallward, *Badiou: A Subject to Truth* (Minneapolis: University of Minnesota Press, 2003), 130.

11 Badiou, *Being and Event*, 429 (emphasis added).

12 Badiou, *Being and Event*, 339.

13 Badiou, *Being and Event*, 339.

14 Alain Badiou, *Manifesto for Philosophy*, trans. Norman Maderasz (New York: State University of New York Press, 1999), 104 (translation modified).

15 Badiou, *Being and Event*, 401.

16 Cohen himself notes that his proof "is easy in the sense that there is a clear philosophical idea. There were technical points, you know, which bothered me, but basically it was not really an enormously involved combinatorial problem; it was a philosophical idea," Paul Cohen cited in Akihiro Kanamori, "Cohen and Set Theory," *The Bulletin of Symbolic Logic* 14, no. 3 (2008): 375.

17 As Badiou puts it, Cohen's method of forcing demonstrates how it is, in fact, entirely possible "to determine under what conditions such or such a statement is veridical in the generic extension obtained by the addition of an indiscernible part of the situation," Badiou, *Being and Event*, 410.

18 Looking back on his invention of forcing, Cohen notes how "this idea as it presented itself to me, appeared so different from any normal way of thinking, that I felt it could have enormous consequences. […] How could one decide whether a statement about *a* is true, before we have *a*? In a somewhat exaggerated sense, it seemed that I would have to examine the very meaning of truth and think about it in a new way," Paul Cohen, "The Discovery of Forcing," *The Rocky Mountain Journal of Mathematics* 32, No. 4 (2002): 1092.

19 A. J. Bartlett, *Badiou and Plato: An Education by Truths* (Edinburgh: Edinburgh University Press, 2011), 212.

20 Badiou, *Being and Event*, 410.

21 Badiou, *Being and Event*, 342.

22 Badiou, *Being and Event*, 406.

23 Badiou, *Being and Event*, 394.

24 Badiou, *Logics of Worlds*, 369.

25 Badiou, *L'Immanence des vérités*, 275.

26 As Joseph Dauben notes, "the title of this paper deliberately masks its explosive content" so as to ensure "there was nothing to excite either immediate interest or censure," "Georg Cantor and the Battle for Transfinite Set Theory," *Journal of the Association of Christians in the Mathematical Sciences* (2004): 4, 6.

27 Carl Friedrich Gauss cited in Joseph Warren Dauben, *Georg Cantor: His Mathematics and Philosophy of the Infinite* (Princeton: Princeton University Press, 1990), 120. Cantor himself was well aware of the controversial nature of his work, writing "I realise that in this undertaking I place myself in a certain opposition to views widely held concerning the mathematical infinite and to opinions frequently defended on the nature of numbers," Georg Cantor cited in Ian Stewart, *Infinity: A Very Short Introduction* (Oxford: Oxford University Press, 2017), 104.

28 Cf. "For my part, I think, and I am not the only one, that the important thing is never to introduce entities not completely definable in a finite number of words. Whatever be the cure adopted, we may promise ourselves the joy of the doctor called in to follow a beautiful pathologic case," Henri Poincaré, *The Foundations of Science: Science and Hypothesis; The Value of Science; Science and Method*, trans. George Halsted (New York: The Science Press, 1921), 382.

29 Leopold Kronecker cited in Dauben, *Georg Cantor*, 1.

30 Badiou, *Manifesto for Philosophy*, 103 (translation modified). Cf. "The specificity of Cantor's invention, its radicality, which he himself found fearsome, is not to have mathematized the infinite, but to have pluralized it, and therefore unequalized it," Badiou, *Conditions*, 306. See also Badiou, *L'Immanence des vérités*, 466.

31  Georg Cantor cited in Dauben, *Georg Cantor*, 124.

32  John D. Barrow, *The Infinite Book: A Short Guide to the Boundless, Timeless and Endless* (New York: Pantheon Books, 2005), 87.

33  Georg Cantor cited in Lynn Gamwell, *Mathematics + Art: A Cultural History* (Princeton: Princeton University Press, 2016), 131.

34  John Dawson goes so far as to draw a parallel between Gödel and Charles Darwin, in that "both men made profound discoveries that ran counter to their own prior expectations and that, as each was acutely aware, placed them in conflict with the philosophic spirit of their times," *Logical Dilemas: The Life and Work of Kurt Gödel* (Wellesley, MA: A K Peters, 1997), 266. To appreciate the disruption his theorems caused, we need only consider how in 1930 (one year prior to Gödel's publication), no less than David Hilbert captured the general mathematical sentiment by declaring that "the true reason why [no one] has succeeded in finding an unsolvable problem is, in my opinion, that there is no unsolvable problem. In contrast to the foolish *Ignoramibus*, our credo avers: We must know. We shall know!" cited in Dawson, *Logical Dilemas*, 71.

35  It is, after all Plato who declares (through the character of Sophocles) that if someone "should demonstrate [...] what one is, to be many, or conversely, the many to be one—at this I'll be astonished," Plato, "Parmenides," 363 (129b).

36  Kanamori, *Cohen and Set Theory*, 375.

37  Badiou and Tarby, *Philosophy and the Event*, 11 (emphasis added).

38  William Butler Yeats, "Easter 1916," in *The Norton Anthology of Poetry* (London: Norton, 1983), 881.

# Chapter 7

1  Heinrich Geiselberger, "Preface," in *The Great Regression*, ed. Heinrich Geiselberger (Cambridge: Polity Press, 2017), xii.

2  George Orwell, *Nineteen Eighty-Four* (London: Penguin Books, 1989), 280.

3  Margaret Atwood, "Everybody Is Happy Now," *The Guardian*, November 17, 2007, https://www.theguardian.com/books/2007/nov/17/classics.margaretatwood (accessed 3 October 2018).

4  Kimiko de Freytas-tamura, "Georger Orwell's '1984' Is Suddenly a Best-Seller," *The New York Times*, January 25, 2017, https://www.nytimes.com/2017/01/25/books/1984-george-orwell-donald-trump.html (accessed 3 October 2018).

5  Mahita Gajanan, "Kellyanne Conway Defends White House's Falsehoods as 'Alternative Facts'," *Time*, January 22, 2017, https://time.com/4642689/kellyanne-conway-sean-spicer-donald-trump-alternative-facts/ (accessed 3 October 2018).

6  Brad Tuttle, "Sales of Dystopian Novels Have Been Spiking on Amazon since the Election," *Money*, January 25, 2017, http://money.com/money/4648774/trump-1984-dystopian-novel-sales-brave-new-world/ (accessed 3 October 2018).

7  Orwell, *Nineteen Eighty-Four*, 269.

8  Orwell, *Nineteen Eighty-Four*, 279.

9  Orwell, *Nineteen Eighty-Four*, 279.

10 Badiou, *Briefings on Existence*, 55.

11 Badiou and Tarby, *Philosophy and the Event*, 11.

12 Orwell, *Nineteen Eighty-Four*, 218.

13 Badiou and Gauchet, *What Is to Be Done?* 40.

14 Orwell, *Nineteen Eighty-Four*, 280.

15 Neil Postman, *Amusing Ourselves to Death: Public Discourse in the Age of Show Business* (London: Penguin Books, 1985), 111.

16 Aldous Huxley, *Brave New World* (London: Flamingo, 1994), 216.

17 Huxley, *Brave New World*, 208.

18 Huxley, *Brave New World*, 205.

19 Huxley, *Brave New World*, 205.

20 Huxley, *Brave New World*, 202.

21 Huxley, *Brave New World*, 207–8.

22 Huxley, *Brave New World*, 206.

23 Huxley, *Brave New World*, 216.

24 Georg Cantor cited in Kazimierz Trzęsicki, "How Are Concepts of Infinity Acquired?" *Studies in Logic, Grammar and Rhetoric* 40, vol. 53 (2015): 196.

25 See Thomas S. Kuhn, *The Structure of Scientific Revolutions* (Chicago: University of Chicago Press, 1962).

26 Carlo Rovelli, *The Order of Time*, trans. Erica Segre and Simon Carnell (London: Allen Lane, 2018), 20. Badiou too positions himself firmly in a philosophical tradition that "interrogated science for models of invention and transformation that would inscribe it as a practice of creative thought, comparable to artistic activity, rather than as the organization of revealed phenomena," Alain Badiou, "The Adventure of French Philosophy," trans. Bruno Bosteels, *New Left Review* 35 (2005): 70–1.

27 As Rovelli notes, the power of science lies foremost in "its visionary capacity to demolish preconceived ideas, to reveal new regions of reality, and to construct new and more effective images of the world. This adventure rests upon the entirety of past knowledge, but at its heart is change," Carlo Rovelli, *Reality Is Not What It Seems: The Journey to Quantum Gravity*, trans. Simon Carnell and Erica Segre (New York: Riverhead Books, 2016), 8.

28 Badiou, *Metapolitics*, 145.

29 Badiou and Nancy, *German Philosophy*, 41.

30 As Badiou explains, universality "is always a construction, a procedure, which unfolds in a particular situation or world," and "is always built with materials that are particular," Alain Badiou and Jean-Claude Milner, *Controversies: A Dialogue on the Politics and Philosophy of Our Time*, trans. Susan Spitzer (Cambridge: Polity Press, 2014), 80.

31 Orwell, *Nineteen Eighty-Four*, 229.

32 An interesting point to add here is that, as Freudenthal observes, even though "controversies are pervasive in the history of science," nonetheless, "according to both traditional and contemporary views of science, there are no scientific controversies *sui generis*," Freudenthal, "Controversy," 155. The reason for this stems from our belief in the "classical notion of Science as an achievement of infallibility and absolute truth," which causes us to lose sight of the fact that controversy in fact represents "an 'internal' factor embedded 'necessarily' within the movement of progress," João Lopes Alves, "Legal Controversy vs. Scientific and Philosophical Controversies," in *Traditions of Controversy*, ed. Marcelo and Hang-liang Chang (Amsterdam: John Benjamins Publishing Company, 2007), 210. On this view, science is, strictly speaking, both *incontestable* (i.e., not open to debate) and *complete* (and therefore not a systematic process). Needless to say, this flies in the face not only of our understanding of science as a process of creation—and accordingly, of dispute—but also of *science's own view of itself*. For as Marcelo Dascal points out, "Science manifests itself in its history as a sequence of controversies. These are, therefore, not anomalies but the 'natural state' of science. Controversies are the locus where critical activity—essential for science—is exercised and its norms established, applied, and modified," "The Study of Controversies and the Theory and History of Science," *Science in Context* 11, no. 2 (1998): 153. Indeed, Dascal continues, it is only "by observing and analyzing scientific controversies that the de facto nature of the workings of scientific rationality (or irrationality) can be determined" (153).

33 Robert Hughes, *The Spectacle of Skill: Selected Writings of Robert Hughes* (New York: Vintage, 2016), 128–9.

34 Aldous Huxley, *Brave New World Revisited* (London: Vintage Books, 2004), 48.

35 Postman, *Amusing Ourselves to Death*, xix.

36 We should add to this that Huxley was also writing in the immediate wake of some of the most *creative* events in human history: at the height of artistic modernism, shortly after the publication of Einstein's special and general theories of relativity, and at the dawn of the new age of quantum mechanics. The radical

disruption caused by these events doubtless contributed to the "stabilizing" obsession of his World State.

37 Postman, *Amusing Ourselves to Death*, 4.

38 Marshall McLuhan, *Understanding Media: The Extensions of Man* (Berkeley, CA: Gingko Press, 2003), 17. As McLuhan's biographer Douglas Coupland glosses, "'the medium is the message' means that the ostensible content of all electronic media is insignificant; it is the medium itself that has the greater impact on the environment," *Marshall McLuhan: You Know Nothing of My Work!* (New York: Atlas Publishing, 2010), 13.

39 Postman, *Amusing Ourselves to Death*, 10. Cf. "All media work us over completely. They are so pervasive in their personal, political, economic, aesthetic, psychological, moral, ethical, and social consequences that they leave no part of us untouched, unaffected, unaltered," Marshall McLuhan and Quentin Fiore, *The Medium Is the Massage* (London: Penguin, 1967), 26.

40 Postman, *Amusing Ourselves to Death*, 15.

41 Postman, *Amusing Ourselves to Death*, 27.

42 Postman, *Amusing Ourselves to Death*, 51.

43 Postman, *Amusing Ourselves to Death*, 80.

44 Postman, *Amusing Ourselves to Death*, 16.

45 Postman, *Amusing Ourselves to Death*, 78–9.

46 Postman, *Amusing Ourselves to Death*, 80.

47 Postman, *Amusing Ourselves to Death*, 87.

48 Postman, *Amusing Ourselves to Death*, 111.

49 Postman, *Amusing Ourselves to Death*, 84.

50 Wolff, *Television Is the New Television*, 35.

51 In America, for example, polls have consistently shown a high percentage of people receive their news from comedy shows like *The Daily Show*, *The Colbert Report* and *Last Week Tonight*. See for example Dan Cassino, Peter Wooley, and Krista Jenkins, "What You Know Depends on What You Watch: Current Events Knowledge across Popular News Sources," *Fairleigh Dickinson University's Public Mind Poll*, May 3, 2012, http://publicmind.fdu.edu/2012/confirmed/ (accessed 10 December 2018); Michael Rozansky, "Stephen Colbert's Civics Lesson: Or How a TV Humorist Taught America about Campaign Finance," *The Allenberg Public Policy Center of the University of Pennsylvania*, June 2, 2014, http://cdn. annenbergpublicpolicycenter.org/wp-content/uploads/Stephen-Colberts-Civics-Lesson_release_6-02-14_Final.pdf (accessed 10 December 2018); and Noel Diem, "Comedy or Cable: Where Do Americans Get Their News?" *Law Street*, January 2, 2015, https://www.lawstreetmedia.com/issues/entertainment-and-culture/comedy-cable-americans-get-news/ (accessed 10 December 2018).

52 Richard Greenfield cited in Ken Auletta, "Outside the Box: Netflix and the Future of Television," *The New Yorker*, January 26, 2014, https://www.newyorker.com/magazine/2014/02/03/outside-the-box-2 (accessed 11 December 2018).

53 Wolff, *Television Is the New Television*, 91.

54 Wolff, *Television Is the New Television*, 91.

55 Postman, *Amusing Ourselves to Death*, 105.

# Chapter 8

1 Postman, *Amusing Ourselves to Death*, 24.

2 Northrop Fry, *The Great Code: The Bible and Literature* (Toronto: Academic Press, 1981), 217. Traditionally, this process takes place over an extended period of time, as progressively more and more specific meaning becomes attached to it. To this end, "resonance starts vague and ends precise, or more precise." Northrop Frye, *Northrop Frye's Notebooks and Lectures on the Bible and Other Religious Texts*, ed. Robert D. Denham (Toronto: University of Toronto Press, 2003), 274. Note that this conception of "resonance" differs from the one operative in sociology, where definitions might vary from "the relevance of a cultural object to its audience" (Michael Schudson, "How Culture Works: Perspectives from Media Studies on the Efficacy of Symbols," *Theory and Society* 18, no. 2, 1989: 169) to "the heightened emotions people experience when they discover a novel cognitive fit in the act of solving problems" (Terence E. McDonnell, "Drawing Out Culture: Productive Methods to Measure Cognition and Resonance," *Theory and Society* 43, no. 3–4, 2014: 261. As late as 2017, Terence E. McDonnell, Christopher A. Bail, and Iddo Tavory argue that "despite its broad appeal, the metamorphosis of resonance from a metaphor into a theory remains incomplete," "A Theory of Resonance," *Sociological Theory* 35, no. 1 (2017): 2.

3 Postman, *Amusing Ourselves to Death*, 18.

4 Alan Rusbridger, *Breaking News: The Remaking of Journalism and Why It Matters Now* (New York: Farrar, Straus and Giroux, 2018), xxi.

5 The transformational role Twitter and social media more generally have played in the development of "actual news" is of course well known. Rusbridger, for example, observes that "our generation has been handed the challenge of rethinking almost everything societies had, for centuries, taken for granted about journalism"

(*Breaking News*, xxi), while Ali Nobil Ahmad warns that the platform's role in news reporting is now so great that it is not entirely unreasonable to fear "journalism being reduced to a tool for Twitter," "Is Twitter a Useful Tool for Journalists?" *Journal of Media Practice* 11, no. 2 (2010): 154. Likewise, the extraordinary (positive and negative) influence of social media on the distribution of news is well documented. In terms of news consumption, the 2019 Reuters "Digital News Report" found that "in the United States [...] amongst under-35s only 13% go direct [to a news app], with over half (54%) preferring to go to social media," Nic Newman with Richard Fletcher, Antonis Kalogeropoulos, and Rasmus Kleis Nielsen, "Reuters Institute Digital News Report 2019," *Reuters Institute for the Study of Journalism* (2019): 13, 15, https://reutersinstitute.politics.ox.ac.uk/sites/default/files/2019-06/DNR_2019_FINAL_0.pdf (accessed December 1, 2019).

6  Postman, *Amusing Ourselves to Death*, 78.

7  Postman, *Amusing Ourselves to Death*, 65.

8  Postman, *Amusing Ourselves to Death*, 69–70. An equally (if not more) immediate logical progression can also be drawn between photography and Instagram, for example, concerning its forcing "exposition into the background" and undermining of "traditional definitions of information, of news, and, to a large extent, of reality itself," Postman, *Amusing Ourselves to Death*, 74.

9  Social media has of course long been championed for its democratizing potential. Twitter in particular is often lauded for the way that it "democratizes and shakes up the genteel inertia of modern political dialogue" and "shifts much of the power once hoarded by political establishments back into the hands–or voices–of people," Vann R. Newkirk II, "The American Idea in 140 Characters," *The Atlantic*, March 24, 2016, https://www.theatlantic.com/politics/archive/2016/03/twitter-politics-last-decade/475131/ (accessed December 1, 2019).

10 Badiou, *Being and Event*, 338.

11 Huxley, *Brave New World Revisited*, 47.

12 Huxley, *Brave New World Revisited*, 48.

13 Recall how Roland Barthes conceives of myth as what allows specific significations to appear as "natural" and "self-evident," rather than culturally determined. Or as he himself succinctly puts it, "the very principle of myth" is that "it transforms history into nature," Roland Barthes, *Mythologies*, trans. Annette Lavers (London: Vintage Books, 2000), 129.

14 Postman, *Amusing Ourselves to Death*, 79.

15 Huxley, *Brave New World Revisited*, 48.

16 Postman, *Amusing Ourselves to Death*, 111, 156.

17 While Mond does at one point announce that "we don't want people to be attracted by old things […] we want them to like the new ones" (Huxley, *Brave New World*, 200), we nonetheless recognize the "new" things to which he is referring here as being variations are already-existing distractions (e.g., recently released "feelies").

18 While either of these possibilities clearly *can* be the case—indeed, we ourselves drew directly on the world of social media in our discussion of dissimulative scandal in Part One—in no way does this make it a rule.

19 James Poniewozik, "The Real Donald Trump Is a Character on TV," *The New York Times*, September 6, 2019, https://www.nytimes.com/2019/09/06/opinion/sunday/trump-reality-tv.html?action=click&module=Opinion&pgtype=Homepage (accessed September 7, 2019).

20 Laura Bradley, "Donald Trump's All-Consuming Obsession with TV Ratings: A History," *Vanity Fair*, January 20, 2017, https://www.vanityfair.com/hollywood/2017/01/donald-trump-ratings (accessed 7 September 2019).

21 Ronald Reagan cited in J. Jeffery Auer, "Acting Like a President; or, What Has Ronald Reagan Done to Political Speaking?" in *Reagan and Public Discourse in America*, ed. Michael Weiler and W. Barnett Pierce (Tuscaloosa: University of Alabama Press, 1992), 95.

22 Even prior to his starring role on "The Apprentice," Trump's life represented a form of "reality TV," his ostentatious lifestyle and possessions serving in his own words as "props for the show," where "the show is 'Trump' and it is sold-out performances everywhere," Glenn Plaskin and Donald Trump, "The Playboy Interview with Donald Trump," *Playboy*, March 1, 1990, https://www.playboy.com/read/playboy-interview-donald-trump-1990 (accessed 7 September 2019).

23 Poniewozik, "The Real Donald Trump."

24 Poniewozik, "The Real Donald Trump."

25 The circularity of this process functions as a kind of media "resonance chamber," where Trump's tweets effectively program television news, even while "the ammunition for his Twitter war is television," Maggie Haberman, Glenn Thrush, and Peter Barker, "Inside Trump's Hour-by-Hour Battle for Self-Preservation," *The New York Times*, December 9, 2017, https://www.nytimes.com/2017/12/09/us/politics/donald-trump-president.html?module=inline (accessed 8 September 2019).

26 Susan B. Glasser, "Trump's Wacky, Angry and Extreme August," *The New Yorker*, September 3, 2019, https://www.newyorker.com/news/letter-from-trumps-washington/trumps-wacky-angry-and-extreme-august-twitter (accessed 8 September 2019).

27 To this end, Trump's infamous tweet about his being "the Ernest Hemingway of 140 characters" carries a grain of truth, in that Hemmingway was himself famous for inflating his own legacy, such that "by the 1940s, he was regularly telling 'tall tales' about his war heroism, 'an exaggeration or lie in nearly every sentence,'" Elaine Showalter, "A Hemingway Tell-All Bares His Tall Tales," *The New York Times*, May 25, 2017, https://www.nytimes.com/2017/05/25/books/review/ernest-hemingway-biography-mary-dearborn.html (accessed 8 September 2019).

28 Obviously, there are many other factors that come into play here. We might equally point, for example, to the fact that Twitter does not require identity authentication (leading to increased levels of disinhibition), or to the fact that the reverse-chronological structure of its "feed" invites a synchronic or ahistorical mode of engagement (and this is to say nothing of intentionally controversial online practices like trolling, doxing, hacking, shaming, and so on).

29 Jonathan Freedland, "While You're Looking the Other Way, Trump Is Changing America for Decades to Come," *The Guardian*, December 15, 2017, https://www.theguardian.com/commentisfree/2017/dec/15/trump-changing-america-president-tweets-russia (accessed 8 September 2019).

30 It is interesting to note here Heidegger's own use of the Greek word *polemos*, which he "transforms into a profound ontological concept" and which "must be understood as *confrontation*; only in confrontation do we most fully become what we are: beings summoned to an ongoing interpretive struggle with the meaning of the world—and with the meaning of Being itself," Gregory Fried, *Heidegger's Polemos: From Being to Politics* (New Haven: Yale University Press, 2000), 4.

31 Galen Stolee and Steve Caton, "Twitter, Trump, and the Base: A Shift to a New Form of Presidential Talk?" *Signs and Society* 6, no. 1 (2018): 161.

32 To appreciate the enormity of this cycle, it should suffice to note that the Wikipedia category page for "Trump Administration Controversies" currently lists 102 separate pages, together with four separate sub-categories containing a further 81 pages (in addition to more sub-categories). "Category: Trump Administration Controversies," *Wikipedia*, last modified March 28, 2019, https://en.wikipedia.org/wiki/Category:Trump_administration_controversies (accessed 8 September 2019).

33 Badiou and Tarby, *Philosophy and the Event*, 11.

34 Badiou, *Ethics*, 16.

35 In his 1959–60 seminar on *The Ethics of Psychoanalysis* Jacques Lacan famously proposed that "the only thing one can be guilty of is giving ground relative to one's desire," *The Seminar of Jacques Lacan, Book VII: The Ethics of Psychoanalysis, 1959–1960*, ed. Jacques-Alain Miller, trans. Dennis Porter (New York: Norton, 1992), 321.

36 Badiou, *L'Immanence des vérités*, 265. Simplifying radically, we can roughly equate "finitude" and "infinitude" here with the logics of the state and the real.

37 Badiou, *Conditions*, 234.

38 Badiou, *Ethics*, 79.

39 Badiou, *Logics of Worlds*, 55.

40 Badiou, *Logics of Worlds*, 59–60.

41 Without falling too deep into the rabbit hole, the difficulty here lies in the fact that, since there is no ethics outside of the (post-evental) subject, unethical practice will necessarily involve the corruption of subjectivity. Yet in the case of "terror," we only have the *illusion* of subjectivity; there is no "authentic" subject to corrupt. The question is then: does this make terror *anethical*? Our own answer is that terror, understood as the simulacral perversion of a subjective truth-procedure, can indeed be understood as a subjective position in as much as it does not simply mimic but moreover functions to *negate the very possibility of subjectivity*. In this sense, terror is unethical in that its existence is predicated on the subject and its "purpose" is to render ethics itself impossible. It is for this reason (coupled with its invocation of the fullness of the situation rather than to its void) that we relate terror to the obscure subjective position.

42 Badiou, *Ethics*, 74, 77.

43 Badiou, *Ethics*, 73.

44 Here it is worth noting how Fried sees polemos, which we have already tied to the state's use of controversy, as addressing to us "a question about the meaning of fascism, or, more precisely, about the problem *announced by* fascism"—a problem which is "not behind us but remain[s], alas, very much present," *Heidegger's Polemos*, 4.

45 Maria Karlsson and Måns Wrange, "Scandal Success! The Political Economy of the Art Scandal," in *Scandalous: A Reader on Art and Ethics*, ed. Nina Möntmann (Berlin: Sternberg Press, 2013), 97. Cf. "The divide between the people and its 'other' defines the political nature of populism," Francisco Panizza, "Introduction: Populism and the Mirror of Democracy," in *Populism and the Mirror of Democracy*, ed. Francisco Panizza (London: Verso, 2005), 28.

46 Matthew Wood, Jack Corbett, and Matthew Flinders, "Just Like Us: Everyday Celebrity Politicians and the Pursuit of Popularity in an Age of Anti-Politics," *The British Journal of Politics and International Relations* 18, no. 3 (2016): 592.

47 Clearly Trump's policies and actions have had (and will continue to have) enormous effects on areas like the environment, the economy, immigration, healthcare, etc. Arguably his "greatest" legacy will, however, be ideological, in

an extraordinary intensification of social division and political partisanship. His concerted assault on the media and its relation to truth that has been especially effective in this respect, a 2019 Hill-Harris US survey showing that "51 percent of Republicans polled said they thought of the press as 'the enemy of the people' compared with 14 percent of Democrats and 35 percent of independents who said the same," Tess Bonn, "Poll: One-Third of Americans Say News Media Is the 'Enemy of the People,'" *The Hill*, July 3, 2019, https://thehill.com/hilltv/what-americas-thinking/451311-poll-a-third-of-americans-say-news-media-is-the-enemy-of-the-people (accessed 8 September 2019).

48 Badiou, *Logics of Worlds*, 557. In this sense, Trump does have reason to be obsessed with a "deep state"—albeit not the secretive cabal he imagines it to be. For the *real state*, the ontological expression of power embodied in the capitalist machine and supported by the various "democratic" institutions, lies irremediably beyond his reach, and will continue to function smoothly despite his best efforts.

49 Huxley, *Brave New World*, 200. This kind of happiness, we know, is nothing other than the static experience of "a comfortable, smooth, reasonable, democratic unfreedom," Marcuse, *One-Dimensional Man*, 1.

50 Alain Badiou, *Métaphysique du Bonheur Réel*, 55.

# Bibliography

Adut, Ari. *On Scandal: Moral Disturbances in Society, Politics and Art*. New York: Cambridge University Press, 2008.

Adut, Ari. "A Theory of Scandal: Victorians, Homosexuality, and the Fall of Oscar Wilde." *American Journal of Sociology* 111, no. 1 (2005): 213–48.

Ahmad, Ali Nobil. "Is Twitter a Useful Tool for Journalists?" *Journal of Media Practice* 11, no. 2 (2010): 145–55.

Allern, Sigurd, and Ester Pollack. "Nordic Politics Scandals—Frequency, Types and Consequences." In *Mediated Scandals: Gründe, Genese und Folgeeffekte von medialer Skandalberichterstattung*, edited by Mark Ludwig, Thomas Schierl, and Christian von Sikorski, 146–63. Köln: Herbert von Halem Verlag, 2016.

Althusser, Louis. "Ideology and Ideological State Apparatuses (Notes towards an Investigation)." In *On Ideology*, 1–60. London: Verso, 2008.

Alves, João Lopes. "Legal Controversy vs. Scientific and Philosophical Controversies." In *Traditions of Controversy*, edited by Marcelo and Hang-liang Chang, 209–22. Amsterdam: John Benjamins Publishing Company, 2007.

Apostolidis, Paul, and Juliet A. Williams. "Introduction: Sex Scandals and Discourses of Power." In *Public Affairs: Politics in the Age of Sex Scandals*, edited by Paul Apostolidis and Juliet A. Williams, 1–35. Durham, NC: Duke University Press, 2004.

Aristotle. *The Metaphysics*, translated by Hugh Lawson-Tancred. London: Penguin, 1998.

Aristotle. *Poetics*, translated by Malcolm Heath. London: Penguin Books, 1996.

Atwood, Margaret. "Everybody Is Happy Now." *The Guardian*, November 17, 2007. https://www.theguardian.com/books/2007/nov/17/classics.margaretatwood (accessed 3 October 2018).

Auer, J. Jeffery. "Acting Like a President; or, What Has Ronald Reagan Done to Political Speaking?" In *Reagan and Public Discourse in America*, edited by Michael Weiler and W. Barnett Pierce, 93–120. Tuscaloosa: University of Alabama Press, 1992.

Auletta, Ken. "Outside the Box: Netflix and the Future of Television." *The New Yorker*, January 26, 2014. https://www.newyorker.com/magazine/2014/02/03/outside-the-box-2 (accessed 11 December 2018).

Badiou, Alain. *À la recherche du réel perdu*. Paris: Fayard, 2015.

Badiou, Alain. "The Adventure of French Philosophy," translated by Bruno Bosteels. *New Left Review* 35 (2005): 67–77.

Badiou, Alain. *Being and Event*, translated by Oliver Feltham. London: Continuum, 2005.

Badiou, Alain. *Briefings on Existence: A Short Treatise on Transitory Ontology*, translated by Norman Maderasz. New York: State University of New York Press, 2006.

Badiou, Alain. *The Century*, translated by Alberto Toscano. Cambridge: Polity Press, 2007.

Badiou, Alain. *The Communist Hypothesis*, translated by David Macey and Steve Corcoran. New York: Verso, 2010.

Badiou, Alain. *Conditions*, translated by Steve Corcoran. London: Continuum, 2008.

Badiou, Alain. *Deleuze: The Clamor of Being*, translated by Louise Burchill. Minneapolis: University of Minnesota Press, 2000.

Badiou, Alain. *Ethics: An Essay on the Understanding of Evil*, translated by Peter Hallward. London: Verso, 2001.

Badiou, Alain. *L'être et l'événement*, Paris: Seuil, 1988.

Badiou, Alain. *L'Immanence des vérités: L'être et l'événement, 3*. Paris: Fayard, 2018.

Badiou, Alain. *Lacan: Antiphilosophie 3: 1994–1995*. Paris: Fayard, 2014.

Badiou, Alain. *Logiques des Mondes: L'être et l'événement, 2*. Paris: Seuil, 2006.

Badiou, Alain. *Manifesto for Philosophy*, translated by Norman Maderasz. New York: State University of New York Press, 1999.

Badiou, Alain. *Métaphysique du Bonheur Réel*. Paris: Presses Universitaires de France, 2015.

Badiou, Alain. *Metapolitics*, translated by Jason Barker. London: Verso, 2005.

Badiou, Alain. *Plato's Republic: A Dialogue in 16 Chapters*, translated by Suzan Spitzer. New York: Columbia University Press, 2012.

Badiou, Alain. *Pornographie du Temps Présent*. Paris: Fayard, 2013.

Badiou, Alain. "In Search of the Lost Real." In *Badiou and His Interlocutors: Lectures, Interviews and Responses*, edited by A. J. Bartlett and Justin Clemens, 7–16. London: Bloomsbury, 2018.

Badiou, Alain. *Second Manifesto for Philosophy*, translated by Louise Burchill. Cambridge: Polity Press, 2011.

Badiou, Alain. *Theoretical Writings*, edited and translated by Ray Brassier and Alberto Toscano. London: Continuum, 2004.

Badiou, Alain. *Theory of the Subject*, translated by Bruno Bosteels. London: Continuum, 2009.

Badiou, Alain, and Barbara Cassin. *There's No Such Thing as a Sexual Relationship: Two Lessons on Lacan*, translated by Susan Spitzer and Kenneth Reinhard. New York: Columbia University Press, 2017.

Badiou, Alain, and Elizabeth Roudinesco. *Jacques Lacan: Past and Present*, translated by Jason E. Smith. New York: Columbia University Press, 2014.

Badiou, Alain, and Fabien Tarby. *Philosophy and the Event*, translated by Louise Burchill. Cambridge: Polity Press, 2013.

Badiou, Alain, and Jean-Claude Milner. *Controversies: A Dialogue on the Politics and Philosophy of Our Time*, translated by Susan Spitzer. Cambridge: Polity Press, 2014.

Badiou, Alain, and Jean-Luc Nancy. *German Philosophy: A Dialogue*, edited by Jan Völker. Cambridge, MA: MIT Press, 2018.

Badiou, Alain, and Marcel Gauchet. *What Is to Be Done?: A Dialogue on Communism, Capitalism, and the Future of Democracy*, translated by Susan Spitzer. Cambridge: Polity Press, 2016.

Barnes, Jonathan. *Early Greek Philosophy*. London: Penguin Books, 1987.

Barrotta, Pierluigi, and Marcelo Dascal (eds.). *Controversies and Subjectivity*. Amsterdam: John Benjamins Publishing Company, 2005.

Barrow, John D. *The Infinite Book: A Short Guide to the Boundless, Timeless and Endless*. New York: Pantheon Books, 2005.

Barthes, Roland. *Mythologies*, translated by Annette Lavers. London: Vintage Books, 2000.

Bartlett, A. J. *Badiou and Plato: An Education by Truths*. Edinburgh: Edinburgh University Press, 2011.

Basinger, Scott, Lara Brown, Douglas B. Harris, and Girish J. Gulati. "Preface: Counting and Classifying Congressional Scandals." In *Scandal! An Interdisciplinary Approach to the Consequences, Outcomes and Significance of Political Scandals*, edited by Alison Dagnes and Mark Sachleben, 3–28. London: Bloomsbury, 2014.

Baudrillard, Jean. *The Gulf War Did Not Take Place*, translated by Paul Patton. Bloomington: Indiana University Press, 1995.

Baudrillard, Jean. *The Perfect Crime*, translated by Chris Turner. London: Verso, 1996.

Baudrillard, Jean. *Simulacra and Simulation*, translated by Sheila Faria Glaser. Ann Arbour: University of Michigan Press, 1994.

Becker, Jo, Adam Goldman, and Matt Apuzzo. "Russian Dirt on Clinton? 'I Love It', Donald Trump Jr. Said." *The New York Times*, July 11, 2017. https://www.nytimes.com/2017/07/11/us/politics/trump-russia-email-clinton.html (accessed 12 April 2019).

Bernays, Edward. "The Engineering of Consent." *The Annals of the American Academy of Political and Social Science* 250, no. 1 (1947): 113–20.

Bernays, Edward. *Propaganda*. New York: Ig Publishing, 2005.

Blumentrath, Jan. "Interview with Jordan Feldstein." *HitQuarters*, October 30, 2013. https://web.archive.org/web/20140209042751/http://www.hitquarters.com/index.php3?page=intrview/2013/October30_17_1_48.html (accessed 9 March 2018).

Bonn, Tess. "Poll: One-third of Americans Say News Media Is the 'Enemy of the People." *The Hill*, July 3, 2019. https://thehill.com/hilltv/what-americas-thinking/451311-poll-a-third-of-americans-say-news-media-is-the-enemy-of-the-people (accessed 8 September 2019).

Bradley, Laura. "Donald Trump's All-Consuming Obsession with TV Ratings: A History." *Vanity Fair*, January 20, 2017. https://www.vanityfair.com/ hollywood/2017/01/donald-trump-ratings (accessed 7 September 2019).

Brown, Milton. *The Story of the Armory Show*. New York: Joseph Hirshhorn Foundation, 1963.

Bulik, Mark. "Picasso and the 'Eccentric' Cubists." *The New York Times*, February 2, 2015. https://www.nytimes.com/times-insider/2015/02/02/1911-picasso-and-the-eccentric-cubists/ (accessed 5 March 2018).

Burkhardt, Steffen. "Scandals in the Network Society." In *Scandalogy: An Interdisciplinary Field*, edited by André Haller, Hendrick Michael, and Martin Krauss, 18–44. Köln: Herbert von Halem Verlag, 2018.

Canel, Maria Jose, and Karen Sanders. *Morality Tales: Political Scandals and Journalism in Britain and Spain in the 1990s*. Creskill, NJ: Hampton Press, 2006.

Cantor, Georg. *Contributions to the Founding of the Theory of Transfinite Numbers*, translated by Philip E. B. Jourdain. New York: Dover Publications, 1955.

Capelos, Tereza. "Scandals and Blame Management, Political." In *The Encyclopedia of Political Science*, edited by George Thomas Kurian et al., 1511–13. Washington: CQ Press, 2011.

Cassino, Dan, Peter Wooley, and Krista Jenkins. "What You Know Depends on What You Watch: Current Events Knowledge across Popular News Sources." *Fairleigh Dickinson University's Public Mind Poll*, May 3, 2012. http://publicmind.fdu. edu/2012/confirmed/ (accessed 10 December 2018).

Chung, Eugenia. *Beyond Infinity: An Expedition to the Outer Limits of the Mathematical Universe*. London: Profile Books, 2017.

Chotiner, Isaac, and Daniel Golden. "An Investigative Journalist on How Parents Buy College Admissions." *The New Yorker*, March 12, 2019. https://www.newyorker. com/news/q-and-a/an-investigative-journalist-on-how-parents-buy-college-admissions (accessed 13 March 2019).

Chrisafis, Angelique. "Attack on 'Blasphemous' Art Work Fires Debate of Role of Religion in France." *The Guardian*, April 18, 2011. https://www.theguardian.com/ world/2011/apr/18/andres-serrano-piss-christ-destroyed-christian-protesters (accessed 3 March 2018).

Clemens, Justin. *Psychoanalysis in as Antiphilosophy*. Edinburgh: Edinburgh University Press, 2013.

Cohen, Paul. "The Discovery of Forcing." *The Rocky Mountain Journal of Mathematics* 32, no. 4 (2002): 1071–100.

Cohen, Paul. *Set Theory and the Continuum Hypothesis*. New York: W. A. Benjamin, 1966.

Coupland, Douglas. *Marshall McLuhan: You Know Nothing of My Work!* New York: Atlas Publishing, 2010.

Dascal, Marcelo. "The Study of Controversies and the Theory and History of Science." *Science in Context* 11, no. 2 (1998): 147–54.

Dauben, Joseph Warren. "Georg Cantor and the Battle for Transfinite Set Theory." *Journal of the Association of Christians in the Mathematical Sciences* (2004): 1–17.

Dauben, Joseph Warren. *Georg Cantor: His Mathematics and Philosophy of the Infinite*. Princeton: Princeton University Press, 1990.

Dawson, Jr., John W. *Logical Dilemmas: The Life and Work of Kurt Gödel*. Wellesley, MA: A K Peters, 1997.

Debord, Guy. *Situationist International Anthology*, edited by Ken Knabb. Berkeley, CA: Bureau of Public Secrets, 2006.

Debord, Guy. "Situationist Manifesto." In *100 Artists' Manifestos: From the Futurists to the Stuckists*, edited by Alex Danchev, 347–50. London: Penguin, 2011.

Debord, Guy. *The Society of the Spectacle*, translated by Donald Nicholson-Smith. London: Zone Books, 1995.

De Duve, Thierry. *Kant after Duchamp*. Cambridge, MA: MIT Press, 1996.

De Duve, Thierry. *Pictorial Nominalism: On Marcel Duchamp's Passage from Painting to the Readymade*, translated by Dana Polen. Minneapolis: University of Minnesota Press, 1991.

De Freytas-Tamura, Kimiko. "Georger Orwell's '1984' Is Suddenly a Best-Seller." *The New York Times*, January 25, 2017. https://www.nytimes.com/2017/01/25/books/1984-george-orwell-donald-trump.html (accessed 3 October 2018).

Deleuze, Gilles. *Difference and Repetition*, translated by Paul Patton. London: Continuum, 2004.

Deleuze, Gilles, and Felix Guattari. *What Is Philosophy*, translated by Hugh Tomlinson and Graham Burchill. New York: Columbia University Press, 1994.

Descartes, René. *Meditations on First Philosophy with Selections from the Objections and Replies*. Edited and translated by John Cottingham. Cambridge: Cambridge University Press, 1996.

Diem, Noel. "Comedy or Cable: Where Do Americans Get Their News?" *Law Street*, January 2, 2015. https://www.lawstreetmedia.com/issues/entertainment-and-culture/comedy-cable-americans-get-news/ (accessed 10 December 2018).

Dredge, Stuart. "Global Music Sales Fell in 2013 Despite Strong Growth for Streaming Services." *The Guardian*, March 18, 2014. https://www.theguardian.com/technology/2014/mar/18/music-sales-ifpi-2013-spotify-streaming (accessed 9 March 2018).

Dreyfus, Hubert L., and Patricia Allen Dreyfus. "Translators' Introduction." In Maurice Merleau-Ponty. *Sense and Non-Sense*, translated by Hubert L. Dreyfus and Patricia Allen Dreyfus, ix–xxvii. Evanston, IL: Northwestern University Press, 1964.

Duchamp, Marcel. "Apropos of 'Readymades.'" *Art and Artists* 1, no. 4 (1966): 47.

Duchamp, Marcel. "The Great Trouble with Art in This Country." In *The Writings of Marcel Duchamp*, edited by Michel Sanouillet and Elmer Peterson, 123–6. New York: Da Capo Press, 1973.

Duchamp, Marcel, and Pierre Cabanne. *Dialogues with Marcel Duchamp*, translated by Ron Padgett. New York: Da Capo Press, 1987.

Easton, William B. "Powers of Regular Cardinals." *Annals of Mathematical Logic* 1, no. 2 (1970): 139–78.

Einstein, Albert. "A propos de 'La déduction relativiste' de M. Emile Meyerson." *Revue Philosophique* 105 (1928): 161–6.

Entman, Robert. *Scandal and Silence: Media Reponses to Presidential Misconduct.* London: Polity Press, 2012.

Esser, Frank, and Uwe Hartung. "Nazis, Pollution and No Sex: Political Scandals as a Reflection of Political Culture in Germany." *American Behavioral Scientist* 47, no. 8 (2004): 1040–71.

Farías, Victor. *Heidegger and Nazism*. Philadelphia: Temple University Press, 1989.

Fernando, Gil (ed.). *Scientific and Philosophical Controversies*. Lisbon: Fragmentos, 1990.

Feltham, Oliver. *Alain Badiou: Live Theory*. London: Continuum, 2008.

Florida, Richard. *The Rise of the Creative Class, Revisited*. New York: Basic Books, 2012.

Foucault, Michel. *The Archaeology of Knowledge and the Discourse on Language*, translated by A. M. Sheridan Smith. New York: Pantheon Books, 1972.

Foucault, Michel. *Power: Essential Works of Foucault 1954–1984*, edited by James D. Faubion, translated by Robert Hurley. New York: The New Press, 2001.

Foucault, Michel. *Power/Knowledge: Selected Interviews and Other Writings 1972–1977*, edited by Colin Gordon, translated by Colin Gordon, Leo Marshall, John Mepham, and Kate Sopher. New York: Pantheon Books, 1980.

Foucault, Michel. "The Subject and Power." *Critical Inquiry* 8, no. 4 (1982): 777–95.

Freedland, Jonathan. "While You're Looking the Other Way, Trump Is Changing America for Decades to Come." *The Guardian*, December 15, 2017. https://www.theguardian.com/commentisfree/2017/dec/15/trump-changing-america-president-tweets-russia (accessed 8 September 2019).

Freud, Sigmund. *The Standard Edition of the Complete Psychological Works of Sigmund Freud, Volume XIX (1923–1925): The Ego and the Id and Other Works*, edited and translated by James Stratchey. London: Vintage, 2001.

Freudenthal, Gideon. "Controversy." *Science in Context* 11, no. 2 (1998): 155–60.

Fried, Gregory. *Heidegger's Polemos: From Being to Politics*. New Haven: Yale University Press, 2000.

Friedman, Sy-David, and Radel Honzik. "Easton's Theorem and Large Cardinals." *Annals of Pure and Applied Logic* 154 (2008): 191–208.

Fry, Naomi. "The College-Admissions Scandal and the Banality of Scamming." *The New Yorker*, March 13, 2019. https://www.newyorker.com/culture/cultural-comment/the-college-admissions-scandal-and-the-banality-of-scamming (accessed 13 March 2019).

Frye, Northrop. *The Great Code: The Bible and Literature*. Toronto: Academic Press, 1981.

Frye, Northrop. *Northrop Frye's Notebooks and Lectures on the Bible and Other Religious Texts*, edited by Robert D. Denham. Toronto: University of Toronto Press, 2003.

Gajanan, Mahita. "Kellyanne Conway Defends White House's Falsehoods as 'Alternative Facts'." *Time*, January 22, 2017. https://time.com/4642689/kellyanne-conway-sean-spicer-donald-trump-alternative-facts/ (accessed 3 October 2018).

Gamwell, Lynn. *Mathematics+Art: A Cultural History*. Princeton: Princeton University Press, 2016.

Garrard, John. "Scandals: An Overview." In *Scandals in Past and Contemporary Politics*, edited by John Garrard and James L. Newell, 13–29. Manchester: Manchester University Press, 2006.

Geiselberger, Heinrich. "Preface." In *The Great Regression*, edited by Heinrich Geiselberger, x–xvi. Cambridge: Polity Press, 2017.

Glasser, Susan B. "Trump's Wacky, Angry and Extreme August." *The New Yorker*, September 3, 2019. https://www.newyorker.com/news/letter-from-trumps-washington/trumps-wacky-angry-and-extreme-august-twitter (accessed 8 September 2019).

Gluckman, Max. "Gossip and Scandal." *Current Anthropology* 4, no. 3 (1963): 307–16.

Gödel, Kurt. *On Formally Undecidable Propositions of Principia Mathematica and Related Systems*, translated by Bernard Meltzer. New York: Basic Books, 1962.

Gödel, Kurt. "What Is Cantor's Continuum Problem?" *The American Mathematical Monthly* 54, no. 9 (1947): 515–25.

Goldblatt, Robert. *Topoi: The Categorial Analysis of Logic*. New York: Dover Publications, 2006.

Golden, Daniel. *The Price of Admission: How America's Ruling Class Buys Its Way into Elite Colleges—and Who Gets Left outside the Gates*. New York: Broadway Books, 2006.

Groddeck, Georg. *The Book of the It: Psychoanalytic Letters to a Friend*. New York: Nervous and Mental Disease Publishing Company, 1928.

Groys, Boris. *On the New*, translated by G. M. Goshgarian. London: Verso, 2014.

Haberman, Maggie, Glenn Thrush, and Peter Barker. "Inside Trump's Hour-by-Hour Battle for Self-Preservation." *The New York Times*, December 9, 2017. https://www.nytimes.com/2017/12/09/us/politics/donald-trump-president.html?module=inline (accessed 8 September 2019).

Hausdorff, Felix. *Set Theory*. New York: Chelsea Publications, 1962.

Hegel, Georg Wilhelm Friedrich. *Elements of the Philosophy of Right*, edited by Allen W. Wood, translated by H. B. Nisbet. Cambridge: Cambridge University Press, 1991.

Hegel, Georg Wilhelm Friedrich. *The Encyclopedia Logic*, translated by T. F. Geraets, W. A. Suchting, and H. S. Harris. Albany: State University of New York Press, 1991.

Hegel, Georg Wilhelm Friedrich. *The Science of Logic*, translated by A. V. Miller. New York: Humanity Books, 1969.

Heidegger, Martin. *Being and Time*, translated by John Macquarrie and Edward Robinson. New York: HarperCollins, 1962.

Heidegger, Martin. *Parmenides*, translated by André Schuwer and Richard Rojcewicz. Indianapolis: Indiana University Press, 1992.

Hepp, Andreas, Stig Hjarvard, and Knut Lundby. "Mediatization—Empirical Perspectives: An Introduction to a Special Issue." *Communication* 35, no. 3 (2010): 223–8.

Herman, Edward, and Noam Chomsky. *Manufacturing Consent: The Political Economy of the Mass Media*. New York: Pantheon Books, 2002.

Holan, Angie Drobnic. "In Context: Donald Trump's 'Very Fine People on Both Sides' Remarks (Transcript)." *Politifact*, April 26, 2019. https://www.politifact.com/truth-o-meter/article/2019/apr/26/context-trumps-very-fine-people-both-sides-remarks/ (accessed 5 May 2019).

Horkheimer, Max, and Theodore Adorno. *Dialectic of Enlightenment: Philosophical Fragments*, edited by Gunzelin Schmid Noerr, translated by Edmund Jephcott. Stanford, CA: Stanford University Press, 2002.

Howarth, Sophie, and Jennifer Mundy. "Marcel Duchamp: Fountain 1917, Replica 1964." *The Tate*, revised August, 2015. https://www.tate.org.uk/art/artworks/duchamp-fountain-t07573 (accessed 1 May 2018).

Howkins, John. *Creative Ecologies: Where Thinking Is a Proper Job*. St Lucia: University of Queensland Press, 2009.

Howkins, John. *The Creative Economy: How People Make Money from Ideas*. London: Penguin Books, 2013.

Hughes, Robert. *The Shock of the New: Art and the Century of Change*. London: Thames & Hudson, 1980.

Hughes, Robert. *The Spectacle of Skill: Selected Writings of Robert Hughes*. New York: Vintage, 2016.

Husserl, Edmund. *Cartesian Meditations: An Introduction to Phenomenology*, translated by Dorian Cairns. The Hague: Martinus Nijhoff Publishers, 1982.

Huxley, Aldous. *Brave New World*. London: Flamingo, 1994.

Huxley, Aldous. *Brave New World Revisited*. London: Vintage Books, 2004.

Jameson, Fredric. *Postmodernism, or, the Cultural Logic of Late Capitalism*. London: Verso, 1991.

Kahneman, Daniel. "Maps of Bounded Rationality: Psychology for Behavioral Economics." *The American Economic Review* 93, no. 5 (2003): 1449–75.

Kahneman, Daniel. *Thinking, Fast and Slow*. New York: Farrar, Straus and Giroux, 2011.

Kanamori, Akihiro. "Cohen and Set Theory." *The Bulletin of Symbolic Logic* 14, no. 3 (2008): 351–78.

Karlsson, Maria, and Måns Wrange. "Scandal Success! The Political Economy of the Art Scandal." In *Scandalous: A Reader on Art and Ethics*, edited by Nina Möntmann, 88–105. Berlin: Sternberg Press, 2013.

Kuhn, Thomas S. *The Structure of Scientific Revolutions*. Chicago: University of Chicago Press, 1962.

Lacan, Jacques. *Autres Écrits*. Paris: Éditions du Seuil, 2001.

Lacan, Jacques. *Écrits: The First Complete Edition in English*, translated by Bruce Fink. New York: Norton, 2006.

Lacan, Jacques. "Monsieur A." *Ornicar?* 21–22 (1980): 17–20.

Lacan, Jacques. *My Teaching*, translated by David Macey. London: Verso, 2008.

Lacan, Jacques. *The Seminar of Jacques Lacan, Book I: Freud's Papers on Technique*, edited by Jacques-Alain Miller, translated by John Forrester. New York: Norton, 1991.

Lacan, Jacques. *The Seminar of Jacques Lacan, Book VII: The Ethics of Psychoanalysis, 1959-1960*, edited by Jacques-Alain Miller, translated by Dennis Porter. New York: Norton, 1992.

Lacan, Jacques. *The Seminar of Jacques Lacan, Book XI: The Four Fundamental Concepts of Psychoanalysis*, edited by Jacques-Alain Miller, translated by Alan Sheridan. New York: Norton, 1998.

Lacan, Jacques. *Le Séminaire de Jacques Lacan, Livre XII: Problèmes Cruciaux pour la Psychanalyse*. Unpublished manuscript. http://staferla.free.fr/S12/S12.htm (accessed 3 March 2019).

Lacan, Jacques. *The Seminar of Jacques Lacan, Book XVII: The Other Side of Psychoanalysis*, edited by Jacques-Alain Miller, translated by Russell Grigg. New York: Norton, 2007.

Lacan, Jacques. *The Seminar of Jacques Lacan, Book XX: On Feminine Sexuality, the Limits of Love and Knowledge*, edited by Jacques-Alain Miller, translated by Bruce Fink. New York: Norton, 1999.

Lacan, Jacques. *The Seminar of Jacques Lacan, Book XIX: ... or Worse*, edited by Jacques-Alain Miller, translated by A. R. Price. Cambridge: Polity Press, 2018.

Lacan, Jacques. *Le Séminaire de Jacques Lacan, Livre XXII: R.S.I.* Unpublished manuscript. http://staferla.free.fr/S22/S22.htm (accessed 3 March 2019).

Lampedusa, Giuseppe di. *The Leopard*, translated by Archibald Colquhoun. New York: Pantheon Books, 1960.

LaFraniere, Sharon. "Paul Manafort's Prison Sentence Is Nearly Doubled to 7½ Years." *The New York Times*, March 13, 2019. https://www.nytimes.com/2019/03/13/us/politics/paul-manafort-sentencing.html (accessed 12 April 2019).

Leva, Michael. *Looking Askance: Skepticism and American Art from Deakins to Duchamp*. California: University of California Press, 2007.

Levinas, Emmanuel. *Totality and Infinity: An Essay on Exteriority*, translated by Alphonso Lingis. The Hague: Martinus Nijhoff Publishers, 1979.

Lévi-Strauss, Claude. *Structural Anthropology*, translated by Claire Jacobson and Brooke Grundfest Schoepf. New York: Basic Books, 1963.

Lippmann, Walter. *Public Opinion*. New Brunswick: Transaction Publishers, 1992.

Lowi, Theodore J. "Power and Corruption: Political Competition and the Scandal Market." In *Public Affairs: Politics in the Age of Sex Scandals*, edited by Paul Apostolidis and Juliet A. Williams, 69–100. Durham, NC: Duke University Press, 2004.

Lucretius. *On the Nature of Things*, translated by Cyril Bailey. London: Oxford University Press, 1910.

Lull, James, and Stephen Hinerman. "The Search for Scandal." In *Media Scandals: Morality and Desire in the Popular Culture Marketplace*, edited by James Lull and Stephen Hinerman, 1–33. New York: Columbia University Press, 1997.

Lyotard, Jean-François. *The Postmodern Condition: A Report on Knowledge*, translated by Geoff Bennington and Brian Massumi. Manchester: Manchester University Press, 1984.

Malevich, Kasimir. "Suprematist Manifesto." In *100 Artists' Manifestos: From the Futurists to the Stuckists*, edited by Alex Danchev, 105–25. London: Penguin, 2011.

Mandell, Hinda, and Gina Masullo Chen. "Introduction: Scandal in an Age of Likes, Selfies, Retweets and Sexts." In *Scandal in a Digital Age*, edited by Hinda Mandell and Gina Masullo Chen, 3–14. New York: Palgrave Macmillan, 2016.

Marcuse, Herbert. *One-Dimensional Man: Studies in the Ideology of Advanced Industrial Society*. Boston: Beacon Press, 1964.

Martel, Diane, and Eric Ducker. "Q&A: Veteran Music Director Diane Martel on Her Controversial Videos for Robin Thicke and Miley Cyrus." *Grantland*, June 26, 2013. http://grantland.com/hollywood-prospectus/qa-veteran-music-video-director-diane-martel-on-her-controversial-videos-for-robin-thicke-and-miley-cyrus/ (accessed 9 March 2018).

McDonnell, Terence E., Christopher A. Bail, and Iddo Tavory. "A Theory of Resonance." *Sociological Theory* 35, no. 1 (2017): 1–14.

McDonnell, Terence E. "Drawing Out Culture: Productive Methods to Measure Cognition and Resonance." *Theory and Society* 43, no. 3–4 (2014): 247–74.

McLuhan, Marshall. *Understanding Media: The Extensions of Man*. Berkeley, CA: Gingko Press, 2003.

McLuhan, Marshall, and Quentin Fiore. *The Medium Is the Massage*. London: Penguin, 1967.

Medawar, Peter. *The Art of the Soluble*. London: Methuen, 1967.

Meillassoux, Quentin. *After Finitude*, translated by Ray Brassier. London: Continuum, 2008.

Merleau-Ponty, Maurice. *Phenomenology of Perception*, translated by Donald A. Landes. London: Routledge, 2012.

Merleau-Ponty, Maurice. *Sense and Non-Sense*, translated by Hubert L. Dreyfus and Patricia Allen Dreyfus. Evanston, IL: Northwestern University Press, 1964.

Meyerson, Émile. *La déduction relativiste*. Paris: Payot, 1925.

Molière, "Tartuffe." In *The Broadway Anthology of Drama: Plays from the Western Theatre Volume 1: From Antiquity through the Eighteenth Century*, edited by Jennifer Wise and Craig S. Walker, translated by Richard Wilbur, 437–67. Ontario: Broadway Press, 2003.

Morales, Mark. "Felicity Huffman Issues Apology over College Admissions Case." *CNN*, April 8, 2019. https://edition.cnn.com/2019/04/08/entertainment/felicity-huffman-statement/index.html (accessed 12 April 2019).

MTV News Staff. "Thanks Miley! 2013 VMAs Shatter Twitter Records," *MTV News*, August 26, 2013. http://www.mtv.com/news/1713119/vma-ratings-record/ (accessed 9 March 2018).

Naumann, Francis. *The Recurrent, Haunting Ghost: Essays on the Art, Life and Legacy of Marcel Duchamp*. New York: Readymade Press 2012.

Newkirk II, Vann R. "The American Idea in 140 Characters." *The Atlantic*, March 24, 2016. https://www.theatlantic.com/politics/archive/2016/03/twitter-politics-last-decade/475131/ (accessed 1 December 2019).

Newman, Nic, Richard Fletcher, Antonis Kalogeropoulos, and Rasmus Kleis Nielsen. "Reuters Institute Digital News Report 2019." *Reuters Institute for the Study of Journalism* (2019). https://reutersinstitute.politics.ox.ac.uk/sites/default/files/2019-06/DNR_2019_FINAL_0.pdf (accessed 1 December 2019).

Nordheim, Gerret von, Karin Boczek, and Lars Koppers. "Sourcing the Sources: An Analysis of the Use of Twitter and Facebook as a Journalistic Source over 10 Years in *The New York Times, The Guardian*, and *Süddeutsche Zeitung*." *Digital Journalism* 6, no. 7 (2017): 807–28.

NPR Staff. "Pharell Williams on Juxtaposition and Seeing Sounds." *NPR*, December 31, 2013. http://www.npr.org/sections/therecord/2013/12/31/258406317/pharrell-williams-on-juxtaposition-and-seeing-sounds (accessed 9 March 2018).

Nye, Joseph. "Corruption and Political Development: A Cost-Benefits Analysis." *American Political Science Review* 85 (1991): 417–27.

Orwell, George. *Nineteen Eighty-Four*. London: Penguin Books, 1989.

Panizza, Francisco. "Introduction: Populism and the Mirror of Democracy." *Populism and the Mirror of Democracy*, edited by Francisco Panizza, 1–31. London: Verso, 2005.

Plaskin, Glenn, and Donald Trump. "The Playboy Interview with Donald Trump." *Playboy*, March 1, 1990. https://www.playboy.com/read/playboy-interview-donald-trump-1990 (accessed 7 September 2019).

Plato. "Apology." In *Complete Works*, edited by John M. Cooper, translated by G. M. A. Grube, 17–36. Cambridge: Hackett Publishing Company, 1997.

Plato. "Parmenides." In *Complete Works*, edited by John M. Cooper, translated by Mary Louise Gill and Paul Ryan, 359–97. Cambridge: Hackett Publishing Company, 1997.

Plato. *The Republic of Plato*, translated by Alan Bloom. New York: HarperCollins, 1991.

Plato. "Sophist." In *Complete Works*, edited by John M. Cooper, translated by Nicholas P. White, 235–93. Cambridge: Hackett Publishing Company, 1997.

Poincaré, Henri. *The Foundations of Science: Science and Hypothesis; The Value of Science; Science and Method*, translated by George Halsted. New York: The Science Press, 1921.

Poniewozik, James. "The Real Donald Trump Is a Character on TV." *The New York Times*, September 6, 2019. https://www.nytimes.com/2019/09/06/opinion/sunday/trump-reality-tv.html?action=click&module=Opinion&pgtype=Homepage (accessed 7 September 2019).

Postman, Neil. *Amusing Ourselves to Death: Public Discourse in the Age of Show Business*. London: Penguin Books, 1985.

Postman, Neil. *Technopoly: The Surrender of Culture to Technology*. New York: Vintage Books, 1993.

Preis, Tobias, Johannes J. Schneider, and H. Eugene Stanley. "Switching Processes in Financial Markets." *Proceedings of the National Academy of Sciences of the United States of America* 108, no. 19 (2011): 7674–8.

Roosevelt, Theodor. "Mr. Roosevelt on the Cubists." *The Literary Digest*, April 5, 1913.

Rossi, Ino. "The Unconscious in the Anthropology of Claude Lévi-Strauss." *American Anthropologist* 75, no. 1 (1973): 20–48.

Rovelli, Carlo. *The Order of Time*, translated by Erica Segre and Simon Carnell. London: Allen Lane, 2018.

Rovelli, Carlo. *Reality Is Not What It Seems: The Journey to Quantum Gravity*, translated by Simon Carnell and Erica Segre. New York: Riverhead Books, 2016.

Rozansky, Michael. "Stephen Colbert's Civics Lesson: Or, How a TV Humorist Taught America about Campaign Finance." *The Allenberg Public Policy Center of the University of Pennsylvania*, June 2, 2014. http://cdn.annenbergpublicpolicycenter.org/wp-content/uploads/Stephen-Colberts-Civics-Lesson_release_6-02-14_Final.pdf (accessed 10 December 2018).

Sanders, Kerry. "Donald Trump: The King of Twitter?" *NBC News*, March 15, 2016. https://www.nbcnews.com/politics/2016-election/donald-trump-king-twitter-n539131 (accessed 27 November 2018).

Sartre, Jean-Paul. *Being and Nothingness: An Essay on Phenomenological Ontology*, translated by Hazel E. Barnes. London: Routledge, 2003.

Sartre, Jean-Paul. *Existentialism Is a Humanism*, translated by Carol Macomber. New Haven: Yale University Press, 2007.

Sartre, Jean-Paul. *Nausea*, translated by Lloyd Alexander. New York: New Directions, 2007.

Schlag, Pierre. "The Problem of the Subject." *Texas Law Review* 69, no. 1627 (1991): 1628–743.

Schopenhauer, Arthur. *The Art of Controversy and Other Posthumous Papers*, edited and translated by T. Bailey Saunders. New York: Macmillan, 1896.

Schudson, Michael. "How Culture Works: Perspectives from Media Studies on the Efficacy of Symbols," *Theory and Society* 18, no. 2 (1989): 153–80.

Schumpeter, Joseph. *Capitalism, Socialism and Democracy*. New York: Harper Perennial, 2008.

Serrano, Andres, and Ben Beaumont-Thomas. "Andres Serrano's Best Photograph: A White Man with Black Skin." *The Guardian*, April 6, 2017. https://www.theguardian.com/artanddesign/2017/apr/06/andres-serrano-best-photograph-interview (accessed 3 March 2018).

Sheridan, Richard Brinsley. *The School for Scandal*, edited by Ann Blake. London: Bloomsbury, 1995.

Showalter, Elaine. "A Hemingway Tell-All Bares His Tall Tales." *The New York Times*, May 25, 2017. https://www.nytimes.com/2017/05/25/books/review/ernest-hemingway-biography-mary-dearborn.html (accessed 8 September 2019).

Simon, Herbert A. *Models of Man: Social and Rational; Mathematical Essays on Rational Human Behavior in a Social Setting*. New York: Wiley, 1957.

Sokal, Alan, and Jean Bricmont. *Fashionable Nonsense: Postmodern Intellectuals' Abuse of Science*. New York: Picador, 1998.

Steiner, Wendy. *The Scandal of Pleasure: Art in an Age of Fundamentalism*. Chicago: The University of Chicago Press, 1995.

Stelios Phili. "Robin Thicke on That Banned Video, Collaborating with 2 Chainz and Kendrick Lamar, and His New Film." *GQ Magazine*, May 6, 2013. https://www.

gq.com/story/robin-thicke-interview-blurred-lines-music-video-collaborating-with-2-chainz-and-kendrick-lamar-mercy (accessed 9 March 2018).

Stepanov, Yuriy, Philip Rinn, Thomas Guhr, Joachim Peinke, and Rudi Schäfer. "Stability and Hierarchy of Quasi-Stationary States: Financial Markets as an Example." *Journal of Statistical Mechanics: Theory and Experiment*, August 2015: 1–19.

Stewart, Ian. *Infinity: A Very Short Introduction.* Oxford: Oxford University Press, 2017.

Stolee, Galen, and Steve Caton. "Twitter, Trump, and the Base: A Shift to a New Form of Presidential Talk?" *Signs and Society* 6, no. 1 (2018): 147–65.

Thompson, John. *Political Scandals: Power and Visibility in the Media Age.* London: Polity Press, 2000.

Thompson, John. "Scandal and Social Theory." In *Media Scandals: Morality and Desire in the Popular Culture Marketplace*, edited by James Lull and Stephen Hinerman, 34–64. New York: Columbia University Press, 1997.

Tumber, Howard, and Silvio R. Waisbord. "Introduction: Political Scandals and Media Across Democracies, Volume I." *American Behavioral Scientist* 47, no. 8 (2004): 1031–9.

Tumber, Howard, and Silvio R. Waisbord. "Introduction: Political Scandals and Media across Democracies, Volume II." *American Behavioral Scientist* 47, no. 9 (2004): 1043–52.

Tuttle, Brad. "Sales of Dystopian Novels Have Been Spiking on Amazon since the Election." *Money*, January 25, 2017. http://money.com/money/4648774/trump-1984-dystopian-novel-sales-brave-new-world/ (accessed 3 October 2018).

Trzęsicki, Kazimierz. "How Are Concepts of Infinity Acquired?" *Studies in Logic, Grammar and Rhetoric* 40, no. 53 (2015): 179–217.

Unattributed. "2016 Academy Award Nominations and Winner for Best Picture." *Box Office Mojo*, February 16, 2017. http://www.boxofficemojo.com/oscar/chart/?yr=2016&view=fulldetail&p=.htm (accessed 5 May 2019).

Unattributed. "The 'Cubists' Dominate Paris' Fall Salon." *The New York Times*, October 8, 1911.

Unattributed. "The Richard Mutt Case." *The Blind Man* 2 (1917): 3–4.

USLegal. "Scandal Law and Legal Definition." https://definitions.uslegal.com/s/scandal/ (accessed 27 November 2018).

Valenti, Davide, Giorgio Fazio, and Bernardo Spagnolo. "Stabilizing Effect of Volatility in Financial Markets." *Physical Review E* 97, no. 6 (2018): 1–9.

Verbalyte, Monika. "Deconstruction of the Emotional Logic of Political Scandal." In *Scandalogy: An Interdisciplinary Field*, edited by André Haller, Hendrick Michael, and Martin Krauss, 62–87. Köln: Herbert von Halem Verlag, 2018.

Vorberg, Laura, and Anna Zeitler. "'This Is (Not) Entertainment!': Media
    Constructions of Political Scandal Discourses in the 2016 US Presidential
    Election." *Media, Culture & Society* 41, no. 4 (2017): 417–32.
Wikipedia. "Category: Trump Administration Controversies." *Wikipedia*, last
    modified March 28, 2019. https://en.wikipedia.org/wiki/Category:Trump_
    administration_controversies (accessed 8 September 2019).
Wolff, Michael. *Television Is the New Television: The Unexpected Triumph of Old
    Media in the Digital Age.* New York: Penguin, 2015.
Wood, Matthew, Jack Corbett, and Matthew Flinders. "Just Like Us: Everyday
    Celebrity Politicians and the Pursuit of Popularity in an Age of Anti-Politics." *The
    British Journal of Politics and International Relations* 18, no. 3 (2016): 581–98.
Yeats, William Butler. "Easter 1916." In *The Norton Anthology of Poetry*, edited by
    Alexander Allison, Herbert Barrows, Caeser Blake, Arthur Carr, Arthur Eastman,
    and Hubert English, 881–3. London: Norton, 1983.
Žižek, Slavoj. *Absolute Recoil: Towards a New Foundation of Dialectical Materialism.*
    London: Verso, 2014.

# Index

www.ingramcontent.com/pod-product-compliance
Lightning Source LLC
Chambersburg PA
CBHW050710280326
41926CB00088B/2908